arranging songs

HOW TO PUT THE PARTS TOGETHER

RIKKY ROOKSBY

For Kay, Robin and Eva – a happy arrangement

Many people can play technically, but it's... how you react to the context. One or two notes can sound brilliant, whereas on their own they're just two notes. Therein lies the craft. You go to a school and learn to play those two notes. But it's your experience, the music you listen to and where exactly you position those two notes. It doesn't have to be 50 notes. You don't see that expressed much in books.

Phil Manzanera of Roxy Music

ARRANGING SONGS
HOW TO PUT THE PARTS TOGETHER

A BACKBEAT BOOK
First edition 2007
Published by Backbeat Books (an imprint of Hal Leonard Corporation)
19 West 21st Street, New York, NY 10010, USA
www.backbeatbooks.com

Devised and produced for Backbeat Books by Outline Press Ltd
2A Union Court, 20–22 Union Road, London SW4 6JP, England
www.backbeatuk.com

ISBN 978-0-87930-896-4

EDITOR John Morrish
DESIGN Lisa Tai

Printed by Colorprint (Hong Kong)
07 08 09 10 5 4 3 2 1

Contents

Preface

Imagine you have just completed writing a song. At this moment it comprises a melody, a lyric, and a chord sequence worked out on guitar or keyboards. Now it's time to record it. But do you know how to arrange it?

Arrangements matter, because a poor arrangement can hamper even a good song to the extent that its true worth struggles to emerge. A good arrangement supports the song and brings out its quality. An inspired arrangement is inseparable from the song itself and becomes a part of how listeners remember it. At its best the art of arrangement transcends mere presentation; arrangement and song fuse into a single entity.

Arrangement concerns the best way of getting your song across, live or in recorded form. It means choosing the right instruments and knowing how to combine them. It also touches on many other practical aspects of music, such as harmony, rhythm, recording, and mixing. Arrangements are often arrived at by default, and many songwriters create them unconsciously; but take care over an arrangement and your song will sound all the better. This book is about arranging and how to do it.

Arranging Songs will help composers put together effective recordings of their material, expand their knowledge of instrumentation, and develop their hallmark sounds. There's information on how to draft an arrangement, how to expand your sense of what an arrangement can do, and how to create new types of arrangement for your songs. The text includes many illustrative references to well-known songs, and there are specially composed audio examples on the CD. Recalling what others have done with arrangements during the past 50 years provides opportunities to recharge your creativity. This book offers a wealth of tips and ideas that will find new life in your own arrangements, whatever style of song you write or play.

RIKKY ROOKSBY

How to use this book

This not a book that needs to be read sequentially; dip straight into any section that interests you. If you feel you get stuck using the same instrumental sounds, browse the many suggested combinations. If you are short of inspiration, try dipping into *Arranging Songs* at random.

The book has nine sections. **Section One** asks what is meant by 'arrangement'. It deals with the particular way the word is used in this book, and other broader issues connected with the subject. **Section Two** examines basic concepts to apply to instrumental parts when arranging and mixing a song. Having thus laid the ground, the book zooms in on the primary instrument of most popular songwriting: the guitar. **Section Three** reviews the use of acoustic guitars in an arrangement; **Section Four** does the same for the electric guitar. **Section Five** looks at guitar effects and the role they can play. **Section Six** provides tips on arranging with the other 'core' instruments: keyboards, bass, and drums. **Section Seven** is an overview of secondary instruments that might feature in an arrangement, including instruments that belong to an orchestra. **Section Eight** examines concepts of arrangement in song structure and mixing. There are 'case study' boxes throughout the book that highlight an arrangement technique in a famous song or the playing of a particular musician.

Arranging Songs is illustrated by a 50-track CD whose contents can be explored either through the detailed commentary track-by-track in **Section Nine** or through the **Index To The CD**. Each audio example includes more than one arrangement technique, theme, or instrument. Watch out especially for those tracks that occur in more than one mix, so you can compare different mixing and arrangement choices.

Arranging Songs also refers to songs by many famous bands and singers. It leans towards classic artists of the 1960s and 1970s, because their music has stood the test of time and they will be familiar to a greater number of readers, and because in some instances they set high standards for songwriting and arranging.

This book concludes my multi-volume series on songwriting, which commenced publication in 2000. To find out more on chord sequences, melody, guitar chords and guitar tunings, and writing songs on keyboards (especially if you're a guitarist), get *How To Write Songs On Guitar* (2000), *The Songwriting Sourcebook* (2003), *Chord Master* (2004), *Melody* (2005), *How To Write Songs On Keyboards* (2005), and *Lyrics* (2006). If you write riff-based songs, *Riffs* (2002) is the most encyclopaedic study ever published about them. To learn more about the elements that make a magical recording, 100 songs from 1960 to the present day go under the microscope in *Inside Classic Rock Tracks* (2001). Information about these titles can be found at www.backbeatbooks.com and www.rikkyrooksby.com.

SECTION 1

What is an arrangement?

An arrangement is the outfit your song wears when it goes out into the world. Good arrangement doesn't rely on a particular line-up of instruments. Even using the most basic rock or pop instrumentation, with guitars to the fore, you can bring new colour and power to your songs by thoughtful deployment of your musical resources.

An arrangement is the means by which you present your song. A song has a certain melody, lyric, rhythm (including a given time signature and tempo), and harmony. But the same combination of these things can be put across in many ways – just as you could go to a fancy dress party in a variety of costumes but remain essentially who you are. The 'garb' in this case is provided by the arrangement. Your song will have a chord progression. Each chord depends on three, four, sometimes five different notes. But those notes could be played on a vast number of instruments. Choosing instruments leads to a particular arrangement.

It is in this general sense of presentation that the word 'arrangement' is used in this book. There is a technical meaning of 'arrangement' to describe an activity that involves writing in musical notation. This is where a piece written for one instrument or group of instruments is re-worked so that it fits a different set of instruments; this may also involve a change of musical genre. For example, a piece for piano and voice is *arranged* (written out) for orchestra, or an orchestral piece is turned into something a four-piece rock band can play. Theoretically, almost any music of any style could be arranged for any combination of instruments and performers.

CLASSIC ARRANGEMENT

When 1970s progressive rock band ELP recorded Aaron Copland's trumpet piece 'Fanfare For The Common Man' they arranged it into a work that could be performed by organ, bass and drums. Similarly, when they recorded the orchestral *Pictures At An Exhibition* they arranged it as a score for the same three-piece line-up. Interestingly, the orchestral score was itself an arrangement. *Pictures At An Exhibition* began as music for solo piano by the Russian composer Mussorgsky, and these piano pieces were arranged for orchestra by the French composer Ravel. Another example of such arranging would be Miles Davis' version of the slow movement of Rodrigo's *Concerto De Aranjuez* for guitar and orchestra, where trumpet replaces the guitar (released on Davis' album *Sketches Of Spain*).

Such drastic changes of instrumentation are often matched by a significant change of musical intent and style. But such technical arrangement is a note-by-note process that is outside the scope of this book. In fact, a whole book could be devoted to the intricacies of most styles of arrangement. Instead, this book approaches the subject from within one broad music genre – that of mainstream pop/rock/soul/folk songwriting, where the aim is to produce a good arrangement of the basic song material using instruments that naturally fit in this broad genre. The most popular composing and performance instrument in this tradition remains the guitar, supported by bass guitar and drums, and keyboards.

Knowing the character of various guitars and amps, etc, makes a difference to arranging.

Looking back on the recording of 'Hot Hot Hot', Robert Smith of The Cure said, "I was trying to be Chic. The singles off that LP [*Kiss Me, Kiss Me, Kiss Me*] were mannered. I used to say to the group, today we're going to be x or y. We had four drum kits set up and three bass amps in the building and loads of vintage guitar amps. We'd pick a sound and do a song. 42 songs in a 30 day period and almost every one of them had a different sound!" Most musicians don't have the luxury of having so much vintage equipment to hand, but samples and digital modelling products make an approximation of such approaches possible.

CONSCIOUS ARRANGING

Arranging a song is a skill many songwriters utilize unconsciously. They are less likely to consciously acquire information about this area of music-making, compared to finding out more on subjects like chord progressions, scales, or how to write lyrics. When recording a new song most songwriters simply draw instinctively on what they know and what is to hand. In a four-piece band with two guitarists, bass and drums, those are the instruments that provide the basis for the arrangement. In fact, even this traditional rock line-up has possibilities for planning an arrangement to get a more interesting result. With conscious arranging you could apply any of the following ideas:

- Leaving out one of the instruments for a section.
- Not using full chords for some sections.
- Not using the guitars to begin with.
- Pulling out the drums during the bridge/middle eight, to make space for a quieter vocal and 'refreshing' the drums for a powerful re-entry on the last verse or chorus.
- Incorporating a passage where the voice is supported by only light percussion and instrumental harmonics.

Any of these adjustments could add colour and power to the song's character.

There are arranging techniques you an use even when you don't have many instruments. A good example would be British rock band Free's perennial hit 'All Right Now' (1970) where the bass guitar is absent from the verse, giving a lift to the chorus when it enters. This was especially useful live (see *Free Live*, 1971), because the band only had one guitarist.

Arrangements form initially around the practicalities of live performance – what the band can comfortably do in front of an audience. This means answering questions such as:

- Who can play what at the same time – as arises when the guitarist can also play a few keyboard chords.
- How complex a guitar part the singer can manage while singing, if he or she also plays guitar.
- Whether the band has the equipment to effectively include acoustic guitar as well as electric.

- Whether the band has hi-tech facilities for triggering sample sounds, playing along to a backing track, etc.

By contrast, arrangement choices for the solo performer, with one instrument such as guitar (two, if they can play harmonica and guitar like Bob Dylan), are simpler. Even so, a good performer will try to vary the sound of the arrangement from song to song by techniques such as:

- Picking.
- Strumming.
- Playing finger-style.
- Playing percussively.
- Playing with a bottleneck.
- Adding harmonics.
- Using a standard capo.
- Using a partial capo.
- Changing the tuning.
- Changing guitar.
- Adding sound-effects like echo, chorus or flanging.

STUDIO/MULTITRACK ARRANGING

The first occasion most songwriters and bands are confronted by issues of arrangement has traditionally been when they make a recording with the option of multitracking and overdubbing. In the past this happened when they booked time in a recording studio. Nowadays, affordable recording technology and computers have made it possible for many people to attempt complex multitrack demos, with anything from four to 24 tracks as standard.

This raises acute questions for the solo songwriter. Having the gear doesn't automatically confer the knowledge of how to use it, as many a fussy and over-crowded demo will prove. Suddenly there are all those empty tracks waiting to be filled with additional sounds. You record a vocal on one track and a guitar on another. But what do you do with the rest? How do you get ideas about building up the recording? How do you know when enough is enough? How proficient do you need to be on other instruments to feel confident about recording with them?

For bands, multitrack recording is not quite so intimidating. Taking the obvious audio map, recording two guitars and bass in stereo will account for six tracks, and if the drummer insists on having 12 microphones dispersed around the kit so every piece of it has a separate track, that will be 18 tracks taken care of. A double-tracked lead vocal, a couple of backing vocals, and two spare tracks for the lead guitar solo, will fill-up a 24-track recording. Some engineers would argue that a decent drum sound is perfectly achievable with four mics (bass drum, snare, overhead and distant). But if you are more stringent about the core instruments (here guitar, bass and drums), having all those available tracks can mean the chance to add other instruments, from keyboards and extra percussion, to brass, strings, and orchestral sounds. The widespread availability of sampled sound, either as hardware (tone banks/sound modules/synths) or software (sample libraries), has vastly increased available instrumental colour, even for home recordings.

THE ART OF ARRANGEMENT

This book deals with aspects of the art of arrangement that do not date. The technology used by songwriters to record their songs has changed considerably in the past two decades and will continue to do so. But the main principles of arranging do not change.

The ability to arrange a song is one of those musical skills that are 'transparent'. It does not draw attention to itself if you get it right. An example of a 'transparent' skill on guitar is the ability to mute four strings while playing octave runs and striking all six strings. With the muting in place two notes are heard accompanied by a percussive noise from the four muted strings; without successful muting there would be many wrong notes. Executed correctly, no one notices what is being done; they only hear a series of octaves. This contrasts with 'opaque' skills, such as playing blindingly fast or wild tremolo-arm bending, that are highly visible.

Arranging well is like the former. If you get an arrangement right, most listeners think, 'what a great song', not 'what a great arrangement'. As we listen, the arrangement invites us to go through it to the power of the song, its melody, progressions and lyrics. Even though it is affecting how we respond to the song on many levels, we are rarely conscious of the arrangement as an entity in itself when we fall under the spell of a song.

As I write this, The Police are on their reunion tour. The Police were a band with an exceptional grasp of arrangement. One of their late 1970s hits, 'Walking On The Moon' was a superb arrangement, not only because it made a virtue out of the instrumental limitation of a power trio (it only has one harmony instrument, the guitar) but because the arrangement graphically portrayed the lyric. Sting had found a great metaphor for the existential weightlessness of being in love – the memory of astronauts bouncing on the moon. The band created a soundscape of echoing guitar and drums that seemed just as weightless and full of space. It had the further advantage of being an arrangement the band could perform live and still sound close to the record. To reflect further on this, imagine 'Walking On The Moon' arranged at the same tempo but in the style of Boston's 'More Than A Feeling', or slightly quicker with continuous chording in the style of The Ramones or The Jam (all bands from the same era) – both possible alternate options. Given the song, most bands would have come up with something more commonplace. The Police's skill was to find a more imaginative presentation for the song.

THE ARRANGEMENT HERITAGE

Arranging is an under-rated skill. There is much awareness, artistry and taste in knowing how to present a song. These are things that really can be learned and improved through careful listening to a variety of music and by grasping the basic concepts outlined in this book. Every good songwriter knows the value of listening back and forth across 50 years of popular music recording, getting to know the landmark styles and artists. There is something to be learned from all of it, no matter what music you play. It is your heritage – so go and possess it. By doing that, you not only benefit in personal knowledge but also help it to live on. Some songwriting and arranging techniques have fallen by the wayside. Not everything carries on into the present. There are things you can re-discover and bring back as a hallmark of the way you make music.

CASE STUDY

KEY-CHANGING

Key-changing is a time-honoured technique that has fallen out of use in much contemporary songwriting, particularly in chart material. Many 1960s songs feature striking key-changes, including The Beatles 'Fool On The Hill' and 'While My Guitar Gently Weeps', and Motown hits like The Four Tops' 'I'm In A Different World' and Stevie Wonder's 'Heaven Help Us All'. In fact, key-changing was taken to dizzy, not to say reckless, extremes on songs like The Toys' 'Lovers Concerto' and The Supremes' 'I Hear A Symphony'. How many of your songs change key? How many might benefit from a key-change? Key-changing can be considered part of the arrangement as well as composing process.

Arranging also involves such skills as:

- Not over-using a sound to the extent that it becomes irritating or ineffective.
- Judging when a sound needs refreshing, reviving an instrument which has been in the mix all the while
- Getting the individual parts to work together, to agree melodically, harmonically and rhythmically.
- Delaying an instrument entry until the right moment.
- Choosing different sounds to give character to a bridge/middle-eight or to illustrate some element of the lyric.

Aside from your basic instruments, it is important to know what other instrumental colours exist and could be used on any arrangement you do. To this end **Section Seven** of this book is devoted to an overview of common additional instruments, explaining their use in popular music. Browse those pages when considering what extra instruments could go on your recording. If you bring in secondary instrumental sounds, other skills involve:

- Knowing where to put these instruments in the mix.
- Knowing which ones will suit which song, and how they fit together.
- Knowing how to write idiomatically so that parts sound realistic even if they are samples played from a keyboard.

This means understanding roughly in what ranges instruments play and what kinds of parts they usually provide. For example, string parts don't sound realistic if they are written in the close triads that can be held down with one hand on a keyboard. They will sound more authentic if the notes are spaced further apart.

It also takes discrimination to know what kind of arrangement suits the character of the song you're recording. A good rule of thumb is to make your accompaniment fit the song: never force a song into a pre-conceived accompaniment. In the former instance, step back and ask what type of song your new composition wants to be. This requires getting a feel for what's there in the initial material of lyric, melody, chord progression and tempo.

If you force a song into an arrangement style foreign to its underlying nature the final result will sound cramped, artificial, clichéd, and/or unintentionally funny. This can be exploited to deliberate comic or satiric effect. Imagine if a heavy rock number like Ozzy Osbourne's 'Shot In The Dark' had originally been recorded in reggae style, or if Metallica had first recorded 'Enter Sandman' with acoustic guitars and mandolin. Clearly, heavy riff material cries out for heavy guitars and a rock beat.

Of course, after the event, when the song has been released in its definitive form, then one could do other arrangements possibly with interesting results. But that is a different arrangement task – a kind of re-arrangement of a known song, or re-imagining of it. That is what happens when people cover a song without trying to emulate the original, but instead give it a new quality or bring out something new in it. But in this book we are concerned with the primary act of arranging to realize the song's identity in the first place. What thinking did Metallica apply to the arranging of 'Enter Sandman' in the first instance?

THE STYLISTIC MEANING OF INSTRUMENTS

Instruments convey not only musical information but stylistic meaning, which, in the context of popular music as a whole, also has to be considered when arranging. When instruments enter an arrangement strategy they bring not only timbres (the tonal character) but a symbolic value independent of any notes they play. To include certain instruments is in itself a gesture of style, and style in popular music counts for a lot. Such choices can say something about how seriously you want the music to be taken, or what genre you want to be seen as belonging in. You may therefore want to take such symbolic meanings into consideration.

For example, even after 50 years, the electric guitar itself retains a rebellious, 'hooligan' air, immediately felt if placed in a classical music context, where it is still widely regarded as not a 'serious' instrument. Despite examples by Deep Purple, Eric Clapton and Frank Zappa, a concerto for orchestra and electric guitar still raises sceptical eyebrows.

In the late 1960s/early 1970s, when rock had its strongest counter-cultural role, many rock musicians and critics had an ideological belief that strings and rock music did not mix. The objection took two forms. First, as a vital component of an orchestra, strings were associated with 'classical' music. There was a troubled relationship between the two musics, since much of the 'classical' music world regarded rock as musically illiterate and unsophisticated. From the moment

Chuck Berry told Beethoven to roll over, rock resented 'classical' as the music of the 'straights', the older generation, and because of its self-validated status as 'high art'.

Secondly, strings were considered a 'sweetener' associated with bland MOR singers and groups whose main motive for recording was commercial. Strings appealed to a 'straight' audience beyond the rock crowd and were mistrusted. No serious bunch of Gibson-toting rock revolutionaries wanted to be vulnerable to the dreaded accusation of 'selling out' and being commercial. Elsewhere in popular music, black soul artists like Etta James felt that strings in an arrangement adulterated rhythm & blues and effectively 'whitened' a record by making it more likely to appeal to a white audience. Peter Buck of R.E.M. is said to have praised John Paul Jones' string parts for tracks on *Automatic For The People* (1992) for being "nonsweet".

The career of Elvis Presley, moving from the early rockabilly Sun tracks to the more orchestrated RCA tracks, was often cited as a grim example of what could happen to rockers who allowed producers to put strings on their records. This feeling shaped the notorious battle over Phil Spector's choral and orchestral overdubs on the Beatles final album *Let It Be*, and the consternation it caused Paul McCartney. This arrangement crime was thought worthy of righting as recently as 2004 when *Let It Be ...Naked* was released, allowing listeners to hear songs like 'The Long And Winding Road' as originally recorded by The Beatles and without the overdubs. In the same year as *Let It Be* raised the eyebrows of rock critics, another counter-culture figure, Marc Bolan of T.Rex, had to be cajoled into putting strings on the songs he was then recording. Ironically, producer Tony Visconti's subtle string parts became a vital component of the group's best music, including hits such as 'Get It On' and 'Ride A White Swan', and made a significant contribution to the Englishness of Bolan's interpretation of American rock'n'roll.

Yet rock itself soon wanted to claim to be art with a capital 'A' just like classical, and was tempted from the mid-1960s to give itself classical trappings. Hence Phil Spector and Brian Wilson's talk of the 45rpm single as a potential 'pocket symphony', and rock bands' willingness to put strings (even whole orchestras) on their more grand recordings (as in The Beatles' 'A Day In The Life', The Moody Blues' *Days Of Future Passed*, and Neil Young's 'A Man Needs A Maid'). Not everyone tuned in to rock was thrilled to find that a Beatles song like 'Eleanor Rigby' or 'She's Leaving Home' had strings on it (or even worse, harp!). It wasn't rock'n'roll, man. It says much about rock's loss of counter-cultural position that few outside the ghettos of metal and punk now bother about losing credibility by arranging strings on a track. There was no outcry when in 2006 George Martin added a string arrangement to George Harrison's demo of 'While My Guitar Gently Weeps' for the *Love* album of Beatles re-mixes. Heading in the opposite direction, the inclusion of strings on songs like 'Fireworks', 'Slowdive', and 'Dazzle' signalled that Siouxsie And The Banshees had grown beyond their punk origins.

The props of classical music continue to possess the power to impress, as can be seen when rock bands film themselves with orchestras, when singers go on television with a rented (miming) string quartet, or when teen idols who want to be taken seriously by covering standards are photographed gazing pensively at pages of music manuscript when in reality they don't read a note. In each case, the 'classical' association of the prop – be it orchestra, violin, or manuscript notation – symbolically conveys the sense that this is a Serious Artist(e) doing something more weighty than ephemeral pop. Such symbolic associations also attach themselves to pieces of recording technology like microphones.

As for the electric guitar, in the mid-1960s Bob Dylan fell foul of his audience's worthy assumptions about the instrument spoiling the purity of folk music and protest song, an objection that culminated in the legendary cry of 'Judas!' at a concert at the Manchester Free Trade Hall. This controversy about the presence of electric guitars in folk also touched the careers of late-1960s groups such as Fairport Convention and Steeleye Span, who did electric arrangements of traditional British folk songs. It was common for such groups to suffer line-up changes when members fell out over whether or not the use of electric instruments, effects or drums, compromised their artistic integrity.

Much of this ideological labelling has gone, but instruments keep certain associations – with styles and eras of music – that are creatively exploited in arrangements. Consciously and unconsciously, music-buyers associate certain timbres with non-musical meanings. Recording, sampling, and emulation technology have made many exotic instruments easily reproducible. Some recent popular music has been about the manipulation of these symbolic identities to evoke the sense of 'cool' attached to certain periods in musical and social history. A musical phrase played low on an electric guitar with a touch of tremolo signifies early 1960s Americana, surf, big cars, teen love over pink milkshakes. A warbly mellotron recorder sample, a stroke of sitar, and a wisp of backward lead guitar mean the Summer of Love of 1967. A fruity analogue synth line suggests big lapels, brutal TV detectives, and the lava lamps of the early 1970s. A saxophone solo suggests night-club sophistication; a nylon-string guitar means 'organic' taverna sincerity and Latin passion; the plaintive reedy call of an oboe means melancholy English pastoral, and so on.

The exotic connotation of non-European instruments is now easily brought into an arrangement. Back in the 1960s you had to make a difficult, tiring, and expensive trip to some far-flung land to capture on tape the sound you wanted from local musicians, as when Brian Jones recorded Moroccan music in the 1960s or when Led Zeppelin recorded with Indian musicians in Bombay in 1972.

These days you can install or upload a software library for 'Pipes, Bells and Drums of Maranisia', and bamboozle listeners into thinking that your three-chord song, which is no more than a re-working of 'Louie Louie', is in fact 'world music'.

ARRANGEMENT, ART, AND COMMERCE

Choice of instruments in an arrangement also relates to your ambitions as a performer. Who do you want to reach with your music? And how many people? As in other areas of songwriting, art and commercial dictates do not always go together. During the arrangement and mixing process, decisions have to be made that balance the requirements of art against the demands of commerce. Typically, you might decide to:

- Add strings.
- Make the drums heavier/lighter.
- Use more/less guitar distortion.
- Choose a piano break or a rap instead of a guitar solo.
- Get female backing singers to do a harmony.
- Have handclaps.
- Use a double bass rather than an electric bass.
- Cut the intro from 16 bars to four bars.
- Put the chorus first.
- Put the bridge in a different key.
- Repeat the chorus three times at the end.
- Cut the coda and fade on the chorus.
- Not end on the key chord.

All these are choices of arranging and mixing that have implications for how accessible you want your music to be. Arrangement is part of that process. We can roughly define the claims of art versus commerce in the following way. The art-inclined approach involves:

- Doing things that are less obvious or immediate.
- Doing things that are less initially audible.
- Doing things that challenge a musical formula or the expectations of listeners.
- Using less familiar and less immediately pleasing sounds and textures.
- Valuing rough edges, mistakes, and accidents.
- Valuing a song's character and identity over its availability.
- Suppressing resemblances to other commercially successful songs.
- Obliging the listener to do some patient and repeated listens before the song fully yields up its meaning.
- Reducing the amount of repetition.
- Increasing the complexity of the harmony.
- Down-playing the role of percussion.

The corresponding vices of the artistic approach are narcissism, obscurity, under-achievement (the deliberate messing-up of a good idea), prolixity, the fetishization of what is ugly, ill-executed and fragmentary, and the valuing of the eccentric over what might speak to many people. There isn't anything inherently revolutionary about being unmusical or lacking technique.

The commercially-inclined approach to arrangement means:

- Doing things that are obvious and immediate.
- Doing things that are clearly audible.

- Conforming to formulas and listener expectations.
- Ensuring that the listener can absorb the song virtually on first hearing.
- Choosing conventionally pleasing sounds and instruments.
- Smoothing away rough edges and removing accidents.
- Increasing the amount of repetition.
- Reducing the complexity of the harmony.
- Providing a clear and emphatic beat.

The vices of the commercial approach are blandness, not allowing for the individuality of an idea, too narrow a sense of what is or could be beautiful, the fetishization of the notion of being smooth and cool rather than intelligent, and the over-valuing of the immediate. Close listening may reveal the weaknesses of a song arranged according to commercial dictates, rather than its strengths.

In commercial arrangements, conscious and unconscious choices make a song resemble others that have been successful. A song's appeal to the greatest number of potential purchasers is valued over its character and singular identity. The history of popular music is littered with instances of people releasing records that are close imitations of a hit in the hope that the audience can be persuaded into buying another song like it. The worst period for this was probably the five years between the end of rock'n'roll and the earliest hits of The Beatles (1958-63) when thousands of songs were recorded with the doo-wop chord sequences of I-VI-IV-V (C-A minor-F-G) or I-II-IV-V (C-D minor-F-G). At one level, people were actually buying what was essentially the same music over and over.

Most genres of songwriting operate within certain compositional, performance and arrangement formulas that help define them. Artistic achievement is possible within these, if you are ready to avoid the first option that comes to mind, and willing to deepen the musicality of the song. The simplest way to do this is to decrease the amount of repetition in a song and increase the number of musical ideas, especially those that are primarily melodic, without getting over-complicated and fussy. This is a tricky thing to judge. No-one gets it right all the time, and indeed often there is no correct answer to balancing the equation.

When seeking a middle way between artistic ambition and commercial ambition, be conscious of how far you wish to compromise.

Arrangements can be judged on whether they fulfil your intentions. If you want a hit at all costs, make arranging decisions that increase the chance of connecting with a mass audience. That means some of those weird 11b9 chords may have to go, as will the four-minute intro and the fretless bass solo, and it may be an idea not to use a tuba, an accordion, and bongos as your main instruments. Commercially, there will always be a central question for solo singer-songwriters: would my songs go over better if I had a rhythm section behind me? Getting a rhythm section made a crucial difference to the careers of Bob Dylan and Marc Bolan.

CASE STUDY

THE EELS' 'NOVOCAINE FOR THE SOUL'

This song has an interesting and unusual arrangement, especially considering it was released as a single. Note these characteristics of 'Novocaine For The Soul':

- **It has strong instrumental contrasts between sections.**
- **It foregrounds discontinuities, in that one section doesn't always flow into the next.**
- **It has an unusual palette of instrumental sound.**
- **It has a misleading intro and a sudden ending.**
- **Alarmingly for the record company, which wanted it to be a hit, 'Novocaine For The Soul' stops entirely for several seconds. "You can't do that," says the executive, "people will think their radio broken, or the D.J. has made a mistake, and what if you're dancing to it? No-one can dance to silence."**

'Novocaine For The Soul' could be re-arranged, keeping its lyric, melody, and chords, into a more commercial radio-friendly song that might have been a bigger hit. It is easy to imagine Nirvana doing a full-blown grunge version, and in fact one way of thinking about the song is that it is effectively a form of unplugged grunge number. But the quirky character of The Eels' original was part of its charm.

An effective arrangement can be also be defined as one:

- That suits the genre of the music you play.
- That fits the commercial and audience expectations of that genre.
- That guarantees immediacy.
- That is reproducible live, or is conceived as a studio concoction.
- That is shaped for mostly artistic reasons to fit the song.

Arrangements can have a deeper creative function. Rather than thinking of them as merely the dressing up of a song, they become part of the song's intention. The paradox is that the harmony of a song can be essentially traditional and the only thing that tells it apart from many others like it is the arrangement. This is one way a performer can draw attention to what they do, or appear revolutionary, even when their basic musical material is as conservative as anyone else's.

An example would be The White Stripes' decision to omit bass guitar and work only with guitar and drums, an idea that perfectly suits their stance of 'garage' authenticity. In their musical world it is always that afternoon when neither so-and-so's brother, who was supposed to play bass, nor the kid from four blocks away, whose family are quite well off and who has a Gibson but can't play it very well, turns up for the rehearsal; but despite that, Meg and Jack say "what the hell" and play on regardless.

ARRANGEMENT AND GENRE – THE MIKE FLOWERS EFFECT

Arrangements and instrumentation do much to define the sound of a particular genre. The point of The White Stripes covering a song like Bacharach/David's 'I Just Don't Know What To Do With Myself' with only drums and guitar is that the instrumentation is primitive compared to the orchestration on Dusty Springfield's original. We are invited to measure the extreme distance between this rendition and that 1960s epic production.

It is only a small step to the deliberate mis-matching of instrumentation and style to make a political point, to have fun, or to satirize. Acts like Hayseed Dixie perform hard rock songs with country instruments in a bluegrass/hillbilly style, and there was Dread Zeppelin's reggae take on Led Zeppelin. This is why, back in the mid-1990s, the Mike Flowers arrangement of Oasis's 'Wonderwall' was funny. It applied a late 1960s easy listening arrangement to a 1990s Britpop song. I have also heard Frankie Goes To Hollywood's 'Relax' arranged and performed as a 1950s big band Frank Sinatra number. Nor should we forget the Temple City Kazoo Orchestra, which performed 'Whole Lotta Love' and The Stones' 'Miss You' using wheezing kazoos. And then there are the notorious versions of Nirvana's 'Smells Like Teen Spirit', performed by Paul Anka and The Ukulele Orchestra Of Great Britain.

Earlier in this section I mentioned the arrangement of classical music by rock bands like ELP, or the use of Gustav Holst's 'Jupiter' theme in Manfred Mann's 'Joybringer'. This is one of the most powerful 'mis-match' arrangements imaginable, since it crosses a powerful musical divide. From one aspect it violates a sense of values, as well as being perceived to be crude. Going in the other direction, orchestral arrangements of classic rock songs invariably sound pompous and grandiose. This is partly because the musical material itself isn't adequate to being transferred across; there aren't enough ideas in the music itself. An arranger of a rock song for an orchestra is faced with the prospect of writing new parts to give the greater number of instruments something to do. The trouble is those parts are not in the original. It is a bit like blowing up family snapshots to 70mm cinematic Technicolor; all the graininess is revealed.

Even within popular music, covers invariably raise interesting questions of arrangement, which is why it is a good move compare cover versions by different artists. This is briefly discussed in **Section Eight**. Bruce Springsteen recently recorded *The Pete Seeger Sessions*, and Bryan Ferry has released a set of Dylan covers. A few years ago there was a whole album of versions of 'Stairway To Heaven', and other Led Zeppelin songs were covered on a CD called *Encomium*. Mojo magazine in the UK often gives away a CD of cover versions of songs by a famous artist or band, so these are worth hunting down. In July 2006 *Mojo* had 15 musicians make a cover version of the entire Beatles album *Revolver* and in March 2007 did the same thing to the *Sgt.Pepper* album.

Sometimes bands cover themselves by releasing an alternate version of a song. Bruce Springsteen does some songs with a band or acoustic or on piano. It is common for bands to put out acoustic versions of their songs or to release demo versions that can then be compared to the final version. One of the leaders in this field is Pete Townshend, who has released many of his demos for Who songs over the years. Doing acoustic versions of songs has become something of a career move, as much as the time-honoured '*Greatest Hits*' or live album. MTV *Unplugged* was a whole series of shows based on the idea of re-arranging songs acoustically. In each case, comparing versions or re-mixes is a good way to learn about the effect of arrangement decisions.

Having reviewed these important general issues it is time to look at some precise basic concepts that apply every time you do an arrangement.

SECTION 2

Basic concepts

To make your arrangements work you need to understand the concept of musical parts. The most important aspects of any part are the contributions it makes to a song's melody, harmony, and rhythm. And having learned to work with the individual strands in your music, you can begin to bring them together, using a number of basic arrangement strategies.

If you have some experience writing and recording songs, you may have already applied some of the following ideas. But it is still important to reflect on them. Their relevance varies from song to song and will be affected by the style of music. In this section we look at two concepts: the idea of a 'part' as a musical event with a number of characteristics, and basic arrangement strategy.

In an arrangement there are many 'parts' – musical events that contribute to the whole song, originating from the lead vocal or the instruments. Each such part possesses a number of qualities. When arranging and mixing you need to be able to check a part for all of these criteria. A part has, or can have:

- A melodic value.
- A harmonic value.
- A rhythmic value.
- Duration.
- Timbre.
- Volume.
- Dynamic profile.
- Presence.
- Symbolic identity.
- Stereo position.

UNDERSTANDING PARTS

It is important to understand the value of the characteristics of individual musical parts, to develop the ability to listen for them and then to compare them when several parts sound together. This is especially important at the mixing stage. Some of these values may clash and that in itself may make an arrangement less effective than it might have been. Let's look at these ten features in more detail.

Remember the first three – melodic value, harmonic value, rhythmic value – by the formula M-H-R. These are the most important of the ten. M-H-R means that an instrumental part in an arrangement has the potential to contribute melody, harmony and/or rhythm. Some instruments naturally possess or express more of one of these qualities than the others. Instruments in an arrangement can also make secondary contributions to to increase the musical content.

- Primarily melodic parts would be provided by lead vocals, lead guitar, and solo instruments

- Primarily harmonic parts come from keyboards and rhythm guitars, sustained string chords, brass chords, etc.
- Primarily rhythmic parts come from drums and percussion.
- Bass guitar has a harmonic role and a rhythmic role, and can also supply melodic interest, as when the bass-line contributes a hook or follows part of the vocal melody.

Let us deal with each part of the M-H-R formula in turn.

Melodic value

An instrumental part has pitch, meaning it is at any moment one of the 12 notes, whether in a low, middle or high octave. In so far as it draws our attention because of the way it moves through a series of pitches, it may have melodic interest. It could be a phrase that we whistle or hum. Even if it is an instrument, not vocals, it can be what is known in music as a 'voice' – a line of single notes following a melodic contour. If this melodic line imitated the actual vocal line then it would reinforce it. This happens when a vocal melody is doubled an octave above the singer by flute or strings. If it is doing something different to the vocals it adds melodic interest. The number of independent melodic parts in a song has a clear bearing on the appeal of the arrangement. An arrangement that features a solo voice over strummed guitar or quarter-note piano chords has one melodic line – the sung melody – and a harmonic 'pad' underneath. It may lack interest because there are no other melodic parts. If added, a solo violin or a harmonica could bring in a second melodic part.

It is possible for an arrangement to have no purely harmonic instruments – ie, no guitars or keyboards – playing full chords. Instead a number of purely melodic lines can suggest the chords even as they start, stop, and follow their individual melodic contours. All contrapuntal music, most notably four-part vocal singing, demonstrates this principle. It is a magical effect, because the musical texture is saturated with melodic direction. Each beat heard vertically is harmonic, ie, makes a chord out of four single notes, but each beat is also melodic, in so far as each line heard horizontally constitutes a melody. This is an under-used texture in popular music. So:

- Supporting parts can double sections of the main vocal melody. This will strengthen it.
- They can also add melodic interest either by functioning as a counter-melody or by creating small independent melody ideas of their own.
- When you perform an overdub, don't just think about whether the notes fit the chord at that point, think about the melodic shape of what you are adding.
- Melody is one of the most memorable aspects of music. In many ways, it is the soul of music. If you want people to remember your songs, melody is the most potent way to do it.

An arrangement will also have a hierarchy of pitches, going from the lowest note (probably in the bass or piano left hand) to the highest. Keep track of where an instrument will fit in this hierarchy. The higher a note the more it will call attention to itself, other factors being equal. During mixing the pitch hierarchy has to be taken into account when balancing the volume of individual parts.

Harmonic value

The pitch of an instrumental part also has another function beyond the melodic. It contributes to the harmony, the chords that underlie the melody at any given point. Although a melody can work unharmonized (as in unaccompanied folk songs) this is rare in popular music. Most people accustomed to harmonized music find a single melody line uninteresting and slightly colourless. When it does happen, it is only in short bursts, perhaps as an intro or in a link section. Dropping back to a single unaccompanied voice can be poignant if it happens after a loud passage. This is why, after the massed power of the last verse, Led Zeppelin chose to end 'Stairway To Heaven' with Robert Plant on his own singing one line of lyric.

A single note, or two notes struck together, has an implicit harmonic value, because without being a full chord such a part will fit with other parts that are full chords. Some parts are explicitly harmonic, namely any instrument which is playing a full chord. The commonest instruments for this task are strummed acoustic and electric guitars, and keyboards such as piano, organ, and some types of synthesizer.

When you first write a song you will probably sing the tune and play block chords underneath. You select chords that flow nicely together and lend an attractive colour to the melody. Remember that any melody note is capable of being plausibly harmonized by at least half a dozen chords, of which at least three will be simple major or minor and in key. Take the note C. It can be harmonized with the chords of C and C minor (as a root note), A minor and A♭ (as a third), and F and F minor (as a fifth). It also occurs in Dm7 and D♭maj7 (as a seventh), B♭sus2 and B♭add9 (as a second/ninth), Gsus4 (as a fourth), and E♭6 (as a sixth).

Another way to realize the power of harmony is to make up a tune over the chords D, G and A (play them in whatever time/bars you wish) and then substitute the chords B minor, E minor and F♯ minor. The melody sounds different with this exclusively minor harmony. Even at a late stage in a recording there is always the opportunity to change a chord to bring a different nuance into a tune. For more detailed information on this see my book *Melody*.

A major or minor chord has only three notes, however many times they are doubled or trebled in an arrangement. (A seventh chord would need a fourth note, a ninth chord a fifth, etc). Once these three notes sound, whether on one instrument or several, that's all you need to establish the harmony for that chord. Of course, the arrangement may not sound full enough, and these three notes may need to be played by many instruments in many different octaves. Guitar chords do this to get more volume and a fuller sound. So an open-string G chord comprises the pitches G B D G B G – three Gs, 2 Bs and a D – and a common way of playing G on the piano would have G D in the left hand and G B D in the right hand an octave higher. But the basic harmony of the bar or bars in which this G chord is heard is unchanged. As long as there is a single G, B and D, we know what the chord is.

This fact has interesting implications for an arrangement. It means that minimal parts can still make a harmonically complete picture. It means that, for example, a complete chord can be sounded by:

- A voice and a bass guitar playing two notes.
- A voice, a bass guitar, and a guitar playing one note.
- Three voices.
- Two guitars and a bass, each playing one note.

There may be times in a song when you want to strip things back this far. This might be to portray something in the lyric, or to refresh the listener's ear after a particularly dense passage that featured many instruments.

Understanding this concept – three notes make a chord – means you know that you can subtract chording instruments like strummed guitars and keyboards from an arrangement/mix without losing the harmony, because the few parts that are left (including a vocal) may imply the missing chords. This is an excellent way to:

- Get 'air' into a mix.
- Make a verse sound different to the others.
- Create an alternate mix of a song that has a viable identity of its own.

If all the chording instruments, with the exception of his acoustic guitar, were mixed out of Dylan's 'Like A Rolling Stone', it would sound quite different. You can even use this technique as part of the arranging process, to find the best way of presenting the song.

Step one: put on the usual strummed chords, possibly doubled on guitar or keyboards, along with bass and drums.
Step two: overdub individual parts with other instruments, including lead guitar, or backing vocals – anything that has a melodic line.
Step three: add a guide lead vocal.
Step four: now mix out all the chording instruments and listen to the result.

Maybe you need them back; maybe you don't. Maybe something more imaginative than strummed acoustic guitar can go into that space.

Listen again to the lead vocal. Is it taking advantage of the harmonic space created by a radically thinned-out chord texture. If you change some of the phrases could they allude to those now absent chords? Would that be better?

Rhythmic value

The rhythm of a song is most obviously expressed through percussion and drums, assisted by the bass guitar in its rhythmic function. How important the rhythmic aspect is in an arrangement varies from one genre to another. If this is a song people will relax and listen to it may be that the melodic and harmonic elements are more important. If it is a head-banging hard rocker or a dance cut then the rhythm is going to be paramount.

Upper parts in guitar and other instruments can also be shaped and phrased so that they too have rhythm or contribute to the over-riding rhythm. Many 1960s Motown and soul tracks feature a high guitar chord played rigidly on the second and fourth beats, in time with the snare drum and other percussive effects such as handclaps or tambourine.

This element of rhythm can also be present in the lead vocal, but some singers are more naturally rhythmic in their phrasing than others who are tuned into the harmonic and melodic value of their notes. Think of the clipped and accented way Michael Jackson sang in the 1980s on songs like 'Billie Jean'; each phrase was peppered with a sequence of gasps and half-stifled cries. And his melodies and the syllables of the lyric were stuttered as though they were an extension of the percussion.

When a part is working well melodically and harmonically, consider whether it can contribute anything to the rhythm of the track. To do this it is especially important to think about the rhythmic effect of any strummed or block chord parts. These may well lack a distinctive rhythmic identity – so make them count for more by giving them one.

Think also about what the drums and percussion are doing. This will emphasize the beat and create space for other things. Check how many instruments you have that are sustaining sounds – sustain supports the harmonic function in an arrangement but it does nothing for the rhythm. The blander the song the less rhythm you will find in it, and the greater number of smooth sustained sounds.

In a band like The Who, the reason why so many of the songs sound powerful is that Pete Townshend's rhythm guitar chords were usually hit with great rhythmic accent. The same is true of Jimmy Page's acoustic guitar work with Led Zeppelin. Even when the band played acoustically the songs retained a certain intensity.

A useful exercise is to construct an arrangement that makes paramount the rhythmic value of everything. That is a good way to sharpen your ears to the effect of rhythm. It takes practice to be able to stop listening to the melodic and harmonic elements of parts and temporarily hear them only as rhythmic gestures.

Hear the whole arrangement/mix as a tapestry of interlocking rhythms and then you can decide if it is coherent or whether some parts are detracting from others by setting up unwelcome cross-rhythms. Some cross-rhythms are great and add to the sophistication of a track, but the effect needs to be monitored. A recording to study from this angle is The Police's 'Spirits In The Material World', especially the synth line part going into the last verse.

Not surprisingly, rhythm & blues and funk artists like James Brown and Funkadelic provide examples of arrangements where rhythmic elements are dominant. Much of that is felt through the drums, percussion, and bass, with guitar and brass stabs. But it can be more instructive to find this in music that is not primarily for dancing.

CASE STUDY

ELVIS COSTELLO AND THE ATTRACTIONS

Many of the songs on Elvis Costello's *Armed Forces* (1979) album, in particular 'Senior Service' and 'Busy Bodies', show how rhythmic patterns between the parts can be sharply contrasted through disciplined part-playing. In connection with arrangement technique, it is interesting to note that The Attractions scrapped their first attempt to record *Armed Forces* because they thought the arrangements sounded too much like a band called The Jags, who The Attractions felt were imitating their sound on the previous album, the new-wave guitar-driven *This Year's Model*. Part of the change that solved this arrangement problem was a greater role for the keyboards and a smaller one for Elvis' guitar. The band's gift for handling any number of arrangement styles was later illustrated on the soul homage LP *Get Happy* (which includes 'Temptation', a fabulous imitation of Booker T And The MGs' 'Green Onions') and the country album *Almost Blue*.

A common rhythmic fault in arrangements is when, at a chord change, one part is syncopated and another isn't. An instance would be where a guitar chord is hit on the off-beat of the fourth beat of a bar, just before the bar-line, supported by a bass guitar note, but the kick-drum misses this by an eighth-note and is hit on the first beat of the next bar. The kick-drum is not supporting the syncopation, and the effect is rhythmically muddy. A second problem occurs when the bass-line runs across the kick-drum rhythm, or where another instrument like piano is also playing a bass-line in the same low register as the bass guitar.

Confusion among parts naturally arises when the parts develop from the players improvising instead of being worked out in notation in advance of a recording session, as was the case in big band and jazz recordings in the 1940s and 1950s, and in 1960s pop sessions using session musicians and orchestral players. There is nothing wrong with developing parts from improvising along with the multitrack or in rehearsal. But the producer – which may be you – must check that a guitarist coming up with what seems like a good idea for a part hasn't cluttered the overall sound.

A notorious example of a part cluttering the arrangement is the inconsistent use of a suspended fourth chord in a mix. Here's how the problem grows:

Step one: guitarists play chords like Asus4, Dsus4, Esus4, quite casually, to add tension and colour. Given four bars of D to play, they find it tempting to add the little finger and introduce a few Dsus4 chords.
Step two: a second guitar is overdubbed and more Dsus4s are introduced, but not in exactly the same places as guitar one used them.
Step three: a keyboard part is added which is a D major chord. The F♯ of this chord clashes with the G in the Dsus4.

Step four: then a melody line is added in a solo instrument and it too has F♯ notes that clash with the Dsus4 chords.

This is a headache, because unpicking this means deciding all over again where the chord will be a sus4 and where not, and making sure that every part agrees. So if you have a suspended fourth chord in *one* of the harmony instruments, make sure all the others have it at that point too. This also applies to the other suspended chord, the second (Asus2, Dsus2, Esus2, etc), though the effect there is not as muddy.

Duration

Having described the M-H-R elements, let's continue down the list. At any given moment a part's notes have a typical duration, varying from very short notes (staccato) to smooth, sustained notes given their full time value (legato). This characteristic is related to rhythm but is not quite the same. Be conscious of which instruments are doing short, long, or something in between.

Changing the rhythmic value of notes in a part can make a big difference to the final effect. There is a telling moment on the recording of 'God Only Knows', captured on The Beach Boys' *The Pet Sounds Sessions*, where one of the musicians suggests to Brian Wilson that the horn motif at just past the one minute mark, where the bridge starts, be played *staccato* (ie, cut off) not *legato* (smooth). This fixes the problem of the loss of energy in the arrangement at this junction, provides a moment of drama after two verses and two hook-lines, and becomes an integral part of the final recording.

Timbre

The timbre of an instrument is part of its individual tone. A strummed 12-string guitar has a light, breezy, rustling metallic sheen that is different to the sound of a six-string guitar. A saxophone has a breathy, velvet quality different in turn from that of a flute. A double bass gives a bass-line a different timbre to a roundwound-strung electric bass. The very high notes on a piano have a percussive, tinkling quality not possessed by notes in the middle of the keyboard. Developing an ear for timbre will enable you to create various combinations of instrumental sound, even within the same instrument family – such as recording a single-coil pick-up electric alongside a guitar with double-coil pickups.

Timbre can be broadly described by descriptive terms such as soft/hard, rough/smooth, clean/distorted, short/sustained, and clear/muted. It is also affected by the way in which an instrument is recorded, whether through an amp, or a microphone, an effects unit, or by direct input into a mixing desk.

Volume

The volume of an instrumental part has two elements: the volume at which the part was initially recorded and the volume it will have in the final mix. The latter can be varied as much as you like, but the former itself will give the part a certain character.

Dynamics

The dynamic of an instrumental part is a feature of the manner in which it was played and is related to expression. This is not the same as volume, which can be altered on a mixing desk. A loud electric guitar played dynamically remains so no matter how much you push it into the background of a mix. So if you are recording a gentle ballad the dynamic of such an electric guitar part may still sound wrong even when it is reduced in volume. You will hear the strings twang and resonate in a way that they wouldn't if they were struck less dynamically. Some instruments change their timbre when they are hit harder, or blown harder.

Presence

The presence of an instrumental part means how often it is audibly present in an arrangement and how much attention it draws to itself. This will also involve what effect it has on an arrangement when it is removed. This sense of presence is also connected with an instrument's symbolic identity.

Symbolic identity

This concept was initially described in the general discussion in **Section One**. It includes the genre associations of an instrument – saxophones for jazz and sophistication, certain organ sounds for gospel/'churchy', nylon guitar for Latin passion/sincerity. Recording an MOR ballad for a veteran crooner you will probably want to avoid a grunge/metal electric guitar sound, just as vibraphone might sound a bit too cocktail-lounge for a punk group.

It isn't that there is anything inherently wrong with any of these instruments, only that in the wider culture and market-place they have acquired certain connotations. It is very difficult for one recording to change these, so when arranging be sensitive to these public connotations of an instrument and whether these carry images that you want to evoke. Some instruments have sentimental associations that might hamper a song, such as Irish or South American pipes, which have, through no fault of their own, kitsch folk and New Age associations. Steel drums evoke the Caribbean. Simon and Garfunkel could put pan pipes on 'El Condor Pasa' back in the late 1960s and it was original. Do this now and you risk your song sounding as though it was sponsored by the Paraguay Tourist Board (not that this stopped The Darkness for the intro to 'One Way Ticket').

Stereo position

In a mix an instrumental part is given a position somewhere in the 180 degree stereo image that stretches from far left through centre to far right. This placing will influence how it blends with, or stands out from, the other parts. Good stereo positioning of a part will help contrast its rhythm, pitch, and timbre with the others. For example, it would make no sense to put all the melodic single-line parts on one side and all the harmonic chordal parts on the other. The guidelines are explained in **Section Eight** on mixing.

BASIC ARRANGEMENT STRATEGIES

Now you have a sense of how a single part within an arrangement can have a melodic value, a harmonic value, a rhythmic value, duration, timbre, volume, dynamics, presence, symbolic identity, and stereo position. Not all of these are equally important or relevant in a given song, but it is worthwhile to know that they have a potential role in an arrangement. The better you are at thinking these issues through *before* you start recording, the faster the recording process and the easier the song will be to mix. If you find yourself taking a lot of time over a mix it may be there is a fault with the arrangement that could have been avoided earlier.

Turning from instrumental parts to the overall effect of an arrangement, it is possible to identify eight basic arrangement strategies. These are subject to variation but are useful generalizations. The majority of the songs you have heard fall into one or other of these. I have identified the eight as:

- Minimal.
- Reproducible.
- Maximal.
- Steady-state.
- Cumulative/subtractive.
- Stepped.
- Dynamic contrast.
- Unplugged/plugged.

These categories say something about the way an arrangement is shaped, how and when the instruments are deployed and to what overall intent.

Minimal arrangement

A minimal arrangement is one in which not only are there very few instruments but they are also played in a minimal style. There is a sense of restraint. Minimal arrangements operate on a 'less is more' attitude, and are not afraid of leaving space in the music. There is often a good use of tension between the music and the spaces where there is less happening. Norah Jones' 'Come Away With Me' is a good example. Tracy Chapman's eponymous debut (1988) featured the singer doing vocals and acoustic guitar live over a rhythm section of bass and drums. The vocals and guitar of Nick Drake's *Pink Moon* (1972) were recorded in two sessions. Bruce Springsteen's *Nebraska* (1982) was made on a 4-track with guitars, harmonica and vocals. David Essex's 'Rock On' was carried mostly by a loud bass-line, vocals, backing vocals, and occasional flickers of strings, and was a very unorthodox adventurous arrangement for a hit single. Other good examples include Fleetwood Mac's 'Songbird' (Christine McVie with piano), 'Landslide' (Stevie Nicks and guitars) and Jeff Buckley's 'Hallelujah'.

One current band whose arrangements are often minimal in instrumentation is The White Stripes, many of whose tracks are cut with vocals, guitar, and drums, and without the bass guitar that would normally glue the rhythm to the foundation of the harmony. Behind their approach lies a certain view of songwriting. Jack White told *Interview* magazine in 2003, 'Songwriting is storytelling, melody, and rhythm, those three components. If you break it down but you keep the three components, then you have what songwriting really is, without excess and overthinking.' Don't forget that in 1993 producer Rick Rubin recorded Johnny Cash singing to his own acoustic guitar accompaniment and 11 of the tracks were released as *American Recordings*.

Oddly enough, a minimal arrangement style can make you more creative than if you had more options. Rock history is littered with bands who disappeared into 48-track high-tech studios for years of overdubbing, only to finish with a record that couldn't match its predecessor, recorded in a fortnight on an 8-track. As Jack White put it, 'Having a huge budget or unlimited time or tracks to make an album, all that opportunity robs you of a lot of creativity, because you're not focused or confined. We purposefully confined ourselves to help us be more focused.' So although minimal arrangements can seem confined they force you to be more creative with what you have. They can also encourage writers to put more creative effort into the song's melody, harmony, and lyric. While it is true that some songs depend on an elaborate arrangement, there is some truth in the adage that says a good song stands out even if played on acoustic guitar or piano.

Even if your entire song is not going to be arranged minimally, it is essential to know how and when to apply the minimal approach to one section of a song. The commonest section to which this is applied is the bridge/middle eight or last verse. The easiest way to achieve it is to pull out the drums and possibly any electric instruments, and/or reduce the number of instruments providing harmony to one. This puts dynamic contrast into an arrangement, refreshing the arrangement, and making the next full section sound even more exciting. Another approach is to arrange the first verse as lightly as you can, as Lenny Kravitz did with 'Fly Away', which has lead vocal, wah-wah slap bass, and drums.

Minimal arrangement allows the voice (and lyrics) to come through clearly – singers feel the benefit of such passages during a gig because they can sing with less force as the band are not playing loudly. If an audience gets involved with a riff delivered with sparse playing it will really get excited when you perform it on full power. Bars of minimal playing at lower dynamic levels let the band play at a quieter dynamic, which makes the next full-on section more dramatic.

CASE STUDY

THE ZUTONS

The currently successful band The Zutons have sections of minimal arrangements in many of their songs. There are stretches where the mix consists only of a vocal, possibly backing vocals, bass, and/or guitar playing the same note, and light percussion such as a hi-hat.

- **'You Will You Won't' begins with only with vocal and drums.**
- **'Confusion' starts with a solo bass guitar, then moves to a verse with vocal and acoustic guitar.**

- 'Nightmare Part III' has opening lines with only bass, drums, and vocal.
- 'Tired Of Hanging Around' sets the first lines of its verse to drums, bass, vocal, and one high guitar part; its chorus is by contrast much fuller.

The first two verses of 'Someone Watching Over Me' are stripped back to single piano notes and melody, with no-one explicitly stating the harmony. The combination of the root note of the implied chords (played on bass, piano, or guitar) with a melody can effectively suggest the three notes of the chord. Imagine a few bars where the implied chord is A minor. If the bass has an A note and the melody starts on a C and rises to an E via a passing note D, this includes the notes A-C-E of the chord of A minor, even if no-one is actually playing that chord.

CASE STUDY

GREEN DAY

Similar examples can be found in a three-piece band like Green Day.

- On 'Pop Rock & Coke' the electric guitars are held back until verse two.
- There are no guitars on the first verse of 'Longview', just a tom-tom drum intro, then bass, then vocal, and the guitars only in immediately before the chorus.
- Verse one of 'She' is drums and bass only.
- The band often use a complete moment of silence where the vocal hook goes – like the title of a song as with 'Welcome To Paradise' and 'When I Come Around'. (Think of the way Kurt Cobain's 'yaaay' cuts through at the end of the chorus of Nirvana's 'Smells Like Teen Spirit'.)

CASE STUDY

THE POLICE

The Police were exceptional at handling space and doing minimal arrangements. Rock trios have to come to terms with having only three people to make some sound. Most approach this by either playing lots of notes and/or by turning everything up to 11 and playing fast (like Motorhead, who also had a singing bassist). The Police went the opposite way and made the musical space inherent in the trio instrumentation for them. This partly arose because of the 'new wave'/reggae axis where the band started. The 'new wave' influence meant that the band focused on short songs, which freed Andy Summers from any obligation to play meandering guitar solos. The reggae influence demanded that for the sake of the rhythm space be left in the music.

Summers' Telecaster chords were stretched out by judicious amounts of chorus, echo, and reverb. Summers experimented playing chords and letting them ring. Sting was a disciplined bassist who could strip his parts down to the minimum. In Copeland the Police had an inventive drummer who could set up intricate cross-rhythms to add sparkle in the percussion and who realised that there could be rhythmic life beyond hitting the snare on beats two and four. There are few moments so rhythmically complex in pop music as the last verse of 'Spirits in the Material World', and the live 'Tea In The Sahara' shows an extraordinary command of musical space typical of the Police at their best.

Reproducible arrangement

> ***"It had to sound like four guys just playing in a room again ... We are a rock'n'roll band, and it just feels kind of logical to turn the amps up and get the drum kit out and bash away."***
>
> Peter Buck on R.E.M.'s approach to recording *Monster*

A reproducible arrangement is one you can replicate live. This need not mean it has to be recorded live in the studio, but it must be simple enough for your band line-up to play it and not miss out important parts. A good recent example would be The Red Hot Chili Peppers' 'Californication'. Much of the song is played by the band's basic line-up of drums, bass, voice, and a clean-toned electric. Apart from this core performance, there are only chorus harmony vocals (presumably duplicated live), a high-pitched soft keyboard pad, and an overdubbed guitar solo. So when the band recorded the song they knew that played live it would sound close to the studio version.

It is common for rock bands to record debut albums based on their current live-set and to keep the overdubs minimal, as with the debut albums by Led Zeppelin, Van Halen, The Jam, and Living Colour's *Vivid*. The Spin Doctors' 'Two Princes' is a good example of a track that is a reproducible arrangement, with only the guitar being overdubbed; the main guitar is stereo. As bands make further albums and develop their studio vision, reproducing their studio sound live gets harder. For some the solution is to tour with hired musicians, or to have backing tracks for some of the parts.

The current technology to do this is more reliable than in the past when bands played live with analogue tapes – a thing attempted by The Who in the early 1970s with *Quadrophenia*. But equipment can fail, and some bands feel their style is cramped by playing along with a backing that has a fixed tempo and no room for improvisation or fluffed cues.

CASE STUDY

RAZORLIGHT

An example of a reproducible sound would be Razorlight's debut album *Up All Night* (2004). The band are post-millennium indie/alt rock with something of a 1970s American new-wave influence. The basic tracks were cut live in the studio and overdubs seem to be minimal. The advantage of this is that with just two guitars in the band they can duplicate their studio sound live. It also leaves plenty of space for enriching the music on later albums. Even so, the songs of *Up All Night* have some nice arrangement touches. For example, Razorlight have a feel for the poetry possible with two fairly clean electric guitars – one doing chords, the other broken chords.

Maximal arrangement

In a maximal arrangement the prime ambition is to make an epic sound. You want a production that will sound huge. No instruments are inherently off-limits. Billy Corgan of Smashing Pumpkins said he liked to go for the "big, grand picture" in sonic terms, and this meant doing many overdubs.

You can hear the fruit of his admiration for Boston and Queen (*Queen II* is one of his favourite albums). Parts of *Siamese Dream* have 20 or 30 guitar overdubs on them. This has been a less fashionable approach in recent years, where rock has been dominated by an amateur/garage ethos that associates the fragmentary with the authentic and cool, and the more polished and arranged with the inauthentic.

The technical question is how to achieve a maximal arrangement with the instruments you have. There's more to a big sound than meets the eye. Don't merely double or treble with the same guitar, always try to find one with a different timbre. If you are recording multiple guitar tracks change the guitar/amp setting each time, and/or change the chord positions. This is touched on in **Section Three**. It is possible to create a big sound without having lots of instruments. Many groups discover in the studio that, contrary to expectations, 15 guitars hammering a riff doesn't sound 15 times better than one playing it.

Maximal arrangements/productions that go beyond just a rock instrument line-up include George Harrison's 'What Is Life' and 'My Sweet Lord', The Beatles' 'All You Need Is Love', Barry Ryan's 'Eloise', Martha Reeves And The Vandellas' 'Dancing In The Street', David Bowie's 'Life On Mars', The Righteous Brothers' 'You've Lost That Lovin' Feeling', The Walker Brothers' 'Make It Easy On Yourself', Wizzard's 'Ball Park Incident', Dusty Springfield's 'I Only Want To Be With You', and Mercury Rev's 'Holes'.

CASE STUDY

PHIL SPECTOR'S WALL OF SOUND

The founding father of the maximal arrangement in popular music was Mr Wall Of Sound, Phil Spector, whose early 1960s productions for the likes of The Ronettes, The Crystals, and Ike and Tina Turner (especially 'River Deep Mountain High') were hugely influential on artists like The Beach Boys and The Beatles. His method for getting a big sound relied on two basic elements: the first was deploying the maximum number of musicians he could cram into the studio. This was because in those days there was very little opportunity for multitracking. Individual parts, such as a bass-line or chording, would be doubled or trebled by players. Second, the production also made judicious use of an echo chamber. In later times, as multitracking increased, a small group of musicians, such as a four-piece rock band, could emulate a big production themselves by recording more parts. However, the more parts in an arrangement the more care has to be taken so they don't get in the way of each other, and the more complex the mix will be.

Steady-state arrangement

A 'steady state' arrangement is one in which instrument profile and dynamics stay fairly constant throughout. This may be chosen because the genre of music does not require or expect sudden changes of level or contrasting sections. It may be chosen because the real focus of the song is the lyric and nothing is done to change this. Such a description can make the 'steady state' arrangement sound bland, but it is possible to make it generate tension. One example would be Thin Lizzy's 'The Sun Goes Down' where there is a driving bass line over a minimal drum pattern with an insistent quarter-note side-stick beat. Over the top are guitar triads and some sustained synth lines. The listener is made to feel that something dramatic is about to happen and it never does. Another instance would be Bob Dylan's 'Knocking On Heaven's Door', where the steady-state arrangement enacts the lyric's sense of defeat. Other examples include The Verve's 'This Time', The Smiths' 'How Soon Is Now', and David Gray's 'Come Away With Me Honey'.

Cumulative/subtractive

A cumulative arrangement is one where the song grows and expands as it proceeds. This will make each verse and chorus slightly stronger than the previous one. It is a satisfying strategy because it builds all the time to a climax; we sense that the most exciting part will be heard toward or at the end. We wait in growing suspense and if the song is a good one the wait will prove to have been worthwhile. It is by far the commonest arrangement approach, and in fact acts as a default for record producing. The cumulative effect can be achieved by various means such as:

- Introducing new chords or a greater rate of chord change.
- Moving toward a key change.
- Adding more instruments.
- Adding electric instruments on top of acoustic.
- Making the melody higher in pitch.
- Making the vocal style more forceful.
- Widening the pitch range, from lowest note to highest.
- Increasing the overall dynamic level.
- Making the beat/percussion more persistent.
- Increasing the tempo.

A good example of a cumulative arrangement is Gene's 'Olympian', about which singer Martin Rossiter said, "The idea with 'Olympian' was to have a theme and variations. We'd probably have executed it better now. I think it's well enough done to work at that length. It still raised a few hairs. I like the repetition. There are eight cycles, three low, four high and one to drop down to give a sense of restraint. We don't need to invest in every rock cliché. The dynamics in pop can often lack a little grace. You know, pianissimo [very soft] one second and fortissimo [loud] the next."

CASE STUDY

CASE STUDY: U2'S 'WITH OR WITHOUT YOU'

U2's 'With Or Without You' is a fine cumulative arrangement, demonstrating that even at the height of their stadium phase the band's sense of arrangement was ahead of most bands. It has a repetitive chord progression that is treated to a dynamic in which the song starts quiet and slowly builds to a roaring climax at about 3.03, dies away, and then has a partial recovery. It has an arch form that is greater than the individual verses and choruses.

In 1987 The Edge told *Guitarist*, "I now see that one of the great things is being able to do something original within a cliché." To appreciate the skill of this arrangement, first look at the musical building blocks. When it is not hovering on a D chord, 'With Or Without You' comprises a single four-bar sequence of D-A-B minor-G (I V VI IV). But at no time are the four chords fully articulated. Most bands would have had a couple of acoustic guitars strumming their way through these changes. U2 avoid this. Instead the chords are implied in the musical space between the bass root notes and The Edge's guitar parts – none of which are straightforward full chords.

A song can have an overall structure as well as a specific one made up of traditional sections. Over-arching form and cumulative arrangement go well together. You have to decide that there is one special point to which in some way the song will build. This is what even disparate songs such as

Frank Sinatra's 'My Way', Jefferson Airplane's 'White Rabbit', Pink Floyd's 'Careful With That Axe, Eugene', Radiohead's 'Creep' and 'There There' have in common. In 'Stairway To Heaven', rock music's greatest example of cumulative arrangement, the first climactic moment is reached on the D chord at the start of the fanfare section, immediately before the guitar solo, the second is at the end of the solo, and the third when Robert Plant hits the high held note on 'roll'.

On a smaller scale, the idea of proceeding by accumulation applies to shorter sections within a song, especially the intro, bridge and the coda. Jefferson Airplane's 'She Has Funny Cars' has a cumulative intro in which drums, maracas, guitar, bass, second guitar and finally vocals enter one after another.

By contrast the subtractive arrangement is a rare form, in which a song starts at its maximum state of expansion and gradually thins out. It can be achieved by:

- Slowing the tempo.
- Removing instruments from the mix.
- Heading from maximal to minimal within a single arrangement.

It is difficult to do, and anti-commercial in so far as it disappoints the listener's expectation that a song will build toward a conclusion, not move away from it. A less severe version is where a coda is noticeably quieter after the song has built toward a climactic final chorus. The challenge is to avoid a sense of artistic anti-climax even if the arrangement has deliberately avoided a sonic climax. If not the stuff of which hit singles are made or exciting live tracks, nevertheless it does have artistic possibilities. If you have a lyric about a romance that starts promisingly but slowly unravels, or about a situation in life where it feels you took a turn that seemed right only to find that the road peters out in the middle of nowhere, this arrangement strategy might work.

Cumulative or subtractive arrangements can also be created by large-scale graduated increases and decreases in speed. In an age of click tracks, the eminently musical arts of the localized accelerando and rallentando – speeding up slightly and slowing down slightly at transition points – are often forgotten. These devices can also be employed through whole sections as part of the structure of a song. Siouxsie and The Banshees songs like 'Pull To Bits' and 'Voodoo Doll' are good examples.

Stepped arrangement

A stepped arrangement is one in which a song uses two or three sections which are each identifiable by their contrasted dynamic level and instrumentation. The song alternates between these, stepping up into one and back down into the previous. This is similar to the dynamic contrast but not as forceful. The Yardbirds' 'For Your Love' is a good example from the mid-1960s, with its minor key verse dominated by the incongruous juxtaposition of harpsichord and bongos, and its rock'n'roll bridge in a major key. It could also be done in such a way that a song has a single stand-out section that is markedly different to the rest.

CASE STUDY

TRACY CHAPMAN'S 'FAST CAR'

Another example of this kind of stepped arrangement is Tracy Chapman's 1980s hit 'Fast Car'. The verses feature acoustic guitar and bass; the choruses are given a mild lift by the full drum-kit entering, with the acoustic guitar changing to strumming chords. The emphasis of the song is on the narrative lyric, to which the delicate two-bar acoustic guitar riff provides a mildly hypnotic accompaniment. The verses with their subdued dynamic level create tension.

This type of arrangement can also go in waves, as in the case of The Beatles' 'No Reply' where the title phrase is sung with greater emphasis and louder acoustic guitar chords, but the song itself keeps sinking back to the earlier dynamic level.

Dynamic contrast

The intention of a dynamic contrast arrangement is to create a musical shock, usually by a sudden switch of volume level and intensity, far beyond what you would get from a stepped arrangement. This is contrast with a capital D for Deafening. The entire arrangement is constructed around this moment. Drums are central in achieving the requisite change of intensity. The drum entrances on Phil Collins' 'In The Air Tonight' and Kate Bush's 'Leave It Open' are typical ways of creating this effect. It will then be a matter of how many times this happens in the song.

A good example is Fleetwood Mac's early hit 'Man Of The World' which proceeds as a quiet ballad until when it hits an F♯ minor and E minor chord and the drums come in. Bad Company's 'Feel Like Makin' Love' contrasts a loose, relaxed country feel in the verses with a more headbanging riff-based chorus. The Who's 'Behind Blue Eyes' has several verses and choruses of bass, vocal, acoustic guitar, and block harmony backing vocals, before erupting into a typically explosive Who bridge. Coldplay's 'Yellow' has moderate contrasts between sections. You can hear it in a commercial form on Wheatus's 'Teenage Dirtbag' where the heavy guitars are retained for the chorus, and in the violent contrasts of Sum 41's 'Fat Lip' where at 1:40 the arrangement thins out to a vocal singing 'Don't count on me', over a picked clean electric guitar, until 2:00 when there is a massively loud re-entry. Radiohead's '2+2=5' and 'Paranoid Android' both have huge and explosive shifts in volume and intensity. For this arrangement style listen also to The Pixies' *Surfer Rosa* (1988) and Slint's 1991 album *Spiderland*.

CASE STUDY

NIRVANA

Grunge made frequent use of dynamic contrasts, nowhere more so than Nirvana's 'Smells Like Teen Spirit'. It is worth revisiting because it was the song that popularized the arrangement trick of extreme dynamic contrast. The song goes from loud and thick to soft and sparse, and back again. During verse one Cobain sings over a bass line that is still playing the roots of the chords from the riff (one way to get more mileage out of a chord sequence). On the verse the chords are implied, not stated. The guitar plays only two notes (a fourth, C-F). Each chorus erupts with distorted multitracked guitars. 'Lithium' is another example of a song with quiet verses – bass and voice, or minimal guitar and voice – and wall-of-noise choruses.

One point to make about this quiet verse/loud chorus arrangement approach is that it naturally suits a power trio. When you have three instruments, only two of which are generating notes, you have to find a way to get some variety into the sound. Power trios are largely defined by their tolerance of, and way of dealing with, 'holes' in the live mix. Some do everything they can to cover them up. But the Nirvana approach is to exploit the 'holes' by foregrounding them. So instead of struggling to make a huge noise all the time, arrange parts of a song so they are carried by less than your full instruments. Notice also that the vocals in 'Teen Spirit' are low and muted on the verse, but higher-pitched and screaming on the chorus.

Even if you don't arrange a whole song this way, it makes a very good intro tactic, as Led Zeppelin's 'Over The Hills And Far Away' demonstrates. That begins with folk-like 6- and 12-string acoustic guitar parts before exploding into electric rock via four fiercely accented chords struck by drums, electric guitars, and bass. The studio version is good, but for the full effect seek out the live version on *How The West Was Won*.

Unplugged/plugged

An unplugged arrangement is the presentation of a previously arranged electric song in an acoustic format. This usually means minimising electric guitars, bass, and drums. It could mean taking everything down to a single instrument and voice. If you want to treat one of your songs to this approach you have to isolate what are the crucial musical elements, in terms of melody, chords, and rhythm (presumably the lyrics remain the same). How few instruments and what types of instrument do you need in order to make the song work?

The mistake with this arrangement strategy is simply to copy the tempo and dynamics of the original. Far better to take it as an opportunity to do something new, perhaps turning an out-and-out rock song into a blues or a ballad. Sometimes this means a change of genre. The famous 1990s MTV series offers plenty of examples of what can be done with this. The series was sparked off by public response to an acoustic rendition by Bon Jovi of 'Wanted Dead Or Alive' in 1989. Eric

Clapton's acoustic version of 'Layla' replaced the blistering angst of the electric version with a gently swinging, mournful take. Neil Young turned 'Like A Hurricane' into a song for organ and harmonica. Nirvana did acoustic versions of grunge songs like 'On A Plain'. It is a pity Jimi Hendrix did not live to give us similar acoustic versions of some of his famous songs (imagine an unplugged version of 'Purple Haze'). Bruce Springsteen's recently released Hammersmith Odeon 1975 concert starts with a piano version of 'Thunder Road', and he has also released a striking blues re-interpetation of 'Born In The USA' – about as anthemic as popular song gets.

The *plugged* arrangement of a song means going in the reverse direction. You take something originally conceived as acoustic and make it electric. The Byrds' cover of Dylan's 'Mr Tambourine Man', Hendrix's cover of 'All Along The Watchtower', Bruce Springsteen's cover of his own acoustic 'Atlantic City' are examples. This often involves an increase in tempo and a more aggressive angle on the lyric. Bob Dylan has done many electric versions of his own songs.

Imagine your finished production

Most arrangements fall into one of these eight categories. When you write a song and then come to record it, try to hear it in your head as a finished production. There's a good visualization exercise you can do for this:

Step one: sit quietly somewhere away from any noise, close your eyes, and see an old-fashioned record player.
Step two: imagine you go to a rack of 45rpm singles and pull out one coloured paper sleeve. This is the next song you will write.
Step three: take the record out of its sleeve, put it on the turntable, manually lower the needle onto the run-in grooves, hear the vinyl crackles and pops, and let music begin.
Step four: see how far the song goes before you lose the thread. What kind of arrangement do you hear?

This can be enough to start an idea. It can be adapted so that the record is a song you have written but not yet arranged.

A significant part of arrangement is choosing the instruments that will play it. These fall into two categories. 'Core' instruments in an arrangement are those that will be play much or all of the time. In a rock band the drums, bass and guitars are core arrangement instruments because we expect to hear them carry a song. This doesn't mean that they might not momentarily drop out, but none could stay out for long without a feeling that the performance was incomplete. The choice of core instruments depends on the genre of music. It can go from the acoustic guitar of the lone protest singer to the orchestra necessary to play a symphony. In songwriting we often work from guitars. The next section looks at how to use acoustic guitars in an arrangement.

SECTION 3

Arranging songs with acoustic guitar

The acoustic guitar is the instrument of choice for many songwriters. Used imaginatively, it can also form the basis of a wide range of exciting arrangements.

The acoustic guitar is the most popular instrument for songwriting. It's easy to carry around, and you only need a few shapes and a rudimentary right-hand technique to put some chord progressions together to support a melody. You don't even need to master barre chords – plenty of famous songs require only open-string shapes. This section is a source of ideas for how acoustic guitars can work in an arrangement.

ACOUSTIC GUITAR CONFIGURATIONS

First, let's survey some of the acoustic guitar configurations you could use on a demo:

- Nylon-string 'Spanish' guitar, doubled.
- Nylon-string 'Spanish' + steel-string acoustic ('folk') guitar.
- A third nylon-string for soloing over a 'Spanish' and a steel-string guitar.
- Steel-string acoustic, doubled.
- Steel-string in standard tuning + steel-string in detuned standard tuning.
- Steel-string + steel-string with a capo.
- Steel-string + steel-string in an altered/open tuning.
- Steel-string + steel-string in standard or open tuning (with slide).
- Steel-string + 12-string acoustic.
- 12-string acoustic, doubled.
- Two steel-string acoustics and a 12-string.

Classical or 'Spanish' guitar

A classical or 'Spanish' guitar, strung with nylon strings, is often the guitar many young people first own by default. Classical guitars are always turning up in attics, and secondhand shops. Or they are acquired from a friend or relative whose uncle once tried to learn and gave up years ago, or who brought one back from Torrelominos. More young women than men seem to acquire them this way.

If you are studying classical guitar as well, this may be the only acoustic you have on which to write songs. The nylon-string guitar has the following characteristics:

- In terms of playability the neck of a classical guitar is wider, so barre chords are more of a vertical stretch.
- The fretboard is shorter, and access above the 12th fret is limited unless you have a modern model with a cutaway.
- The action is often higher.

- It has a different tone colour to the steel-string acoustic. It has less sustain, it doesn't sound so bright when strummed, and this softer sound is increased if you don't strum with a pick but use your thumb or the side of your hand.
- Though the nylon-string guitar doesn't cut through as the steel-string acoustic, the darker, mellower tone colour can be effective as a background for other instruments.
- Nylon-string guitars tend to sound better played finger-style.
- They do not lend themselves to string-bending techniques.
- When strummed, chords give a softer impression than on steel-string acoustics, but are potentially muddier.
- With the exception of 'lute tuning' and 'dropped D', nylon-strings don't work well with altered or open tunings.
- There are nylon-string guitars with onboard pick-ups suitable for recording without a microphone or for live performance.

In terms of symbolic identity, the classical guitar can be seen as an 'ethnic' instrument in so far as it signifies Spain and the Mediterranean (think of its association with flamenco music). Its expressive 'signature' is therefore rural life, passion, emotion, seduction, fragility, and sincerity. This symbolic identity is strongly evoked by a classical guitar solo. To get the most tone during a solo playing single notes, use the technique known as the 'rest' stroke. Strike the string with a fairly straight finger, bringing it through the string until it rests on the one immediately lower in pitch. Play close to the bridge for a bright, brittle tone; play on the edge of the soundhole for a neutral sound; play near the end of the fretboard for the mellowest tone (these techniques apply to all guitars, even electrics).

Mason Williams' single 'Classical Gas', Jose Feliciano's cover of The Doors 'Light My Fire', Leonard Cohen's debut album, and The Beatles 'And I Love Her' remain key recordings of the nylon-string guitar in popular music; 'And I Love Her' also includes a solo played on a classical guitar.

If you double the nylon-string guitar in an arrangement, so that you have two tracks of it, you will strengthen the mellow tone it creates. Steel-string acoustic with a nylon-string guitar makes an interesting combination of guitar tone, the brightness of the folk guitar contrasting with the darker classical.

Steel-string acoustic

Also nicknamed a 'folk' guitar, more songs are written on a steel-string acoustic than any other instrument.

- In terms of playability the neck of a steel-string acoustic is narrower than a classical guitar, so barre chords are less of a vertical stretch but may require more pressure.
- The fretboard is longer and joins the body around the 15th fret. Access above this is reasonable, especially with a cutaway.
- The action is often high on cheap models but easier to bring down. Cheap acoustics can make barre chords very hard, especially at the first fret.

- The steel-string acoustic has greater projection than the classical guitar, more sustain, and is generally brighter, especially when strummed with a pick.
- The brighter, metallic tone colour is effective as a background for other instruments or for dominating an arrangement.
- Steel-string acoustics also suit finger-style.
- Strummed chords give a clearer impression than a classical.
- They are more effective with open and altered tunings than a classical.
- Steel-string guitars also come with onboard pick-ups suitable for recording without a microphone or for live performance. Not everyone is a fan. Steve Craddock of Ocean Colour Scene: "DI'd acoustics are horrible, so [ours are] all recorded with a mic, otherwise you don't get the full resonance of the body. After all, the reason for having it on a track is that it's an acoustic guitar, so it's best to keep it unadulterated."

If your strings are light gauge and you have enough strength you can even play single note runs and bend the strings a little.

Stereo guitar

If you only have one guitar and limited recording facilities, the trick for getting more from it is some form of stereo recording. This means that the sound from the guitar on which you play your main accompaniment is in some way split or cloned into two separate parts that will sound different. One of these is going to be subjected to some form of effect to make it sound different to the other, even though it actually originated from the same source. Here are some tips:

- Use two different microphones (they don't both need to be brilliant quality), sending the signals to two separate recording tracks.
- If you have a pick-up on or in the guitar you can send that signal to track two while the microphone captures the acoustic signal on track one.
- This track two signal could be routed through a guitar effects unit before it reaches your recording device.
- Once both tracks are recorded you can change the sound of one by equalisation, a chorus unit, or similar effect, either at the mixing stage or by re-recording onto another track.
- To distinguish the guitars, give one some short echo, or one more distortion.
- At mixing, pan them left and right with different amounts of reverb and you will create the illusion of two guitars.

Note that with this technique you cannot make the guitar on the right play a different rhythm – it will always be the same as the one on the left, unless you add a lot of prominent echo and time the repeats so that they chime with the guitar's dry signal and are in time with the tempo. But this very U2-like sound may not suit your song.

ARRANGING FOR TWO GUITARS

If your recording set-up allows for overdubs you can have an independent second guitar part.

If guitar one is strumming, play sustained chords on guitar two, hit once in a bar, at least for one section of the song. The Strokes' 'Someday' is a good example. Guitar two's role will be to add harmony but not rhythm or melody. Tempo is crucial – the slower the tempo the harder to keep the chord sustaining. Open-string chords, new strings, steady finger pressure, and the properties of your guitar all play a part in making this work. Strum guitar two whenever the music feels like it needs to take off – as in a chorus. This technique works well if guitar one is a high capo part and the sustained guitar two is an open string position. Guitar two can double at the same pitch as guitar one, but higher shapes could also be used. When strumming rhythm guitars, make sure the patterns aren't exactly the same so there's a subtle left-right-left alternation.

With a second guitar, try arpeggiating the chords by fingers or with a pick – this gives a different rhythm, and the arpeggio idea can sometimes suggest a melodic phrase that might then be brought out by other instruments. Then try arpeggiating at a higher pitch. Top three string triad shapes are good for this purpose, or triads on strings two, three, and four.

Chord shapes for second guitar

Assuming that one of the guitars is playing down in first position, the other guitar could use barred chord shapes higher up the neck. You can hear this effect on a Strokes track like 'Soma'. This is rarely much of a gain in terms of notes of a different pitch. An A chord (guitar one) barred at the fifth fret position adds only one higher note (shown in bold) to an open A chord in first position:

String:	6	5	4	3	2	1
Guitar one	–	A	E	A	C♯	E
Guitar two	A	E	A	C♯	E	**A**

A C chord barred at the eighth fret adds only two extra higher notes (in bold) to an open C chord:

String:	6	5	4	3	2	1
Guitar one	–	C	E	G	C	E
Guitar two	C	G	C	E	**G**	**C**

An E chord barred at twelfth position adds three higher notes (in bold) to an open E chord in first position but is difficult to play:

String:	6	5	4	3	2	1
Guitar one	E	B	E	G♯	B	E
Guitar two	E	B	E	**G♯**	**B**	**E**

OPEN AND BARRE CHORDS

This simple chord progression comes to life if you use one guitar to play the open chords on the top line while a second guitar plays the high barre chords on the bottom line.

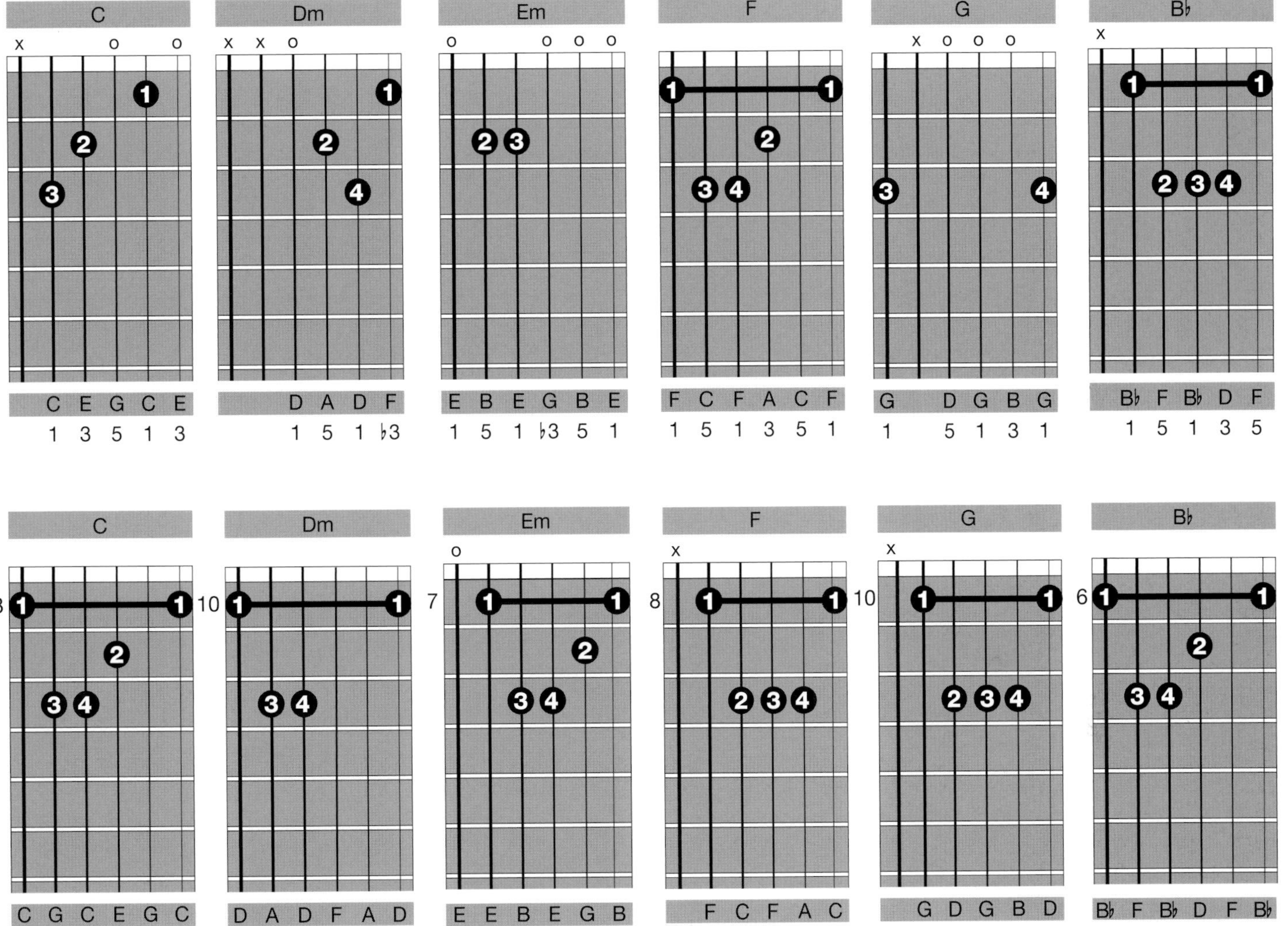

But although using different chord shapes in standard tuning only brings marginal increases in pitch, it is still worthwhile. The change from open to fretted string, and from a thinner to a thicker string, can make a tonal difference. (The use of a capo to achieve the same thing is described below).

Imagine a chord progression using C, D minor, E minor, F, G, and B♭ chords. The box above shows both the open string shapes and higher shapes for a second guitar part.

TRIAD SHAPES FOR GUITAR TWO

Triads, in which each note of a chord is only sounded once, are a clean-sounding alternative to full guitar chords. The figure 1 indicates the root of the chord. Try the progression using triads.

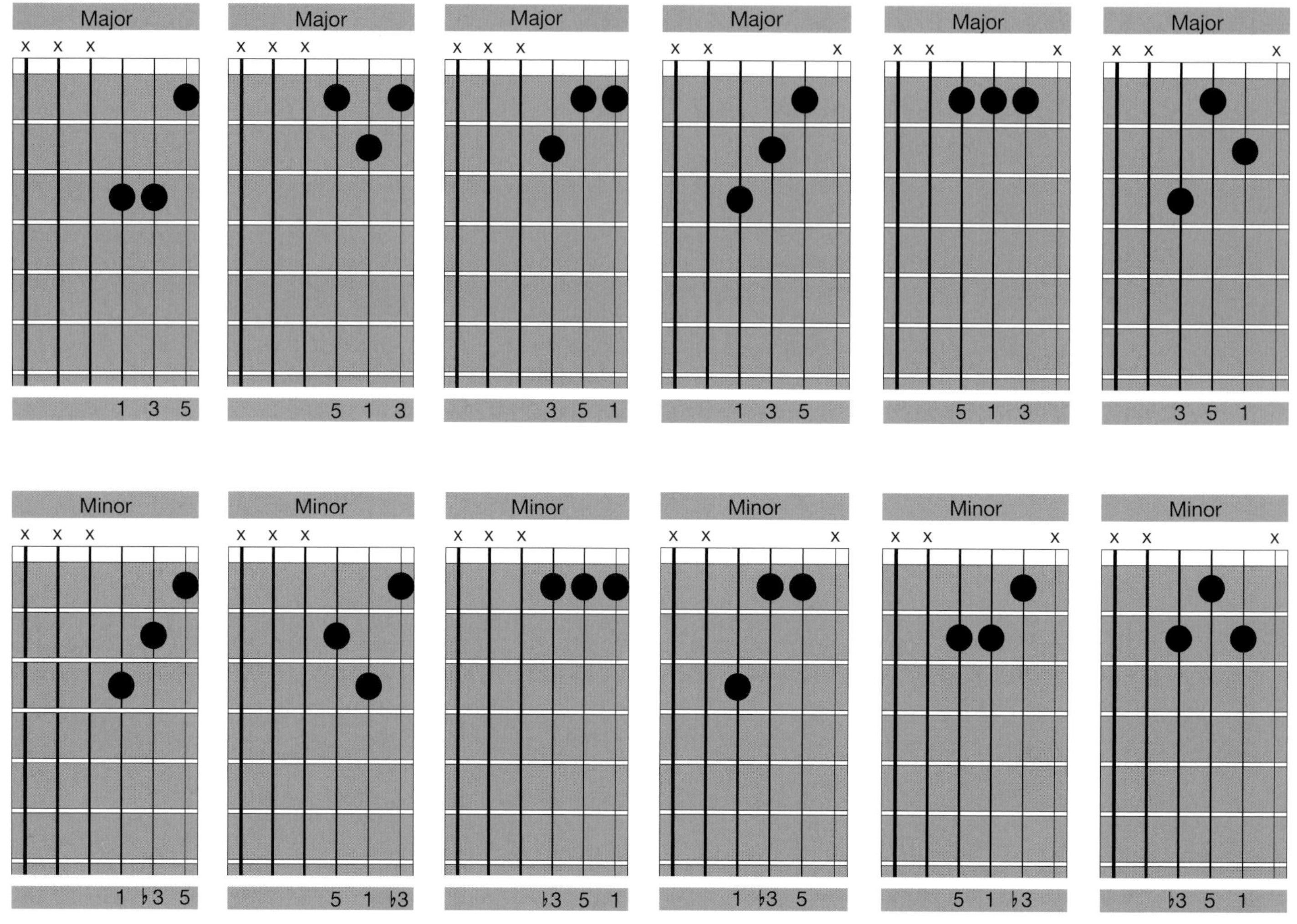

Triad shapes for second guitar

Triads are simple chords with only three notes in them. There are four types: major, minor, augmented, and diminished, of which the first two concern us here (for more on this see the relevant chapter in my earlier book, *Chord Master*). A C major triad has the notes C-E-G and C minor is C-E♭-G. A simple major or minor triad is harmonically complete. The usual guitar chords that you strum take the three notes of a triad and either double or treble them to generate more sound. But triads are handy in their own right (see above). They make excellent second guitar parts where one guitar is already playing full chords. Find the triad equivalents for the previous chord progression in a different part of the neck. On their own they make a good intro, and fills during a verse, especially if played over an open string or arpeggiated (played one string at a time).

CASE STUDY

THE KINGS OF LEON

There are some good triad ideas on the Kings Of Leon's *Aha Shake Heartbreak* (2004):

- **The second track 'King of the Rodeo' is dominated by an A triad located at the 12th fret on the top three strings. This is further coloured by the addition of a high A at the 17th fret on the top string. This stretch is only possible because the frets have got sufficiently narrow by the 12th fret.**
- **An E triad features at the 16th fret in 'Taper Jean Girl' over E-A notes in the bass.**
- **The track where triads really come into play is 'The Bucket'. The initial eight-bar phrase uses a D at the 14th, an A at the ninth (decorated with the little finger turning it into A5) and a G at the seventh decorated by a C♯ at the ninth, making a G ♯4 chord. Under this guitar sequence the bass plays a D pedal note. Between 2:32 and 2:45 a second guitar plays an arpeggio figure derived from the D at the 14th, then a D6 at the 12th and a G6 at the 12th.**
- **The chorus of 'Day Old Blues' has a 12th-fret E triad, ninth-fret C♯ minor, and seventh-fret E triad.**
- **'Four Kicks' has a D triad at 14th and an E minor triad at the 12th.**

If this brief look at triads whets your appetite, have a listen to the spooky 14th-fret B minor triad at the start of Fleetwood Mac's 'Black Magic Woman', 'Sparks' from The Who's Live At Leeds, the intro of 'Blowin' Free' by Wishbone Ash, Siouxsie and the Banshees' 'Arabian Knights', and Led Zeppelin's 'Achilles Last Stand'.

Over the page are two chord progressions shown in both open shapes and matching triads. The first is in a major key and has E, F♯ minor, G♯ minor, A, B, and C♯ minor. The second is in A minor and has A minor, C, D minor, E, F, and G.

CHORDS AS ARPEGGIOS

Where you do have chording instruments (as often you will), always consider the option of replacing block chords (like strummed guitar) with arpeggios. An arpeggio is the notes of a chord played sequentially, up and/or down, in a harmonic ripple that sketches the chord without hitting its notes all at once.

- On guitar, arpeggios can be played finger-style or with a pick.
- They are very effective when played with a sustaining effect like chorus or echo.
- Open chord shapes or an altered tuning maximize open strings.
- On piano the sustaining pedal allows the notes to bleed into each other.

MAJOR CHORD SEQUENCE

This major chord sequence is shown using full chords for guitar one and triads for guitar two. Try arpeggiating the chords for one of the guitars rather than strumming.

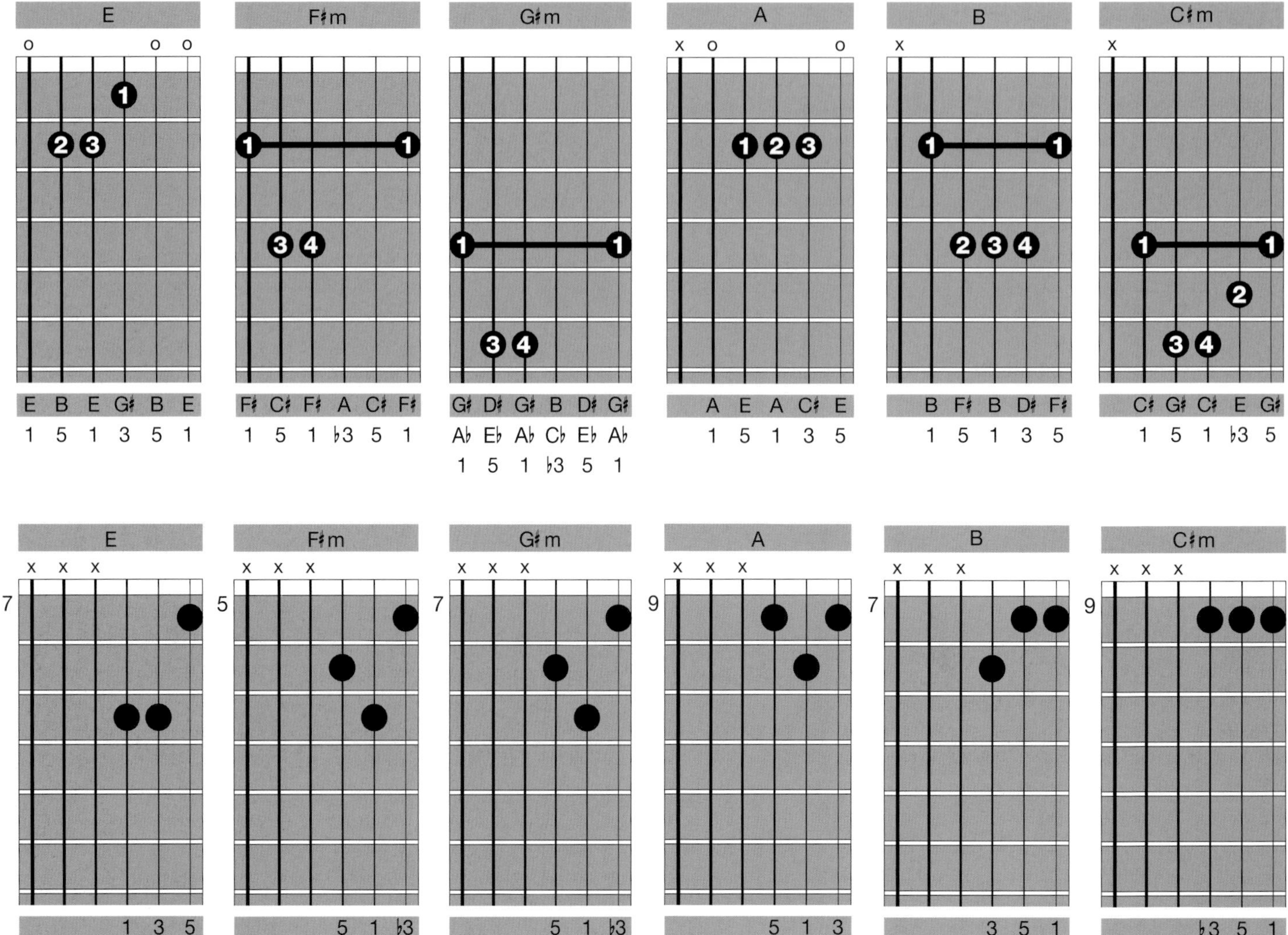

Arpeggiation lends melodic interest to what would have been a vertical chord but performs the same harmonic function. Every arpeggio, especially on a chord change, is a melodic part in waiting. Listen to such changes and you may hear scraps of melody – like a leap of intervals – which can be given to another instrument to actually play. Sometimes an arpeggio can be a riff in waiting, as is the case with Van Halen's 'Ain't Talkin' 'Bout Love'. It can also state part of the melody as on The Strokes' 'Is This It'.

Be cautious when recording block chord parts. The easiest thing is to quickly overdub four

MINOR-KEY CHORD SEQUENCE

This minor-key chord sequence is shown using both full chords and their respective triads, to be played by two guitars. Again, try arpeggiating one set of chords.

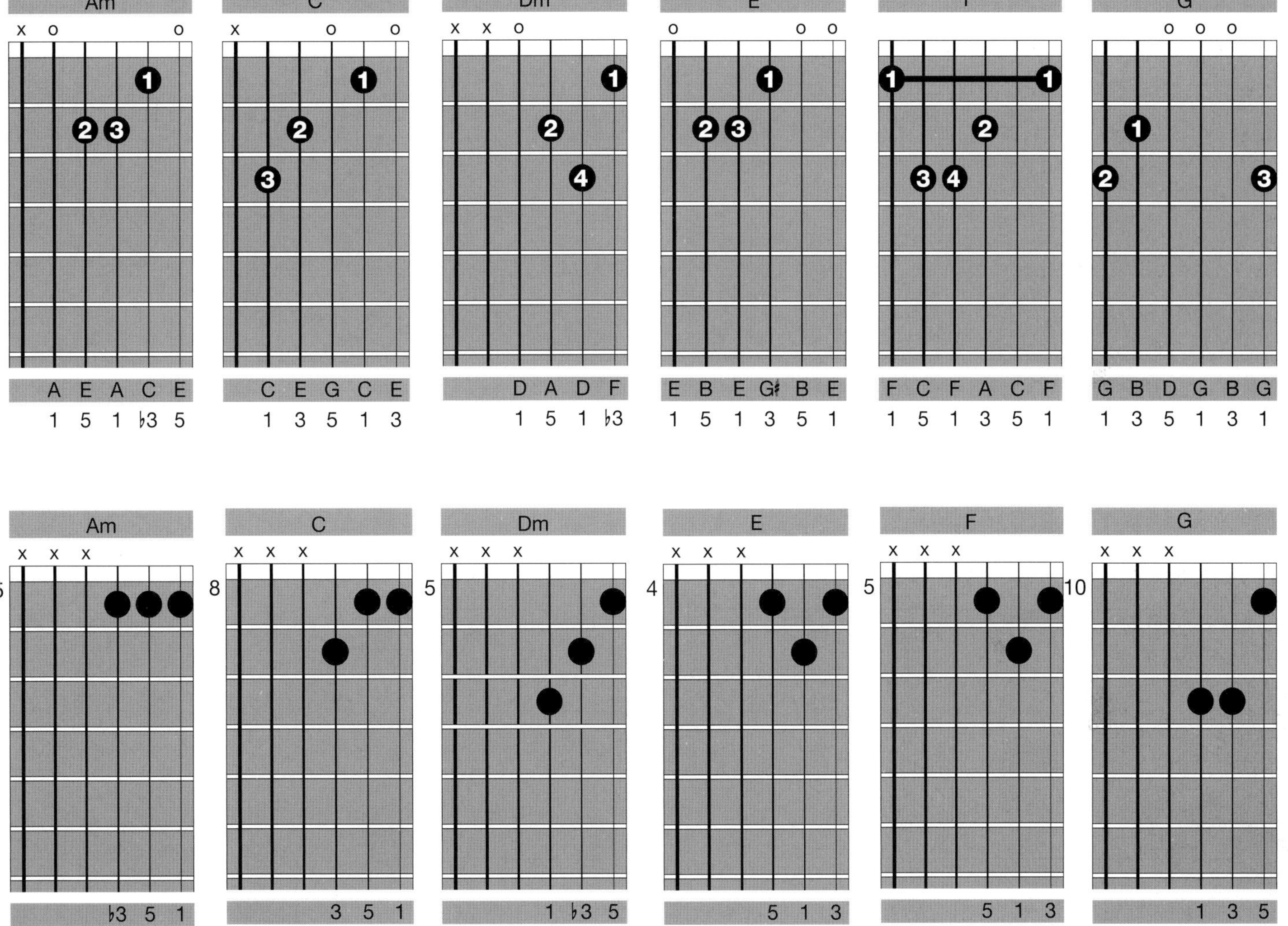

guitar parts on the chord progression, strumming roughly the same rhythm. If you aim for an epic production this may be okay. I remember Peter Frampton telling me about recording multiple acoustic guitar overdubs on George Harrison's *All Things Must Pass* album, where there would be huge numbers of instruments. Too many block chord parts can make the arrangement sound uninteresting and lumpy, and miss the chance to get more melodic parts or 'voices' into the music. If you do use more than one block instrument (multiple guitars and/or keyboards):

- Consider where it stands in pitch with the other(s).
- Try not to double at the same pitch too much; spread the sound out.
- Upward is usually better than lower down. Chords below the range of the guitar will make the mix muddy and trespass on the bass-line.
- Higher-pitched chords can be made ethereal because they can take greater amounts of reverb in the mix-down and thus be placed in the distance.
- Choose chordal instruments that have contrasting timbres – clean versus distorted, smooth versus rough, etc.
- Use a clipped rhythm on some chord parts rather than a continuous one.

The arpeggio guitar-playing on The Smiths' 'This Charming Man' and 'Wonderful Woman' results in a guitar counter-melody all the way through; any strummed harmony guitars are a long way back in the mixes.

PLECTRUM OR FINGERSTYLE?

When thinking about chords and arpeggios, consider the effect your strumming technique has on your guitar sound. Straight finger-style playing:

- Suits slower, gentler acoustic material (the fast finger-picking in country styles like bluegrass requires an accomplished technique and may be distracting to sing over).
- Is used to arpeggiate chords.
- Works well in a minimal arrangement but may get buried if the arrangement has many instruments.

Playing with a pick:

- Provides volume and definition for chords, riffs, and single note runs.
- Can produce a more even sound when strumming.
- Can approximate some finger-picking if you hold a pick to play bass notes and play the upper notes with second and third fingers. This is handy for changing from finger-style to a strummed section and back again.

Choosing a hard or soft pick when recording acoustic guitar makes a difference. A soft pick produces a percussive clicking noise that can be enhanced by equalisation if necessary. This is noticeable on a track like Coldplay's 'Parachutes'. When the other instruments are in place the sound of the guitars may not be separately audible (though their chords are still contributing to the harmony) but the click will. An example is the left and right guitars on The Smiths' 'Suffer Little Children'.

PERCUSSIVE RHYTHM

On up-tempo tracks there is the possibility of the guitars generating a percussive rhythm. This is good if you don't have percussion or drums available. Generally, rapid strumming automatically results in a percussive effect, as on 'Pinball Wizard' or The Moody Blues' 'Question'. More specifically, it is done in various ways by which the strings are banged against the fretboard, or the guitar body itself is tapped. Flamenco is a specialized guitar style that makes a big feature of such percussive playing. The strum pattern is punctuated by beats where the chord is struck while muted. Just as the pick hits the strings there is a downward movement of the strumming hand, which bangs the strings against the frets even as it mutes the strings.

ARRANGING AND CHOOSING A KEY

When a song is completed but not yet recorded, you have the option to transpose it at the last minute into a different key. This could be desirable because:

- The key makes the melody go too high or too low for your voice.
- You have too many songs in that key already. This becomes important when planning the track running order on an album, as it is not a good idea to have too many tracks in one key, or placed next to each other.
- The key may not be as effective in the style of music of the song.

Some keys suit some instruments more than others. Eb is not a good key for either guitar or bass because it has the highest key note, 11 semitones (half-steps) above the open bottom string (assuming you don't detune by a semitone). Effective keys for the guitar allow for the open strings, which increase the resonance of chords; they are also keys with fewer barre chords. During chord-changes the open strings ring, whereas changing in a sequence of barre chords the sound breaks each time you lift your fingers off the fretboard.

The guitar is suited to C, G, D, A and E among the major keys (with their respective minors). These are the keys with the least barre chords and the most opportunity to do open string fills. Given what has been said about the importance of open strings, it comes as no surprise to discover that R.E.M.'s favourite keys are probably E, D, and E minor with G, C, and A not far behind. Muse's nervy, solipsistic angst is partly expressed through their liking for writing songs in minor keys (E minor, D minor and G minor seem to be favourites). The majority of songs on Franz Ferdinand's debut album are in minor keys, which is unexpected given the overall high-energy feel of their debut album.

Using a capo

A capo is a small mechanical device, an artificial fifth finger that never gets tired holding a barre, fixed temporarily at a given fret. This little gadget has made some significant contributions to popular music. Don't let anyone tell you that it is a 'cheat'. Hundreds, if not thousands, of famous songs owe their sound to the fact of the guitars on the recordings being capoed. The Darkness's 'Love Is Only A Feeling' makes fine use of high-capoed acoustics that are brought back toward the end of the track on their own. You can also hear capoed guitars on Travis's 'Driftwood', Radiohead's 'No Surprises', and from further back Simon and Garfunkel's 'Mrs Robinson' and Bob Dylan's 'Positively 4th Street'. The capo is important to multitracking guitars on many songs by The Smiths and The Who, including where electric guitars are featured.

- As an arranging device, a capo is very useful when multitracking guitars. Here are some of the things you can do with it:
- A capo changes the tone of a guitar. Once it reaches the sixth or seventh fret the guitar sounds different. With the loss of low bass notes and the addition of more high notes, the guitar takes a small step toward the mandolin's territory. This in itself will make it sound different to a non-capoed guitar track.
- New chord shapes are possible when the capo is high enough up the neck to enable you to stretch a greater number of frets than would be possible in first position.
- A capo is the easiest way of changing the key of a song so that it better suits your voice. Imagine a song in G major with the progression G-C-D-E minor. The chords are simple but let's say for the sake of argument the key is too low for you to sing. By fixing the capo at the third fret you can play the same open-string shapes but are now singing a minor third higher in B♭ major (the true pitch of the chords now being B♭-E♭-F-G minor).
- The main use of a capo is to make it easier to play in a key that is normally hard for the guitar.

A capo enables a player to reduce the number of barre chords in a piece or song. Imagine we are required to play a chord sequence in the key of E♭ minor – not a comfortable key for guitarists. Putting aside detuning (which is mentioned later), the option with a capo would be place it at frets one, six, or nine to reduce the number of barre chords. It would then be playable with shapes that belong to D minor, A minor or E minor respectively. The following table shows the actual pitch of the eight master-shapes when they are played with a capo.

CAPO POSITION

[Open]	A	C	D	E	G	Am	Dm	Em
Fret one	B♭	D♭	E♭	F	A♭	B♭m	E♭m	Fm
Fret two	B	D	E	F♯	A	Bm	Em	F♯m
Fret three	C	E♭	F	G	B♭	Cm	Fm	Gm
Fret four	C♯	E	F♯	G♯	B	C♯m	F♯m	G♯m
Fret five	D	F	G	A	C	Dm	Gm	Am
Fret six	D♯	F♯	G♯	A♯	C♯	D♯m	G♯m	A♯m
Fret seven	E	G	A	B	D	Em	Am	Bm

This means that when multitracking chordal guitar parts, the capo makes it easy to play a second set of chords higher than the first guitar part, but also to make them have fewer barre shapes to increase resonance. Imagine a song in E major with open string chords. Guitar two could play the same chords using shapes from the key of C with the capo at the fourth fret, or A if the capo were at the seventh:

Guitar one	open shapes	E	F♯m	G♯m	A	B	C♯m
Guitar two	capo fourth fret	C	Dm	Em	F	G	Am
Guitar three	capo seventh fret	A	Bm	C♯m	D	E	F♯m

For an extreme 'doubling' effect, put a capo at the 12th fret and play the same open-string shapes an octave higher. How feasible this is will depend on what type of guitar is used, how good its intonation is above the 12th fret, and what the key is, which determines whether you can get your fingers into the narrow frets. If an acoustic proves impossible for the task, a clean-toned electric guitar on its bridge pickup work will be an acceptable substitute.

This is also a way of approximating the sound of a 12-string if you don't own one. But if you want the open string guitar and the 12th position capo guitar to sound like one instrument the parts must not deviate too much in rhythm, and must be panned to the same place in the stereo image at mix-down. It will sound better if some of the bass frequencies on the capo 12th-fret guitar are reduced.

If a chord sequence in C major in open position is played on a second guitar as if in E major with a capo at the eighth fret, the overall span of sound will be tonally rich. During mixing these guitars would be panned left and right in the stereo image.

There is a considerable degree of pitch over-lap between these shapes and this applies even if you capo at 12th fret in an open chord key. But this doesn't make the capo ineffective since it creates a mix of open and fretted notes plus different shapes that affects the resonance.

Detuning and a capo

One method to heighten the contrast between guitar chords is to have a capo on guitar two and to detune Guitar one by a semi-tone or tone. If the open-string guitar is detuned, it increases the distance between the open and capo positions, and changes the tone of the open string position. Steve Mason of Gene sometimes uses standard tuning a tone down because to his ear it "makes it sound more dense". Here are the eight open-string shapes and their actual pitch as the guitar is detuned:

Open chords	A	C	D	E	G	Am	Dm	Em
Semitone detuned :	G♯/A♭	B	C♯/D♭	D♯/E♭	F♯/G♭	G♯m/A♭m	C♯m/D♭m	D♯m/E♭m
Tone detuned:	G	B♭	C	D	F	Gm	Cm	Dm

For example, imagine writing a song in D♯. The likeliest chords would be D♯, E♯ minor, F minor, G♯, A♯, and B♯ minor. In standard tuning a capo at the first fret would turn these into C, D minor, E minor, F, G, and A minor – far more playable. But another approach would be to detune by a semitone (half-step). This is matched with a capo guitar at the sixth fret in standard tuning. If you wanted to play this higher guitar part on the detuned guitar the capo has to be placed at the seventh fret.

Standard tuning	D♭	E♭m	Fm	G♭	A♭	B♭m
Detune a semitone	D	Em	F♯m	G	Am	Bm
Standard tuning, capo sixth fret	G	Am	Bm	C	D	Em

Now let's try detuning by a tone and going into a minor key. The song is written in the key of C minor, with C minor, Eb, F minor, G minor, Ab, and Bb as chords. A capo at the third fret would make these A minor, C, D minor, E minor, F, and G shapes. But detuning the guitar by a tone would create a much deeper sound. This could be matched with a capoed guitar at the eighth fret (tenth if you played the part on the guitar that was detuned):

Standard tuning	Cm	E♭	Fm	Gm	A♭	B♭
Detune a semitone	D minor	F	Gm	Am	B♭	C
Standard tuning, capo eighth fret	Em	G	Am	Bm	C	D

Admittedly, like many transposing issues, detuning, using capos, and juggling chord shapes and chord pitches run the risk of brain damage! ("Now, this is an A♭ that's a G shape with the capo here but as the guitar is detuned it's really a … aarghh!"). Recording three guitar parts requires playing the same chord progression in shapes that belong to three different keys! Make sure you write them down.

ARRANGEMENTS AND ALTERED TUNINGS

"I have a Trans-Performance Les Paul [which creates instant tuning changes]. It's phenomenal. I've always written in open tunings, ever since I heard Joni Mitchell for the first time; things like open D and G. Then I might make a mistake tuning, or a string gets knocked, or it's drifted way down. Then I don't know what tuning I'm in so I make it up as I go along – which adds different sounds. 'Show Me The Way' was in open G – it starts with the D at the seventh fret."

Peter Frampton

Altered tunings have become increasingly popular with guitarists, though 'altered' does not always mean changing the relationships of the strings to each other. Standard tuning – EADGBE – can go down by a semitone (half-step) or tone step. In particular, lowering standard tuning by a semi-tone or tone is a technique exploited because of the tonal difference it offers. Otherwise, putting one guitar in an altered tuning is an effective way of making it sound distinct from another guitar part. Even a single string alteration can be effective because it may increase the number or position of open strings in the chord. If guitar one is in standard tuning, options for guitar two are:

- 'Lute tuning', third string down to F♯. Good for songs in D and B minor.
- Top string down to D. Good for songs in C, G, D, A and E, A minor, E minor, B minor.
- Fifth string down to G. Good for songs in G, G minor, or E minor.
- 'Drop D', sixth string down to D. Good for songs in D or D minor.

The pitch and key of any of these can be further modified by a capo.

If you want to go the whole hog there are full open tunings, ie, tunings in which the open strings make a proper chord. Remember that these can be a headache for live performance (more re-tuning or the need for extra guitars open-tuned and ready). The advantages of open tunings include:

- Increased sustain and resonance.
- Single barre one-finger major chords (or minor, if a minor tuning).
- Unique chord shapes.
- Opportunity to combine open strings with scale figures (octaves, thirds sixths).
- Fuller harmonic effects.
- Good for finger-picking and bottleneck playing.

One of the most popular is open G (DGDGBD). If guitar one were in open G, guitar two could be standard tuning, capo at seventh fret, with the shapes of C major. Another popular open tuning is open D (DADF♯AD). It has a deeper resonance than open G, owing to the lowest string, D, being the key note. It would combine well with a standard-tuned guitar playing in the key of D. A third guitar could be standard tuning, capo at the seventh fret, chord shapes in the key of G, which would provide lots of extra high notes.

Altered tunings have a big effect on the type of songs you write and consequently on how they are arranged. If you want to investigate this, seek out albums by Crosby, Stills, And Nash (with or without Neil Young), Joni Mitchell, *Led Zeppelin III*, English songwriter Nick Drake, or Pierre Bensusan. Songs like Joni Mitchell's 'Big Yellow Taxi', The Beatles' 'Blackbird', and Stephen Stills' 'Love The One You're With' are indebted to the altered tunings involved. It is said that British folk guitarist Davy Graham in the early 1960s invented DADGAD tuning the better to imitate some North African music, as can be heard on the album *Folk, Blues And Beyond*.

Another master of altered tuning is John Renbourn, who was part of folk-rock band Pentangle in the mid 1960s. During an interview I did with him we got around to the subject of tunings and flexibility. He commented, "If you take DADGAD, it's fine if you're playing in related scales round D, right? Or close ones – you could play in a mode on A. Pierre Bensusan plays quite a lot in C using DADGAD. But it seems you're making things more difficult for yourself if you want to use an open tuning and play the same type of harmonic music that would be suitable for EADGBE. The opposite applies, too. If you're in standard and you want to play something that's purely in one mode or has an even more limited note grouping then sometimes you have notes that are inessential in the tuning. So why have them?

"I can just about manage [to sing] an octave in B. So if I want to sing a certain folk song I adjust the tuning. If I drop the G to F♯ ['lute tuning'] that helps. I could then play things effectively. You begin the process of changing one string. Then you think, ah well, this piece has got a strong C♯ in it, so why don't I just drop the D string a semitone (half-step)? Then you find you've got a nice accompaniment for the words and a few guitar phrases that roll together and sound good without you singing them. Then you begin to find your way round the tuning ... Most of the tunings I use are neither major nor minor. If I use open G, open D, one in A, or open C it is just to play pieces that are specifically in a major key and fit."

Capos and altered tunings

Here are some advantages of using a capo with an altered tuning:

- A capo can raise the pitch of an open or altered tuning to the desired key. This is a sensible way to take the strain off the neck. Open A (EAEAC♯E) and open E (EBEG♯BE) are popular open tunings on electric guitar, but they require tuning a number of strings above standard pitch, risking string breakage and neck strain. Many players don't like doing this on an acoustic with heavier strings. Tuning to open G and open D (the equivalents a tone down) and putting a capo at the second fret is a good compromise.
- A capo brings a second guitar in open tuning up to the correct pitch for a song that is played with guitar one in standard tuning. For a song in E, guitar one plays standard open shapes, guitar two is in open D tuning with a capo at the second fret.
- If you like open tunings and play live, a capo is one way to get several songs from the same tuning, but still varying the key and without slowing proceedings by constant re-tuning. Song one is in open G, song two is in A (open G tuning, capo second fret) and Song three is in C (open G tuning, capo fifth fret).
- A capo can help you cheat in the studio if you have a song in an altered tuning and want to do a key-change. Imagine being in an altered tuning in the key of A major and half way through the song you want to change key up a semitone (half-step) to

B♭. The problem is that the A major section uses distinctive open-string chord-shapes and these cannot be replicated with barre shapes. So another guitar part is recorded for the second half of the song with the capo at the first fret. You still have the open tuning but it is now sounding in B♭. Unfortunately, this will not be reproducible live.

- Capos also help with transposing key for the sake of a singer. This applies to altered tunings as well. Let's say you have a song in open D tuning (DADF♯AD) and that's a good key for you to sing but not for the new vocalist who has joined your band. She wants to sing it in G, a fourth higher. Perhaps the song might be moved into open G tuning (DGDGBD). You try this and find some of the best chord shapes are lost. Instead, the solution might be to go back to open D and capo at the fifth fret.
- Further arranging effects are possible, in standard and altered tuning, if you use a non-standard capo. Partial capos hold down three strings at a time instead of all six. The 'Third Hand' capo allows the clamping of any combination of string at a given fret. For more information on these capos see my book *The Guitarist's Guide To The Capo* (Artemis, 2003).

ARRANGING WITH 12-STRING GUITAR

A 12-string guitar is a wonderful instrument, providing it is comfortable to play. The first time you strum an acoustic 12-string is a startling experience. First, the body is bigger than a six-string. Second, there doesn't seem to be any room between the strings. Your fretting hand tries to find the spaces between the strings on the fretboard, and your strumming hand feels like it's trailing across the strings on the inside of a piano. Finger-pickers notice this even more, with the additional challenge of plucking two strings at once. But most persevere, because the 12-string acoustic has a shimmering sound with high notes where you don't normally hear them. And like someone temporarily blinded by the sun, you find you can't touch a six-string for weeks after because it seems uninteresting by comparison.

The idea of doubling strings to get more sound from an instrument goes back centuries. From that it was a small step not only to double the strings but to make them an octave higher to increase the pitch range.

The standard way to tune a 12-string is to have the top two strings tuned to the same pitch (EE, BB) and all the others tuned in octaves (eE, aA, dD, gG). Notice that the higher pitched string is physically the higher of each pair. The string that gives the most trouble in practice is the octave above the G. If the guitar is lightly strung, this will be an 0.08 gauge string tuned up to the G above a guitar's top E. A very thin string at high tension, this is the one that snaps most frequently. Some owners eventually get fed up with this and treat the G string the same as the top two strings; ie, with two Gs at the same pitch. Alternatively, tune the entire 12-string a semitone or a tone below standard pitch. This relieves tension on the neck, lessens string breakage, and may make the guitar easier to play. Concert pitch can be restored with a capo at the first or second fret.

- Use a 12-string in an arrangement if you want to add to the guitar texture without thickening it.
- When playing a 12-string guitar, hit the pairs of strings evenly, especially if using a pick on single note runs or finger-picking. (Some players who play folk-style on 12-string prefer finger-picks.)
- A capo on a 12-string further increases the number of high notes.
- Detuned 12-string can be even richer.
- In songs that imitate of otherwise evoke non-Western music, 12-string guitars can sound exotic – as in the case of Robert Plant's 'Calling To You'.
- 12-string guitars are great for arpeggio figures, alone or doubling a six-string. Putting a 12-string arpeggio clean over distorted low-pitched guitars is like seeing stars against a purple storm cloud.

Songs that feature acoustic 12-string prominently include Led Zeppelin's 'Tangerine', David Bowie's 'Queen Bitch' and 'Space Oddity', Boston's 'More Than A Feeling', The Eagles' 'Hotel California', the intro of The Band's 'The Weight', and many songs by The Smiths. There's a memorable sequence in the film *Jimi Hendrix*, released in the early 1970s, in which Hendrix plays 'Hear My Train a-Comin' on a detuned 12-string.

Nashville tuning

One unconventional way of using a 12-string is to take off the lower string of each octave pair. Steve Craddock of Ocean Colour Scene said the band had a fondness for it: "We used Nashville tuning for some tracks, where you take a 12-string and take off the normal octave strings. It's definitely on 'The Song Goes On'. In fact, we've used it on the last couple of albums. There's a track on *One For The Modern* called 'Jane She Got Excavated' – I did an electric Nashville tuning part for it for the intro so we've been using it for quite a few years. It's got a different kind of ring and sustain to it. And it doesn't take up a lot of room in a track."

Unconventional chord voicings/12-strng effect

If you don't own a 12-string another means for getting more resonant guitar texture is to layer into the recording chord shapes that contain open strings as additional harmonic notes, or open strings as unison notes. Opposite are some chord boxes that do this.

UNUSUAL CHORD VOICINGS

Using these unusual chord voicings, which incorporate open strings for additional harmonic notes, can help you to approximate the sound of a 12-string guitar or just create a more resonant guitar texture.

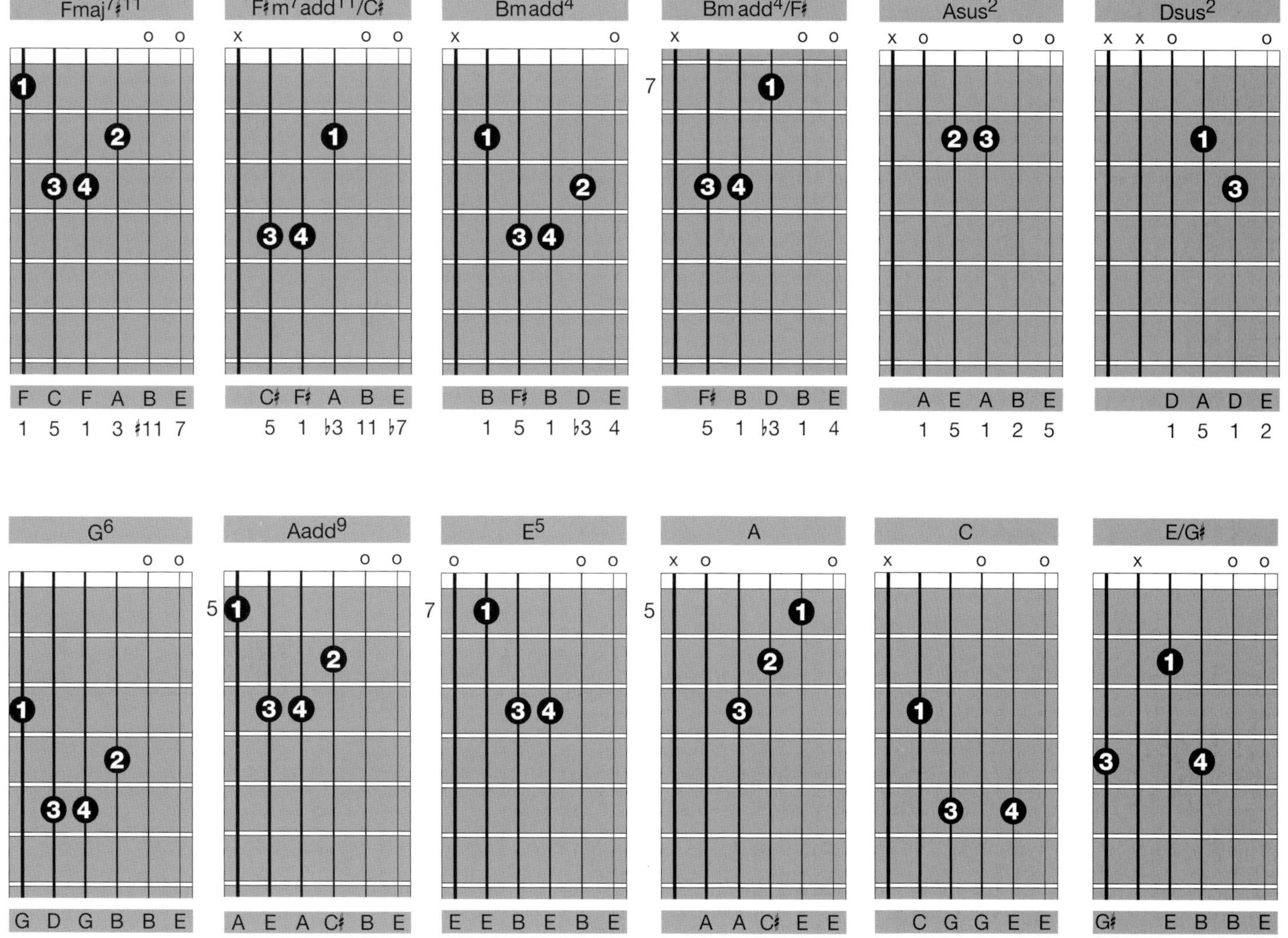

CASE STUDY

PETER BUCK OF R.E.M.

I like rhythm guitar; I don't like too much fiddling around ... I like interesting choral voicings ... When I write songs I purposely write parts that make good songs but are also where I can do different things and not expose my limitations. I use quite different chord voicings to most people ...

The most important component of Buck's guitar style is his use of open strings, either in chords or in riff-like figures involving two or three notes. One of the distinctive qualities of his rhythm guitar is his chord voicings. Many feature unusual combinations of open strings against fretted strings. Often the top E and B strings are used as drones. Buck told *Guitar World* in 1996, "I always seem to come back to using very simple chords with lots of open droning strings."

Take the first two chord boxes shown on the previous page (Fmaj7♯11 and F♯m7 add11). As these shapes move up the neck they form differing relationships with the open E and B strings. Some of the resulting chords are beautiful enough to set a song going. As you change chords listen for how the open strings ring between changes. Chorus and delay bring the notes out. In terms of Peter Buck's playing with R.E.M., you can hear the following:

- **F♯m7 add11, along with Amaj9 and G6, is heard in the verse of 'Near Wild Heaven'.**
- **The B minor add4 occurs in 'Cuyahoga'.**
- **Some of these open string chords work double a note at the same pitch, thus creating a 12-string effect. Listen to the G6 produced at the third fret by an E shape (as in 'Can't Get There From Here').**
- **Buck's love of lush chords, often minor, is an essential ingredient of the richness of the chorus to 'What If We Give It Away'.**
- **With numbers like 'Driver 8', 'The One I Love', 'Losing My Religion', and 'Bang And Blame' in mind, Buck explained that especially with E minor "you're only fretting two strings. So you have all those open strings resonating, making a real nice harmonic overlay that you don't get with a barre chord."**

HARMONICS AND ARRANGEMENTS

Harmonics are high, soft notes created by touching a string at certain points on the neck but not pressing it onto the fretboard. To create a harmonic, touch the string right over the metal fret, not behind it. Strike the string and pull your finger away to let the string ring. The strongest harmonics are at frets 12, seven, five, and four or nine. They pitch as follows:

- 12th fret gives the note an octave above the open string.
- Seventh fret gives the note an octave and a fifth above the open string.

- Fifth fret gives the note two octaves above the open string.
- Fourth or ninth fret gives the note two octaves and a major third above the open string.

To get these harmonics when you have a capo on the fretboard simply add on to the above fret positions how many frets the capo has been placed. In an arrangement, guitar harmonics:

- Make effective higher pitch decorations during instrumental links.
- Can be part of a riff.
- Can mark the transition between one section and another.
- Can add ambience to thinner-textured sections.
- Are strengthened by double-tracking, chorus, phasing, echo and/or reverb.
- In standard tuning, the top three strings' harmonics give E minor (12th and fifth frets), B minor (seventh fret), and G♯ minor (fourth or ninth frets) triads.
- In standard tuning, the second, third, and fourth strings' harmonics give G (12th and fifth), D (seventh), and B (fourth or ninth) triads.

There are prominent harmonics in Television's intro to 'Prove It', R.E.M.'s 'Feeling Gravity's Pull', Led Zeppelin's 'Dazed And Confused' (intro, through a wah-wah pedal), U2's 'Pride (In The Name Of Love)', and The Rolling Stones' 'Wild Horses'.

OTHER STRINGED/FRETTED INSTRUMENTS

This section has focused on acoustic guitar, but there are other related acoustic stringed instruments to be aware of in case you want to include one in an arrangement. They often have a strong symbolic identity, may not be easy to record (assuming you can play one), and also may not sound right played off a keyboard. One instance is the **pedal steel guitar**, which is associated with country music, with its sweet sustained notes and prominent vibrato, and well-suited to reverb and echo. Its traditional use can be heard on an album like The Dixie Chicks' *Wide Open Spaces*. The more imaginative use of this instrument would be in contexts where the listener doesn't expect to hear it, such as U2's *How To Dismantle An Atomic Bomb* (where it is played by producer Daniel Lanois).

The **banjo** features in a number of folk, country, and trad jazz styles. Sound-wise it is to acoustic guitar what the harpsichord is to the piano. It features on tracks like Mungo Jerry's 'In The Summertime' for a jugband effect, Dexy's Midnight Runners' 'Come On Eileen', R.E.M.'s 'Wendell Gee', and Led Zeppelin's version of the traditional folk song 'Gallows Pole'. Another famous folk-related instrument is the **mandolin**. Like the banjo, it has little sustain, which is why its notes have to be struck frequently or picked rapidly to create the illusion of sustain. It sits very well in an arrangement with acoustic guitar, occupying as it does a higher pitch range. In terms of symbolic identity, the mandolin suggests romance, poverty, and the outcast. It features on R.E.M.'s 'Losing My Religion' (composed on mandolin), Led Zeppelin's 'The Battle Of

Evermore', and 'That's The Way', and Bruce Springsteen's 'Atlantic City'. The Smiths' 'Please Please Please Let Me Get What I Want' has a mandolin break as a coda.

The **ukulele**, beloved of George Harrison, evokes 1930s performer George Formby and 1960s singer Tiny Tim . It has a child-like, irreverent character, wholly unpretentious, and like the mandolin has little sustain so has to be strummed continuously. You can hear it adding light relief to the fade of The Beatles' 'Free As A Bird', on Queen's 'Good Company', and The Who's 'Blue, Red and Grey'.

Going further afield, instruments like the **balalaika** and **bouzouki** instantly suggest Greece, Eastern Europe, and Russia. Peter Buck apparently wrote R.E.M.'s 'Monty Got A Raw Deal' on a bouzouki at about three in the morning in a hotel room in New Orleans. Further afield still, there is the **sitar** (stringed, though not with a conventional fretboard), which in the mid-1960s came to symbolize the allure of Indian spirituality. George Harrison's study of the sitar led it to appear as an exotic instrument on The Beatles' 'Norwegian Wood', 'Love You To', and 'Within You Without You', as well as in the background of 'Lucy In The Sky With Diamonds' and 'Getting Better'. On Traffic's 'Paper Sun' a sitar is panned right and left toward the end of the song. It is also heard on The Rolling Stones' 'Paint It Black'.

The **Coral Sitar electric guitar** was devised as a guitar substitute for the sitar and features on many 1960s recordings with its distinctive nasal twang. Like the mellotron (and 1980s drum machines) although it is an imitation instrument, it is still played in arrangements to evoke the period in which it was first heard. You can hear a Coral sitar guitar on Red Hot Chili Pepper's 'Behind The Sun', Smashing Pumpkins 'Luna', solo on the intro of The Supremes 'No Matter What Sign You Are', and in the back of the mix on The Verve's 'Bitter Sweet Symphony' and The Darkness's 'One Way Ticket'.

Having reviewed the role of the acoustic guitar in an arrangement, and a variety of techniques to employ with it, it is time to do the same thing for the electric guitar.

SECTION 4

Arranging songs with electric guitar

The electric guitar is the central instrument of most rock and pop music. Its capacity for sustaining chords, and the wide range of effects available for it, offer a vast range of arrangement possibilities.

The electric guitar is a huge part of most rock and pop arrangements that also feature drums. Its first advantage when playing with a rhythm section is sheer volume. It has greater powers of sustain than an acoustic, and this sustain means the electric can provide effective harmonic support for someone to sing over without strumming all the time. With an enormous range of sound-processing devices available to alter its tone, the electric guitar offers vast possibilities in arranging that go far beyond the acoustic guitar's role as a chord-provider. This section provides ideas for how electric guitars can be used in an arrangement.

First, here are some classic electric guitar combinations:

- Single-coil pick-up with one or two acoustics.
- Double-coil pick-up with one or two acoustics.
- Double-coil with a second guitar with a single-coil or mini-humbucker.
- Electric fifths played clean or distorted under acoustic guitars.
- Electric six-string with electric 12-string.
- Twin lead guitars.
- Electric in standard tuning + electric detuned.
- Electric in standard tuning + electric with capo.
- Electric in standard tuning + electric in open or altered tuning.

STEREO ELECTRIC GUITAR

In a power trio or quartet (guitar, bass, drums, possibly plus a vocalist), if you want to record a song without overdubs, there is the challenge of how to arrange it effectively.

One way to mix such a song is to plan for the guitar to be on one side, the bass on the other, with drums and vocals central. This is featured on concert recordings such as The Who's *Live At Leeds*, where it suits the fact that John Entwistle often played quasi-guitar lines in a higher register than usual for bass. But this type of mix means that if either the bass or guitar stops playing the mix is lop-sided, and the middle of the stereo image lacks the lower impact of bass notes combining with the drums.

An alternative approach is to record the electric guitar part in stereo and treat one side differently to the other. The same technique recommended with acoustic (with a short echo) will work but with an electric there's the option to make one side clean and the other distorted, or use two types/levels of distortion. The former sounds good on chord parts, but won't work so well on a lead break.

ARRANGING WITH TWO ELECTRIC GUITARS

> ***"Carlos plays the clean on-beat rhythm guitars and I play all the other stuff. Like on 'TVC15' – those weird whiney things – that's me. I double or trebled the part. They put it in a spot where it's audible but you've got to listen, and so that guitar part creates an atmosphere. The beauty is that those overdubs don't synchronize."***
> Earl Slick on sharing guitar duties with Carlos Alomar on David Bowie's *Station To Station*

This is the most popular combination of electric guitar sounds. Here you are spoilt for choice when it comes to tone. A three single-coil pickup Stratocaster (or similar) provides five different tones from its selector switch, and these can be further changed by winding the tone control up or down. A two double-coil pickup Les Paul (or similar) provides three tones from its toggle switch, which can be further altered by turning the tone controls up or down. Recall that a whole generation of electric guitarists in the 1960s and 1970s were obsessed with the fuzzy mellow tone Eric Clapton extracted from a neck position humbucker on Cream songs like 'Sunshine Of Your Love' and 'SWLABR'. In his footsteps came Mick Ronson, who also often favoured the mellow front humbucker when overdriven, as heard on David Bowie albums such as *The Man Who Sold The World* (1970), *Ziggy Stardust* (1972), and *Aladdin Sane* (1973).

Even with just those two electric guitars, that gives many different sounds – even before we get to a consideration of effects units, levels of distortion, amps or amp-modelling, recording via a microphone or by going straight in to the desk, etc. Consider also the tonal possibilities of recording less familiar guitar makes and models. The distinctive guitar tone on an Elvis Costello track like 'Watching The Detectives' owes much to his Fender Jaguar, and think also of the wiry lead of Springsteen's Fender Broadcaster, or Leslie West's distorted Gibson Les Paul Junior with Mountain, and other distinctive guitar tones from instruments made by Gretsch, Danelectro, and Rickenbacker.

Many of the rules about capos and altered tunings apply equally to the paired electric guitar combination. There are some new options in the tuning area because you can tune up a little more than would be advisable on an acoustic.

PLAYING ELECTRIC RHYTHM

When you put electric guitar into an arrangement it is important to realize there are a number of playing options. These can have a substantial effect on the rhythmic tidiness of the arrangement. So let's review them.

Reinforcing lines

An electric guitar part doesn't have to mean chords. One distinctive use for an electric guitar in an arrangement is not to provide harmony but to put in or emphasize single-note melodic lines. In songs like The Beatles' 'Help', T.Rex's 'Metal Guru', David Bowie's 'John, I'm Only Dancing', Catatonia's 'I Am The Mob', Queen's 'In The Lap Of The Gods', some of the guitar parts are single-note phrases, accentuating the root notes of the chords. The electric guitar has such a strong presence that single notes can sound very full. On Queen tracks like 'Bohemian Rhapsody' big guitar chords are not needed because of what the piano part provides. As the piano has a wide pitch range, from low in the bass, it would be easy for the guitar to be redundant if it played as it would in an arrangement with only guitars. This was clearly a significant arranging issue that Queen had to think through to make the most of their instrumental options. So never underestimate the power of a single-note low-pitched electric line, as the transition at the end of Oasis' 'Live Forever' illustrates, going into the guitar solo proper, where it plays the three-note phrase C-B-A with real drama.

Electric arpeggio playing

The greater sustain of the electric guitar, coupled with sound effects such as echo and chorus, makes arpeggiating chords even more effective than on an acoustic. Played without distortion, such arpeggiating is typical of the 'jangle' style of guitar playing heard on recordings by such bands as The Smiths and early R.E.M. Remember that an arpeggio is a melody in waiting. Be ready to capitalize on any melodic ideas that emerge from an arpeggiated chord sequence. In The Jam's 'Man In The Corner Shop' the guitar arpeggiates the chords and plays part of the vocal melody. This technique provides a ready contrast with other sections of a song where the chords are strummed. Sum 41's 'Fat Lip' has a good example of this after the second chorus.

The Cure's 'It's Friday I'm In Love' has acoustic guitars provide the basic harmony but pulled right back so you're more conscious of their strumming than their notes. Electric guitars arpeggiate across the top more loudly. John McGeoch made an arpeggiated chord sequence the guitar hook of Siouxsie and the Banshees' 'Spellbound' (*Ju-Ju*), and the intro riff of The La's 'There She Goes' is doing the same. Electric guitars arpeggiate chords in the verses of Springsteen's 'Thunder Road'. With greater sustain you can choose patterns that have notes struck with less frequency.

STRUMMING VERSUS SUSTAIN

Even the finest acoustic guitars have comparatively short sustain. It's a factor that has shaped guitar technique. Why do guitarists strum? Why have alternating thumb finger-picking? It isn't only because these create rhythm. Such techniques generate a wash of sound, and, in the case of finger-picking, a harmonic backdrop for a melody. Think of the mandolin, which has little sustain. Almost as soon as a note is struck it fades away. Hence the characteristic mandolin technique of rapid strumming of a single note with a tightly-gripped pick. You can approximate this high on the guitar's top string, as is heard during the guitar solo in Radiohead's 'Paranoid Android', the first solo in Thin Lizzy's live 'Still In Love With You', and Muse songs like 'Sunburn', 'Showbiz', and 'Citizen Erased'. The rapid strum is a substitute for sustain.

To increase it, guitarists experimented with string gauges (heavier strings mean more tone) and altered tunings. The development of the electric guitar in the 1940s and 1950s marked a big step forward in the quest for sustain. Then came feedback. High volume levels and a guitar facing the amp could coax a single note into maintaining its initial volume. The trick was to keep the note from breaking into a higher overtone. Feedback is an unpredictable beast, and it doesn't solve the problem of achieving sustain at low volume.

Technology brought some solutions. Guitarists discovered compression – a staple effect in the studio for many years before stomp-box makers shoe-horned the relevant circuitry into a small metal box called a compressor/sustainer. Compression brings the signal up by a certain ratio as the note dies away. Electric players can also get extra sustain with distortion boxes. Many patches in a MIDI guitar effects unit like Roland's celebrated VG8 system have very long sustain, imitating that of bowed instruments. Synth guitar chords are sustained effectively on a Police track like 'Secret Journey'.

An acoustic guitar is strummed during a chord progression to maintain the harmony at a certain volume. If a guitar has greater sustain you don't need to keep strumming, you can play a chord and let it ring. This is one technique you are more likely to use on electric than acoustic. This means the percussive striking of the strings need not get in the way of the voice. Just let the chords hang. This works well with two electrics, where one plays sustained chords and the other strums, as in the verses of Thin Lizzy's 'The Boys Are Back In Town', or over a strummed acoustic, where the contrast in rhythm is accentuated by the tonal difference in the guitars. On Television's 'Guiding Light' a guitar on the left plays arpeggios, the one on the right plays accented clipped chords on beats two and four – there is no sustained chording for the first part of the verse. Similar things are all over The Strokes' *Is This It*. Listen to the way the rhythm guitars work on Kate Bush's 'King Of The Mountain'.

A popular electric rhythm technique is to hold down a barre chord – the shapes A, A minor, E and E minor in barre form – and play only the lower strings slightly muted. This can be used during a verse, and then for the chorus you take off the muting and open up with fully resonant chords hitting all the strings. Another approach favoured in soul and rhythm and blues bands is where a chord is fretted high on the neck and played with a cutting treble tone on the second and fourth beats of the bar (or similar). You can hear this on Dylan's 'Visions Of Johanna'. These chords have no sustain, but are designed to work more as part of the rhythm section than the harmony. From this we can deduce the following:

- The shorter the duration of a chord the more its harmonic value is reduced and its rhythmic value increased.
- The longer the duration of a chord the more its harmonic value is increased and its rhythmic value decreased.

FINGERSTYLE ELECTRIC

The sound of your electric playing will be affected by whether you use a pick and what kind it is, and also if you use your fingers. Not only the tone, but the songwriting riffs and ideas of players like Mark Knopfler of Dire Straits and Jeff Beck were shaped by the fact that they played with their fingers. The lead fills on Dire Straits tracks like 'Sultans Of Swing', 'Lady Writer', and 'Where Do You Think You're Going' are coloured by the sound of strings being rolled, pulled up, or snapped by the fingers. This can also be done on acoustic but the point is that on the electric these nuances are more audible – even the tone of a single bent note can sound different if played with a finger in contrast to a pick. You can hear this on CD tracks 31-32.

Electrical electric guitar

Playing an electric guitar as if it were merely an amplified acoustic is a bit of a waste of resource. Assuming the song requires it, aim to find a way to suggest the 'electrical' nature of the electric guitar. When it comes to rhythm playing, listen to the way Neil Young plays the chord sequence of 'Alabama' from *Harvest*. Instead of strumming all the strings at once, he breaks them up into splintered fragments of two or three at a time. This is more dynamic and textured, more electric, and more interesting to listen to. The same approach can be heard on Elvis Costello's 'I Want You', the verses of Led Zeppelin's 'Bring It On Home', on T.Rex songs such as 'Jitterbug Love' and 'Baby Strange', and the verses of David Bowie's 'John I'm Only Dancing'. A more elaborated version of this style is heard on Jimi Hendrix's quieter songs such as 'Wind Cries Mary' and 'Little Wing'. At the extreme end of this are players like Jonny Greenwood of Radiohead and Tom Morello of Rage Against The Machine.

Jack White of The White Stripes has the knack of emphasising the electrical-ness of the electric guitar. After all, solid-body electrics date from a time of sci-fi B-movies, cars with fins, and space rockets. They ought to sound like they've been shipped from Mars, not like merely louder acoustic guitars. Jack White's playing often has this space-age grit, as on the saturated distortion 'Dead Leaves and the Dirty Ground', and in the feedback that squawks at every chance in 'Aluminum'.

ELECTRIC 12-STRING

The electric 12-string was popularized by Rickenbacker. It was on the Beatles first visit to the USA, in 1964, that George Harrison was given only the second 360-12 model ever made. He got the guitar in February and used it immediately for recording the LP *Hard Day's Night* on songs like the title track and 'You Can't Do That'. Among other famous makes of electric 12-string were models from Vox and Fender, which produced its Electric XII with a body that resembled its Jaguar and Jazzmaster.

The more well-known Gibson 6- and 12-string twin-neck guitar was first produced in the late 1950s but didn't catch on until the early 1970s when its association with such players as John McLaughlin (Mahavishnu Orchestra), Charlie Whitney (Family) and Jimmy Page turned it into the rock equivalent of the Lancaster bomber, or to change the frame of reference, King Arthur's sword Excalibur. The young Arthur only had to pull the sword from the stone, whereas players of this monster have to lift a weight equivalent to the sword *and* the stone. Later dismissed as the ultimate guitar pose and a sure indication of lumbering prog-rock stupidity, the twin-neck has certain unique musical possibilities of its own, connected with sympathetic resonance, which even a 12-string can't produce (check out Dan Ar Bras' album *Music For The Silences To Come*). And the public can't see you using one during a recording session!

The electric 12-string:

- Gives a steel-bright version of the shimmering quality of the acoustic 12-string.
- Amplified, can generate an extraordinary wall-of-sound if played with strummed chords.
- Is usually recorded clean, rather than distorted. Effects like distortion, chorus or flanging should be used lightly or it will sound muddy.
- Produces its own 'chorus' effect by being tricky to tune. The slight de-tuning creates the effect that chorus was originally designed to reproduce.
- Can sound great clean with lots of reverb – if the 'wet' part of the signal is much greater than the 'dry' you can get lovely ghostly guitar tones. Listen to Dave Mason's 12-string contribution to Hendrix's 'All Along The Watchtower'. Strumming several open string parts in this way can enhance the natural overtones from the strings.

The classic way of playing the electric 12-string is by picking chords into rapid arpeggios – the style that Roger McGuinn used in the Byrds (on tracks like 'Turn Turn Turn'), and Peter Buck demonstrated with the I.R.S-era R.E.M. This allows the octave strings to be fully appreciated. It's unusual for people to attempt to play guitar solos on an electric 12-string and certainly string-bending is not much of an option beyond half a step. McGuinn took a memorable solo in The Byrds' 'Eight Miles High', emulating John Coltrane's sheets-of-sound saxophone playing.

The 12-string lends itself to playing melodic phrases – of course in octaves – such as the one that opens The Byrds' 'Mr Tambourine Man'. And heavy single note riffs on the lower strings get instant octave-doubling, as on Led Zeppelin's 'Living Loving Maid'. This has an interesting effect on 'power-chord' fifths.

The bottom three strings alone can generate an equivalent chord to all six on a six-string. This means low triad shapes become the equivalent of a six string chord.

As an example, hold C on the fifth string third fret, E♭ on the fourth string first fret, and play the G string open. On a six string, this gives a C minor triad. On a 12-string it produces the equivalent of playing a standard C minor barre chord at the third fret. Out of the movement of these triads can come different harmonic progressions and ideas to what you might normally create on a six-string.

Electric 12-strings have graced songs like The Beatles 'Any Time At All' and 'You Can't Do That', many songs by The Byrds, and the live version of Led Zeppelin's 'The Song Remains The Same'. Family's 'In My Own Time' has an arresting intro of discordant chords played on 12-string electric guitar with echo to the left.

TWIN LEAD GUITAR

For the first decade after their invention, bands with two guitars tended to split the parts into rhythm and lead guitar. One of the guitars laid down chords if the other played a melody (as in The Shadows) or soloed. The twin lead concept was born when someone realized both guitars could play a melody over the bass, with the chords only implied. How? Simple: only three notes make a complete chord (a triad). If the bass guitar takes the root and the guitars play the third and the fifth of the chords, hey presto! A complete chord. In an arrangement, twin lead guitar offers the following main options:

- It supplies implied chords.
- It provides chord/melody parts over background chord strumming.
- It provides link or solo passages with twin lead moving in parallel.
- Multitracking makes it possible to go on adding guitar lines at different octaves.

The key intervals for twin lead are thirds, sixths or either plus an octave, or octaves. The thirds and sixths will be a mixture of minor and major intervals because a harmonized scale naturally involves both. Here are some examples in C major:

C major in thirds						
E	F	G	A	B	C	D
C	D	E	F	G	A	B
C major in sixths						
A	B	C	D	E	F	G
C	D	E	F	G	A	B
A minor in thirds						
C	D	E	F	G	A	B
A	B	C	D	E	F	G
A minor in sixths						
F	G	A	B	C	D	E
A	B	C	D	E	F	G

Other intervals, like fourth or fifths, are possible at the beginning or end of phrases, to reinforce the underlying chord.

CASE STUDY

THIN LIZZY

Thin Lizzy came out of Ireland in the early 1970s, as a trio led by a bass player who sang, with two hit singles, 'Whiskey In The Jar' and 'The Rocker'. With two different guitarists, 'The Boys Are Back In Town' in 1976 took them back into the charts, and for a while they were a top-flight concert attraction. A typical Thin Lizzy song was arranged so that the guitarists played fifths ('power-chords') and single-note riffs in unison or at different octaves through the verses and choruses. Then there would be links where the guitars broke into parallel phrases of harmonized twin lead. Played at high volume this produced a full enough sound and looked dead impressive. This is best heard on any compilation with tracks like 'Waiting For An Alibi' and 'Don't Believe A Word', or *Live and Dangerous* (1978), though the lesser-known 'Wild One' or 'Soldier Of Fortune' are impressive in the lead guitar layering.

Thin Lizzy weren't the first band to explore the possibilities of twin lead. The Yardbirds, The Beatles ('And Your Bird Can Sing'), Fleetwood Mac's *Then Play On* (1970), and Wishbone Ash had all explored the style. In the 1970s The Eagles 'Hotel California' used twin lead to state the harmony during the verse before the carefully orchestrated coda. You could pull out all the harmony instruments playing chords, such as the acoustic guitars, and the harmony would still be clear. The harmony on the verses of Led Zeppelin's 'Ten Years Gone' is carried by orchestrated lead guitar lines. Brian May of Queen has filled many tracks with multiple lead guitars. Boston's 'More Than A Feeling' and Television's 'See No Evil' both have twin lead, despite the fact the bands belong to different rock genres. More recently it was a central feature of albums by The Darkness.

ALTERED TUNINGS AND ELECTRIC GUITAR

Altered tunings are less common on electric guitar than acoustic because the former are less often finger-picked, and because the sonorities of altered tuning chords are easily obscured in loud, amplified contexts. The more parts you place around an altered tuning the more the effect of that tuning is lost. One way to counter this would be to double the guitar part and keep the guitars to the front of the mix. Alternatively, if there are particular intervals and voice-leading parts peculiar to the tuning emphasize these by getting other instruments to play them.

Altered tunings can also sound mushy on electric. However, in the 1990s bands like Sonic Youth, Soundgarden, and My Bloody Valentine made altered tunings a central feature of their music. The Darkness' guitar textures are sometimes created via alternate tunings. Dropped D tuning (DADGBE) features in 'Growing On Me', 'Christmas Time', and 'The Best Of Me'. 'How Dare You Call This Love?' uses EADGBD and 'Holding My Own' is 'double dropped D' (DADGBD), the same tuning Neil Young featured on 'Cinnamon Girl'.

Coldplay use altered tunings on 'Yellow' (EABGBD♯) and 'Trouble' (EADGBD). Billy Corgan of Smashing Pumpkins has used standard tuning down a semi-tone, or dropped D, as on 'Silverfuck',

'Hummer', and 'Jellybelly'; 'Sweet Sweet' is a pretty and simple ballad with the tuning EGDGBE. Other variant tunings include E♭A♭D♭GB♭E♭ for 'In The Arms of Sleep' and E♭A♭D♭G♭A♭E♭ for 'Farewell and Goodnight', both from the *Mellon Collie* set.

Here are some tunings suitable for electric guitar and tips on how to use them in an Arrangement.

- In so far as they are more resonant than standard tuning, altered tunings can take up a lot of aural space in an arrangement, especially if distorted. Therefore such a track may not need very many guitar parts.
- Detuning by a semitone or tone can help the vocalist pitch notes in certain keys.
- Detuning also decreases string tension, making it easier to bend strings and bend them further.
- Lowered bass strings lend themselves to heavy riffs. Tony Iommi was also a pioneer of de-tuning. On the Sabs' third album Master Of Reality he succumbed to the evil lure (!) of D♭ major by detuning a tone and a half on 'Children Of The Grave', 'Into The Void', and 'Lord Of This World', and used the same approach for the later 'Supernaut', 'Cornucopia', 'Snowblind', 'Sabbath Bloody Sabbath', 'A National Acrobat', and 'Killing Yourself To Live' (though the key centre there is G♭).
- Drop D tuning turns the lowest three strings into a power chord that can be played with one finger.
- Open A (EAEAC♯E) and open E (EBEG♯BE) are popular electric tunings, especially for blues/bottleneck playing.

As with acoustic guitar tunings, consider how you might handle any songs written in altered tunings when playing live.

PART-PLAYING

> ***"We had a very good producer from the second album onwards, Chris Thomas, who had worked with The Beatles, he'd come from doing* Dark Side Of The Moon, *subsequently did the Sex Pistols. I learned an incredible amount from him about part-playing in recording. With Chris it was: look for the gap, don't play over the vocal, less is more. You learned how to position things – just as all the great Motown stuff has incredible position and texture. All the parts add up to something greater, it all locks in."***
>
> Phil Manzanera of Roxy Music

One of the central skills of arranging is understanding the concept of part-playing. It is natural when putting down more than one guitar track to get into that particular performance and do more than is needed. But what makes a single instrumental part interesting may create a mess in the overall mix. This is where restraint and imagination is needed. At about 18 Billy Corgan of Smashing Pumpkins realized that what was important was to put the emphasis on the songs rather than the guitar-playing. As he told *Guitar World*, "guitar playing, in and of itself, does not mean a whole heck of a lot. But guitar playing within the context of great music and great songs is a big deal."

You have to keep your ear on the big aural picture, on what the final effect of the arrangement will be. Resist the temptation to add too many details to a single part. If you do that with all of them there will probably be too much going on and the music will sound congested. This applies to extra notes, fills and rhythm patterns.

An example of skilful part-playing would be the rhythm guitar technique of putting a staccato chord on beats two and four in time with the snare drum. This is heard on many Motown tracks, such as R. Dean Taylor's 'Gotta See Jane' and Smokey Robinson and the Miracles' 'I Second That Emotion', The Turtles 'You Showed Me', and 'It's A Man's Man's Man's World' by James Brown. A syncopated version of the same guitar idea can be heard on The Verve's 'Sonnet' and Blur's 'The Universal', both tracks evoking a 1960s pop sound.

Often part-playing requires you to do very little and stick to it. On Television's 'See No Evil' the guitar on the left side of the mix plays only one chord during the intro; the more interesting parts, the twin lead and arpeggio figures, are heard on the right. Similarly, on the intro to Cream's 'Badge' Eric Clapton plays only muted percussive guitar, allowing Jack Bruce's bass-line to have centre-stage.

GUITAR FILLS

> ***"Steve Cropper is probably my favourite guitarist of all time. You can't think of a time when he really ripped off a hot solo, but he just plays perfectly."***
>
> Peter Buck

One particular part-playing discipline is the art of the guitar fill. A guitar fill is a short, melodic phrase, placed between vocal phrases or other solo instrumental lines. It can have a harmonic function if it strengthens the chords, and/or a rhythmic function. 1970s funk often features short guitar fills that support the rhythm. Guitar fills can be played using common scale patterns and bends, or a series of thirds and sixths – a favourite signature of Steve Cropper on records like Otis Redding's 'Dock Of The Bay'. Sixths can also be heard on Percy Sledge's 'When A Man Loves A Woman', on Coldplay's 'Yellow', on the double-time section of Led Zeppelin's 'The Lemon Song', in the first verse of Dire Straits' 'Sultans Of Swing', and on Pulp's 'Sunrise'.

Fills can also be provided by keyboard and other instruments. Such fills often act to provide an answer phrase for the previous vocal line, or to answer another instrumental phrase.

At the opposite extreme, in the late 1960s the high profile of the guitar virtuoso and the improvisatory jam meant that guitar players were sometimes permitted to play lead lines all the way through a track – as is heard on tracks by Jefferson Airplane or Crosby Stills Nash and Young.

This could be very distracting from the lead vocal, and also had the effect of taking drama from the main solo and partially erasing the differences in the arrangements of various song sections.

ARRANGING A RIFF

A riff is a short (one to four bars) musical phrase heavily featured in a song so that it becomes a significant point of interest. In many rock numbers the guitar riff is as much a hook as the chorus melody. It may replace chords altogether (think of Led Zeppelin's 'Whole Lotta Love'). In rock music it focuses the energy of the song. Many riffs are pitched in the lower register of the guitar, though there have been famous riffs played on the higher strings (think of Alice Cooper's 'School's Out' or U2's 'With Or Without You').

Riffs are popular because they are short, repeated, and stick in the mind. Musicians like them because once you've got a riff together the whole band can get behind it and you have an instant feeling of musical unity. The guitar plays a riff in unison with the bass and then breaks away to solo while the bass keeps the riff going.

When it comes to writing riffs consider the M-H-R formula. Whether on guitar or keyboards, riffs have:

- A harmonic element (what chords they imply, if any).
- A melodic element (which intervals they use).
- A rhythmic element (how they fit with the drums).

To consider these in order, riffs are usually in single notes, fourths, fifths, or octaves. These can be combined in any way. The bridge riff in Led Zeppelin's 'Good Times Bad Times', for example, combines fourths and fifths. Deep Purple's 'Smoke On The Water' is in fourths only. Ocean Colour Scene's 'The Riverboat Song' riff is in single notes. Cream's 'Sunshine Of Your Love' is a combination of chords with a scale-like riff. If whole chords are played in a sufficiently punchy rhythm and repeated in short loops they can be considered riffs too, as in the chorus of Boston's 'More Than A Feeling', The Who's 'I Can't Explain' and 'Substitute', and The Jam's 'In The City'. Led Zeppelin's 'Achilles Last Stand' combines triads with single notes on its main riff.

Riffs can also be built from a scale – usually in rock the pentatonic majors and minors, with the blues scales and the addition of extra chromatic notes if you want to get really slinky. The bridge of Blind Faith's 'Presence Of The Lord' is pentatonic minor based. Franz Ferdinand use an arrangement texture where single-note guitar lines work with the bass to imply the chords, as on 'Take Me Out'. This is reminiscent of the same effect in 'Cascade' by Siouxsie & the Banshees on *A Kiss In The Dreamhouse*, and you can hear similar figures on early Cure tracks.

Rhythmically, the best riffs are often doubled by the bass and their rhythm patterns coincide with what the drums are doing. The vintage trick is to leave a gap where the snare drum is hit and play around that. That's why some of the best riffs you will write will come playing with a drum loop, a drum machine, or drummer. Hearing a rhythm is the best way to spark a good riff that's punchy.

When it comes to arranging riffs, playing a riff on acoustic guitar makes an effective means to introduce a riff in a song while saving the electric guitars for a potent entry later on. The riff in the verse of Radiohead's 'Paranoid Android' is heard initially on acoustic guitar. Another approach is to arrange a riff to be played by both clean and distorted guitars. Here are some typical multitrack possibilities for arranging a riff:

- Stereo electric guitar + bass guitar one octave below.
- Two electrics in unison pitch, placed left and right.
- Two electrics one octave apart.
- Second or third electric placed a third above (harmonized riff).
- Second or third electric placed a tenth – an octave and a third above (harmonized riff).

Riffs can also be transposed, so they start on a different note but keep their pitch shape and rhythm. You can hear this in Franz Ferdinand's 'Cheating On You' at 1:57, where the main riff is transposed up two tones, or in the bridge of Hendrix's 'In From The Storm', where the scale riff is transposed from A to B to C.

It is worth listening to Led Zeppelin's 'The Wanton Song' to experience the power of a well-timed riff doubling when the second guitar comes in at the end of the guitar solo.

Eric Clapton's 'Layla' riff owes some of its power to being heard in three different octaves, low, middle and high. That riff is interesting also because although the first seven-note phrase is the same in all parts, the second phrase of five notes is actually three different parts. The top is played with bent notes, the middle phrase is a counter-melody, and the lowest guitar plays fifths.

There is also the arrangement approach of having a riff that alternates with a vocal line, as on Ten Years After's 'Love Like A Man', Fleetwood Mac's 'Oh Well', Led Zeppelin's 'Black Dog', and The Cult's 'Automatic Blues'.

GUITAR SOLOS

> ***"I'm not a technically proficient guitar player. I'm about what it means at the moment, the attack of it and the attitude. I don't sit at home trying to learn how to play scales and try to be as fast as I can. I just care about the emotion that comes out of it, I suppose!"***
>
> Jack White, The White Stripes

> ***"I find writing solos very boring. For the solo in 'Save Me I'm Yours', I tried thousands of things. I tried a wah, third and fifths, slide, all types and then eventually settled on that repeat delay effect. We put it into Pro Tools and had it fire from all directions. It's picking up the tempo of the song and then it doesn't bludgeon you. Sometimes you have to think about these things. People assume you always do it off the cuff."***
>
> Steve Mason, Gene

If you are arranging and recording a rock number, chances are you will think of including a guitar solo. Here are some relevant considerations:

- Does a guitar solo suit the song? Would the solo be better played on another instrument? Could there be two instruments sharing the solo, or dividing it between them?
- What can the solo contribute to the meaning of the lyric or the emotion of the song? Does the music have an emotion other than, "Listen to me play another solo, faster than the last one"?
- What kind of guitar tone is needed?
- Can the solo develop from a musical idea previously heard in the song? The solo on Electric Soft Parade's 'Empty At The End' begins with part of the verse melody.
- How will it connect with the sections immediately before and after?
- Would it appropriate to your music to have an 'anti-solo' solo, as on 'Smells Like Teen Spirit'. On that track the usual rock guitar clichés are avoided, and making it clear that technique is not its concern, the solo reproduces the verse melody, with some of the notes slurred and bent. After 1980s speed-metal playing, it was a way for grunge to say "I can't widdle and I don't care".

In a moment we will look at some useful scale patterns for lead solos. But first, it's worth realising that many great solos sound that way not so much because of what the lead guitar plays as the context that is created for it. Factors such as the richness of the chord progression the solo goes over, and the way it has been arranged, plus the rhythm of the music, have a big role in providing opportunities to play an expressive guitar solo.

Here are some tips for constructing a guitar solo:

- Devise a memorable opening phrase and a memorable finish that brings the solo to a fitting conclusion.
- Shape the solo like a mini-story.
- Think in phrases and don't be afraid to repeat them. Listen to the repetition in the breaks on R.E.M.'s 'Disturbance at the Heron House', 'Strange', and the tasteful lead solo of 'The Flowers Of Guatemala'.
- Bends, pre-bends, slides, grace notes, hammer-ons, pull-offs, pinch harmonics, vibrato, tremolo arm pitch-shifts, can add colour to your playing.
- Don't think only in scales – solos can also draw on arpeggios, broken chord ideas, octaves, open drone strings, consecutive intervals, etc. Listen to the double-stops in Hendrix's 'Wind Cries Mary'.
- Some guitar solos owe more to feedback, noise and sound-effects than notes – a kind of painting with sound. Matthew Bellamy's solos with Muse don't have much use for single pentatonic/blues-rock phrases. The solos are short, not especially melodic, and use effects and noise to paint with sound. Andy Summers' feedback solo on The

Police's 'Bring On The Night' and Marty Willson-Piper's break on 'Rhythm Of Life' by All About Eve are two more examples.

- Use octaves or unison bends to emphasize a phrase.
- Double or triple-track very high phrases if they happen at a climactic moment.
- Try recording several takes of the solo and then play them all back at once. Solos played by more than one guitar at a time feature on Roxy Music's 'Street Life', Eric Clapton's 'Bell Bottom Blues', Wishbone Ash's 'Throw Down The Sword', Black Sabbath's 'N.I.B.', Fleetwood Mac's Then Play On, and Grant Lee Buffalo's 'Fuzzy'.
- Both Free's 'Little Bit Of Love' (guitar phrase at 1:29) and Roxy Music's 'Pyjamarama' have lead guitars that don't quite fit together.
- The indie/new wave solo (see Franz Ferdinand, Arctic Monkeys, Razorlight) is typified by few bends, no long sustain or much overdrive, no fast runs, and, most importantly, single notes picked several times before the run moves on. This style of lead allies the solo more to the underlying rhythm and harmony of the track, rather than playing independently of it.
- Think of the solo as a melody. Earl Slick: 'I did get stuck in a thing years ago of playing a bit too much and mindlessly. I enjoy it more now when I get into something more 'ambient' – for want of a better word. If you think about all the records you listen to over the course of time what do you remember? You remember the line in 'Satisfaction', you don't remember Keith's solos note for note on those earlier blues things the Stones did. You remember the Hendrix solo on 'Little Wing' because it was like a melody.'

Which scales do I use?

Choice of scale depends on the style of the music and the chord progression. Check the chord progression and see how many chords it contains (if any) that don't belong to the key. Analyze those problematic chords to find which notes they contain which are off key. You can then either avoid those notes in those particular bars, play an arpeggio based on that chord, or play a scale that fits it. Most simple chord progressions can be played over with a single scale, albeit with more than one pattern for that scale on the neck.

Here's an example: The chord sequence for a guitar solo consists of D, G, A minor, and C, the song being in the key of D major. The D major scale is D E F♯ G A B C♯; but A minor and C contain C natural not C♯. The C♯ would clash. D Mixolydian is D E F♯ G A B C and that will fit over all the chords with no problem. D pentatonic major – D E F♯ A B – presents no clashes. The D pentatonic minor – D F G A C – will also work, with the F natural giving a blues flavour which the others would not.

Here are the ten most useful scale types. The notation/tab gives two patterns for each – one with the root note on the sixth string and one with it on the fifth string. This covers a good part of the neck.

Remember that as long as you don't run out of frets, these patterns can be moved up or down an octave. They can also be transposed onto any other note from A by moving up or down the neck to find the root note you want.

SCALES FOR SOLOING

9. A major
10. A major
11. A mixolydian
12. A mixolydian
13. A natural minor (aeolian)
14. A natural minor (aeolian)
15. A harmonic minor
16. A harmonic minor

Pentatonic minor

In rock, blues and soul the most popular scale is the **pentatonic minor**. It is a more 'forgiving' scale than some others. In certain musical situations if you have the right pentatonic scale it is easy to avoid hitting 'bum' notes. In C the notes are C E♭ F G B♭. As a pattern of semitone (half-step) intervals, or frets, think of this as 3-2-2-3. It has a distinctive tough sound played over a sequence of major chords. Try a 12-bar or a progression where each note of the scale is turned into a major chord. It also fits most minor key progressions. But if the progression is major key with its standard major *and* minor chords you have to be careful, as the pentatonic minor will clash with the minor chords. Playing E pentatonic minor over E, A, and B chords sounds bluesy, but not pleasant if F♯ minor, G♯ minor and C♯ minor chords are involved.

'Blues' scale

By adding one note to the pentatonic minor we get what is known as the **blues scale**. The extra note is the flattened fifth, giving the scale C E♭ F G♭ G. You can get this extra note either by fretting it or bending up the note one a fret back. There's a slight difference in the effect.

Pentatonic major

The next most popular form of scale is the pentatonic major, whose notes in C are C D E G A (2-2-3-2). In comparison to a pentatonic minor, the major seems happy, bright and upbeat. You cannot use this scale in a minor key. C D E G A sounds fine over any of the six primary chords of C major, namely C, D minor, E minor, F, G, and A minor.

Major 'blues' scale

We can get a major blues scale adding a flattened third to the pentatonic major: C D E♭ E G A. This adds an unexpected 'spice' to it. As with the previous blues scale, the flattened third is produced by bending and other times by fretting.

Major scale

This scale is the basis for most Western music. It consists of seven notes arranged in a sequence of intervals: tone, tone, semitone, tone, tone, tone, semitone (whole-step, whole-step, half-step, whole-step, whole-step, whole-step, half-step). In frets this is 2-2-1-2-2-2-1. If we take C as our starting note the notes for a scale of C major would be C D E F G A B C. The pentatonic major is merely an abbreviated version of the full major, with notes four and seven dropped. The major scale lends itself to many musical situations. It won't give you the 'tough' tone of the pentatonic minor, but it will add interest to an otherwise pentatonic solo in a major key.

Mixolydian

The Mixolydian is a major scale with a flattened seventh: C D E F G A B♭. Since blues music uses lots of flattened sevenths this is a common scale. It also enables you to replace the worse than useless diminished chord on the seventh note of the scale with a major chord on the flattened seventh. This produces classic rock progressions like C B♭ F. Simply take any major scale pattern, locate the seventh notes and move them back a semitone (half-step). It is often found in 1950s rock'n'roll solos by guitarists such as Chuck Berry.

Natural minor

This is the most common minor scale for soloing. In C minor this would be C D E♭ F G A♭ B♭. The pattern of intervals is 2-1-2-2-1-2-2. It adds two notes – D and A♭ – to C pentatonic minor which can be very expressive, bringing a new dimension to the sound of the pentatonic minor.

Harmonic minor

This is the second type of minor scale. It involves one change from the natural minor, the seventh note raised a semitone (half-step) to B. This results in a large one-and-a-half tone jump between notes six and seven (A♭-B), which gives the scale an unusual flavour. In rock the harmonic minor is exploited either for a neo-classical effect or for an 'Eastern' sound. A harmonic minor scale will fit in a minor key where chord V is major, as in the chord sequence A minor-G-F-E. You can hear the harmonic minor on Muse tracks like 'Sunburn', 'New Born', 'Muscle Museum', 'Micro Cuts', and 'Darkshines'. In rock the harmonic minor makes a powerful statement that runs counter to rock's roots in blues.

Dorian scale

The Dorian scale is C D E♭ F G A B♭ – a natural minor scale with the sixth note sharpened. This gives the Dorian a slightly more 'angular', tense quality. The sharpened sixth is not quite as 'depressed' as the sixth found on the natural minor scale. This has always been a favourite of Santana. The Dorian mode on C suits a C minor-F chord change. It would not fit a C minor-F minor change for which you would need C natural minor. If you have a chord sequence with C minor, F minor, and G minor you need the natural minor; if the chords are C minor, F minor, G, the harmonic minor will be useful, and if you see an C minor-F change it's the Dorian you want.

Phrygian scale

This is the natural minor with a flattened second: C D♭ E♭ F G A♭ B♭. It has a distinctive Spanish sound, and is heard in flamenco music. On the guitar it is particulary effective when based on the note E (E F G A B C D E), as this allows for phrases built on some of the open strings. Robert Smith used this scale when playing with Siouxsie And The Banshees on a track called 'Bring Me The Head Of The Preacher Man'.

OCTAVES

Until the 1990s octaves were comparatively little used by rock players. They tended to be a jazz guitarist's method for fleshing out melodies before taking solos. The octave riff of Hendrix's 'Fire' or, in the late 1970s, the brief octaves that Scott Gorham threw into the guitar break on Thin Lizzy's 'Dancing In The Moonlight' were, in rock songs, unusual. In the 1990s they became more popular, as rock guitarists sought new musical figures beyond pentatonic scales. Matthew Bellamy of Muse often works with octaves, as in the intro of 'Sober' and in 'Fillip'. Billy Corgan of Smashing Pumpkins liked playing octave figures high up the neck over a droning open E string, as 'Cherub Rock' shows.

On Foo Fighters' *One By One* the main ingredient of the lead guitar work is octaves. On *One By One* there are octaves on the intro to 'Overdrive', and at the start of 'Low', with rapidly strummed octaves on the right at 3:14-40 during a solo. At the end of 'Times Like These', octaves on the left reinforce the chord changes.

There are four useful octave shapes. (In this notation we are reading from bottom E to top E, with x indicating an unplayed string.) Try these:

Fifth fret octave E: x7xx5x
Fifth fret octave A: xx7xx5
Fifth fret low octave A: 5x7xxx
Fifth fret octave D: x5x7xx

There are other shapes, but these are the easiest to move around. The first two are held down with the first and third finger on the fretting hand and played with a pick and a finger. The lower two positions can be struck just with a pick if you use your first finger on the fifth-fret bass note to mute the x string that comes between. The finger on the seventh fret can then mute all the strings higher than it – that way you can mute the four strings you're not using but hit all six to give your octave a percussive quality. String-muting is an example of an invisible guitar technique – no-one notices if you're doing it right! – and important to learn when handling electric guitar at high volume, when the instrument is a much livelier beast.

Octaves can be used in the following ways:

- To emphasis a melody or a guitar fill.
- To play riffs over an open string that resemble the sound of an open tuning.
- To thicken a lead phrase, as can be heard toward the end of Grandaddy's song 'Crystal Lake', from *The Sophtware Slump*.

In the next section we proceed to guitar effects and how these change the way a guitar part fits in an arrangement.

SECTION 5

Arranging and guitar effects

When you use electric guitars in an arrangement, you need to consider what effects to use and how well suited they are to your song. Effects can form a crucial part of your sound.

"The great thing about effects is that they change the way you hear the guitar, thereby changing the way you react to the guitar. The most mundane licks can turn into something completely different with the right effect."

Billy Corgan of Smashing Pumpkins)

When guitars are added to an arrangement, or when an arrangement is created around them, there are many choices available as to what type of guitar sound is recorded. It is important to know about the main electric guitar effects, so you can choose the one that fits the song.

Some effects will also help you fill out the sound. Here's Alex Lifeson of Rush, reflecting on life as a guitarist in a power trio: "It's always been a challenge for me to fill the sound as much as possible from the guitar angle and that's why we brought keyboards into the band at an early time, to add another dimension. But it was refreshing for me to work on this last record without them filling the sound. We approached the record like that and it was fun. On stage it's the same thing. I try to fill out as much of the basic sound … Effects are one road you can take to get that depth and width – chorus and delays and syncopations with the drums. They create the bigger sound that Rush is known for. It's natural for me to think in those terms and develop suitable guitar parts." I asked if he meant things such as arpeggios and chords with open strings ringing? "Exactly – that is it."

VOLUME-BASED EFFECTS

Distortion

In rock music, distortion is the most important effect that modifies the electric guitar. Distortion originated in the sound of valve amps being overloaded. It was the genie in the bottle of that particular analogue technology back in the 1950s. The solid-body guitar could not generate sound on its own and needed an amplifier. Valve-tube technology already existed, so it was adapted to make amps for electric instruments. But many players found themselves competing with the considerable volume level of an unamplified drum kit. They turned up their amps and the signal distorted. At first some players merely tolerated this, but eventually many decided it suited the raw character of the rock'n'roll, electric blues and rhythm and blues they played. When amps were manufactured with transistor technology, which doesn't distort in the same way, designers had to find a way to emulate the distorted sound. Eventually circuitry was designed so that various degrees of distortion could be achieved at low volumes as well as high. The distortion beast had been tamed.

Distortion changes a guitar tone by:

- Thickening, compressing and dirtying the tone, partly as a result of boosting overtones, which are part of the original note but not normally heard.
- Increasing the sustain of the notes, which is especially useful for any single-note phrases.
- Decreasing the separation of notes within a chord – the notes 'bleed' into one another.
- Increasing the sensitivity of the strings to left and right hand finger movements and picking sounds.
- Decreasing the effectiveness of more complex chords – this is why many rock guitar parts are comprised of bare fifths.
- Boosting the volume of natural and artificial harmonics.

There are many different types, verging from mild overdrive to heavy metal saturation, and related types such as fuzz, which has its own character rather than being only another degree of intensity on that scale. The uses of distorted guitar in an arrangement are:

- To add power and aggression in most rock styles.
- To make intervals such as fifths ('power-chords') sound fuller.
- To add sustain to single notes or chords.
- With slightly overdriven guitar parts positioned behind acoustic guitars to give them greater strength and to fill out the sound.
- Using fuzz, to evoke guitar tones of the 1966-71 era (as with Hendrix's fuzzface pedal).
- To reinforce a single stereo guitar part by adding more distortion to one side of the signal than the other. This, with a short echo, heightens the illusion of two guitars, as on the chorus of Coldplay's 'Shiver'.

I hear many demos where the guitars are over-distorted for the style of music, and even where it is right for the genre you may need less distortion on chord-playing than you think. Try under-distorting your guitar rather than over-doing it, at least at first. Many classic rock records dominated by distorted guitar have less distortion than we imagine. Distortion has a habit of taking up a lot of frequencies in a mix, and since it compresses the signal it can also make guitars in a mix sound less dynamic. Conversely, a clean guitar part can lend harmonic focus if the other guitars are low and distorted.

Violin-toning

Imagine the sound-wave of a guitar note on a graph: the instant the note is struck is the moment of maximum volume, and then there's a downward curve as the note dies. Unless time itself reversed we would normally never hear a guitar note that got louder. One way to reverse this is to manipulate the volume of a guitar note as soon as it is played. This is called 'violin-toning' because the sustain of the note mimics a bowed string.

To do this, wind the volume on the guitar off, play a note and then quickly turn the pot back up (how far and fast depends on how loud your amp is). Bingo! The sound-wave is reversed, the note starts inaudible and fades up. There's no percussive click when the note is struck, and the ear is more conscious of the sustain in the sound. How easy it is to manipulate the volume pot depends on the layout of your guitar controls. Some players use the little finger. The effect sounds great with reverb and delay, especially if entering with a bend. If you find this difficult and have enough volume try hammering-on the notes you want with the fretting hand and use your picking hand to turn up the volume.

Leslie West's duet with himself on the live side of Mountain's *Flowers Of Evil* and on the intro of 'Pride And Passion' is a good example. Jan Akkerman of Dutch progressive rock band Focus was a master of violin-toning. If I had to pick out a few highlights of Akkerman's playing with this technique I'd go for the track 'Focus' on *In and Out of Focus*, a masterpiece of restraint where Akkerman confines himself to violin-toning a few notes over the repeated B minor-D change.

Violin-toning is also a way of imitating 'backward' guitar, provided the last note of every phrase is cut off extremely quickly. 'Backward' guitar is a tape effect discussed in **Section Eight**.

Volume pedal

A volume pedal does the same thing as violin-toning but you control it with your foot. It's not an 'effect' in the same way as distortion, wah-wah, chorus, or phasing. But a volume pedal can be a highly musical tool, if one with a limited range of uses. It's not the sort of effect you'd play on more than a couple of numbers. As you move the pedal from the full back position (volume off) downwards the volume increases. In terms of playing, you have to train your foot to automatically bring the pedal back after each note in order to use the volume swell on the next. Striking the note at the right moment is critical. The note won't be immediately audible, so if you hit a note with the pedal in the volume 'off' position and you're on the beat, as the volume comes up you'll be heard as 'late'. If you want the chord to swell on the beat, then you have to hit it fractionally early.

Johnny Marr made great use of the pedal to play weeping chords on The Smiths' 'Well I Wonder' on *Meat Is Murder* (1985), as did George Harrison on The Beatles' 'I Need You' and 'Yes It Is', and Lindsay Buckingham on Fleetwood Mac's 'Dreams', where the volume-pedal guitar phrases defined the character of the whole song.

Violin-toning and volume pedals:

- Take away the percussive attack of the guitar, softening it.
- Work well with pre-bends, echo and reverb.
- Give a more expressive quality to chords, and enable chords to be sounded without strumming.
- Give the guitar a vocal, expressive quality – singers, after all, can increase the volume of a note. Mark Knopfler's majestic lead playing on Dire Straits''Brothers In Arms' has a number of swelled notes.

Tremolo circuit

Not to be confused with the tremolo ('whammy') arm on some electric guitars (which actually creates vibrato, an alteration in pitch), the tremolo circuit creates a shimmering effect by rapidly blocking a signal and then letting it through again. Such circuits were often fitted to cheap amplifiers in lieu of a reverb unit. Famous examples of its use include the verses of Led Zeppelin's 'Immigrant Song', the intro of The Beatles 'You Like Me Too Much', the bridge of Roy Orbison's 'Pretty Woman', the Association's 'Never My Love', and the last verse of Green Day's 'Warning'. Chris Isaacs' 'Wicked Game' lovingly recreates a late 1950s arrangement with mellow tremolo guitar. The Smiths' 'How Soon Is Now' is one of the greatest exercises in tremolo not only because the effect is foregrounded throughout, but also because it takes the sound away from its 1950s associations and gives it a different emotional charge.

Peter Buck added a distinctive clean tremolo phrase to 'How The West Was Won And Where It Got Us', and it was featured on the *Monster* album on tracks like 'Crush With Eyeliner', 'What's the Frequency, Kenneth?', and 'I Took Your Name'. The guitar break on Black Rebel Motorcycle Club's 'As Sure As The Sun' has vicious tremolo splintering the notes. The Arctic Monkeys' 'Riot Van' features a tremolo guitar solo.

If you think of using tremolo:

- Be aware of its 1950s associations if the guitar tone is clean.
- It can sometimes be synchronized with the tempo of the song.
- The effect is more noticeable on sustained chords rather than single notes.
- It can be highly effective if included in small doses rather than a lot.
- It is effective with pitch-shifted chords and feedback.

TIME-BASED EFFECTS

Chorus

> ***"Chorus has been important [to me] for a long time. Remember the original Boss stompbox chorus – the heavy metal one with a vibrato switch as well as the chorus. I fell in love with that. I used a Roland JC120 [amp with chorus built-in] for Farewell To Kings and that turned me on to that sound."***
>
> (Alex Lifeson of Rush)

Chorus is a guitar effect that appeared in the late 1970s. It has a smooth, rich quality, and as its name suggests emulates the small pitch variation that occurs when a number of the same instruments play together. A string section in an orchestra generates its own 'chorus' naturally because of the minute variations in pitch between the players, causing people to describe a 'lush' string sound.

Chorus changes a guitar tone by:

- Thickening and smoothing the tone, creating the illusion of two guitars instead of one.
- Increasing the sustain of notes, which is good for chord and arpeggio playing, and situations where you don't want sustain through distortion.
- Helping non-rhythmic chordal work, whereby the guitar can function more like a harmonic 'pad' and doesn't need to be strummed so often.
- Helping a clean guitar 'sit' with keyboard pad sounds/parts.
- Adding fullness to partial ('broken') chords and intervals – but it also works with complex chords.
- Boosting the volume and presence of natural and artificial harmonics.

As with distortion, there are many types of chorus, and the intensity of the chorus effect can be controlled, from mild to noticeably out of tune. The uses of chorus in an arrangement are:

- Chorus helps the guitar blend with keyboards by taking off its rough edges and increasing sustain.
- To make chords sound smoother, but with less treble.
- It adds richness to barre chords, so they don't sound so different from open string chords.
- It gives depth and sustain to arpeggio figures.
- Slightly chorused clean electric parts can be positioned with acoustic guitars to fill out the sound.
- Chorus works well with effects such as echo and phasing.

Chorus suits genres where the guitar parts are clean and smooth. It doesn't particularly suit rock guitar, and any parts where you play clipped chords or need dynamic punch. It needs sustained playing to reveal its quality. It creates a mushy tone if combined with distortion (listen to Jimmy Page's guitar with The Firm in the early 1980s), which is an acquired taste.

Phasing and flanging

> ***"If you hold the notes it gives more chance for the sound to come through. On 'Psycho Twang' I used a flanger, took the guitar signal out and left the flanged part in – it's only the effect you hear."***
>
> Earl Slick, guitarist with David Bowie

Phasing and flanging are similar effects to chorus but more noticeable. They can be loosely described as a 'wooshing' noise which cycles up and down the frequencies. The speed and depth of this c2cling can be altered.

- Strong flanging or phasing is impressive on chords or arpeggios. Listen to the intro and outro of Led Zeppelin's 'Achilles Last Stand', or the bridge of Badly Drawn Boy's 'Something To Talk About'.
- Both effects add sustain, especially to barre chords, as can be heard on David Bowie's Station To Station album and Big Star's 'The Ballad of El Goodo'.
- Neither works well with rhythmic figures, although 1970s soul used a certain amount of phased riffs.
- They are distinctive sounds and occupy quite a wide frequency band. As a consequence they are best used sparingly. The guitar solos on Hendrix's 'House Burning Down', The Isley Brothers' 'That Lady', Ash's 'Goldfinger', Suede's 'Animal Nitrate', and Roxy Music's 'In Every Dream A Heartache' are either phased or flanged.

There is also studio-generated track-wide phasing which is applied to an entire mix. The Supremes' 'Nathan Jones' and The Small Faces 'Itchycoo Park' are two examples. This technique is associated with psychedelia. Flanging was also featured to get original guitar riffs by UK guitarist John McGeoch on Siouxsie And The Banshees albums like *Ju-Ju* and *A Kiss In The Dreamhouse*. The guitar solo on Smashing Pumpkins' 'Cherub Rock' was flanged using two tape machines (the original way of creating it).

Leslie cabinet/rotary speaker

Related to phasing and flanging is the Leslie cabinet, a rotary speaker through which a musical signal could be fed. This late-1960s effect can be heard on the guitar arpeggio figures in The Beatles' 'Let It Be' and 'Yer Blues', Cream's 'Badge', Badfinger's 'No Matter What', adding fills to Simon and Garfunkel's 'America', Led Zeppelin's 'Night Flight', Blind Faith's 'Presence Of The Lord', The Band's 'Tears Of Rage', and on the intro of Green Day's 'Redundant'. This is an excellent effect to apply to single-note guitar figures like arpeggios whose main function is not rhythmic but harmonic, giving them a plangent sweep and presence.

Echo/delay

Echo has been a guitar effect since the 1950s, when a specific type ('slap-back') characterized rock'n'roll guitar and vocals. It was crucial to the guitar sound and approach of Hank Marvin of The Shadows, the instrumental group that dominated the UK pop scene from 1960-63. Echo can be related to the M-H-R formula described in **Section Two** in so far as it can be exploited for melodic, harmonic or rhythmic reasons. The function of echo in an arrangement:

- Is melodic if it is used on single notes to enhance a phrase. A long synchronized echo can result in the sense of two melodic parts answering each other.
- Is harmonic if the echoed notes extend the presence of a chord or cause part of a chord to over-hang the next.

- Is rhythmic if the echo is synchronized to the beat and tempo, or a suitable fraction thereof, so that the echo returns reinforce the rhythm. The guitar's original signal and echo can double each other or intersect.

Echo/delay is controlled through many parameters, depending on how sophisticated the unit. For instance, imitations of analogue echo allow for gradual degradation of the original signal with every repeat, expressed as a loss of higher frequencies. The three most important parameters ruling echo are:

Volume: the volume of the echo compared to the original note. An echo could be as loud as the original note or it could be much quieter. Make the echo quieter if it is intended only as a background feature.
Delay time: the length of time between the original note and the echo – this varies considerably. Very short echoes are heard as a form of reverb on the original note, ie, an acoustic space, rather than a separate echo. Use this to thicken parts. The longer the echo the trickier it is to manage because it lags behind the music. Very long echoes are suited to ambient instrumental music.
Repeats: a note can echo more than just once. Multiple echoes are also hard to handle in music that is quick moving. They can be treated in stereo so that they 'ping-pong' from left to right and back.

The uses of echo are:

- To lend drama to a phrase. This works especially well with a vocal phrase or a lead guitar lick, as in the case of the first lead guitar phrase towards the end of Bad Company's 'Feel Like Makin' Love'.
- To thicken, deepen or emphasize a sound.
- To create unusual melodic parts.
- To give more body to harmonics.
- To create ambient mixes and guitar parts – see The Verve Urban Hymns album.
- To harmonize a scale run in thirds or in a lead solo, such as that in Thin Lizzy's 'That Woman's Gonna Break Your Heart'.
- To allow a guitar part to answer itself, as in Brian May's echo solo on Queen's 'Brighton Rock'.
- To throw a single guitar across the mix, as in Golden Earring's 'Radar Love', which starts with an impressive use of echo on a guitar riff panned to the right.

CASE STUDY

THE EDGE (U2)

Echo can be far more than mere decoration; it can shape the design of the song and arrangement. U2's core sound was born the day guitarist the Edge got an echo device. Among the units he used initially were the Electro-Harmonix Memory Man and then a TC Electronic Digital Delay. Echo enabled the Edge to side-step accepted ideas of how rock guitar should sound (low overdriven riffs, barre chords, lead solos played on pentatonic scales). He once said, "Really I just started writing with the echo and it all happened ... Parts that would have sounded at best bland without the echo suddenly sounded amazing." U2's album *The Joshua Tree* opens with 'Where The Streets Have No Name', where the intro has the Edge playing a four-note figure on the higher strings. What makes this four-note motif work is the echo. He plays it with a delay timed so that a rhythm is set up between the notes and their echoes. It has rhythmic and melodic interest. Notice that when a delay is set up precisely the percussive clicks of the pick hitting the strings will be in time with the beat, thus doubling the rhythmic quality of the guitar.

This concept of a rhythmic echo riff can also be heard on 'With Or Without You'. At 1.52 into the song is the first appearance of a high-string riff – a fifth opening to a sixth – with lots of delay. Edge's echo-laden guitar style has influenced many other players, as can be heard on Coldplay's 'In My Place', 'Shiver', and 'Don't Panic', and the intro to The Darkness' 'Out Of My Hands'.

PITCH AND FILTER EFFECTS

Tremolo arm/pitch-shifting

Some guitars, most notably the Fender Stratocaster, are equipped with a 'tremolo' arm. This will put a mild vibrato on chords and single notes, which is how Hank Marvin used it as part of his signature sound with The Shadows on tracks like 'Apache'. It can also be used more aggressively to drop the pitch of a note in a perfectly smooth glissando and then return up, as on Van Halen's 'Eruption'. The effect is magnified by distortion. Led Zeppelin's 'For Your Life' gives Page the opportunity to use a Strat and pitch-squiggle the chords with the tremolo arm. It is one of those riffs that put space between chords to allow for the snare-drum to crack through. The tremolo-dropped chord on this track is often panned right across the stereo image. A solo like Ritchie Blackmore's on Deep Purple's 'Smoke On The Water' is typified not only by some energetic string-bending but by extensive tremolo-arm noises.

Pitch-shifting can also be done from a pedal on some guitar effects units. Harmonizers began as crude octave splitters that put another version of a guitar phrase up or down an octave. Then came units that would put any interval above or below, but being unable to change the interval mid-way meant they would always include some out-of-key notes, and they could not always handle bends. Modern harmonizers can automatically adjust to the key or scale you want. Many harmonizers have a slightly robotic tone, but if you are pushed for recording space or time it is a quick method for building up a guitar choir. Others prefer doing it manually. Here's Earl Slick: "I'm not a very precise player; I don't want to be. I like it when things are done off the cuff and not exactly together. I kept mistakes on the record. It's more natural for the music that I play. When I do a take if the notes are bent a little wrong I'll keep it as long as it feels good. On *Zig Zag* 'Isn't It Evening' has two guitars on the opening slightly out of tune. I did it on purpose … didn't bother to tune again the second time. A harmonizer does it perfect. I prefer the manual, imperfect way of doing it."

Wah-wah

The wah-wah pedal, the most popular foot-operated guitar effect, was a mid-1960s frequency filter invention. The idea was an imitation of certain tones trumpet players make with a mute. It has strong symbolic associations with guitar heroes like Eric Clapton – who played one on Cream's 'Tales Of Brave Ulysses', 'White Room', and Blind Faith's 'Presence Of The Lord' – and Jimi Hendrix, whose self-mythologizing anthem 'Voodoo Chile' opens with a wah-wah and muted strings. George Harrison even wrote a song called 'Wah-Wah', after an argument during one of The Beatles' recording sessions.

More generally, the wah-wah pedal is associated with hippy/psychedelic rock (see 'The Witch' by The Rattles) and 1970s soul-influenced crime-film soundtracks, notably Isaac Hayes' *Shaft*. By the 1980s it was regarded as rather uncool. This is caught in Peter Buck telling *Guitar World* about the lead break on 'Stand': 'I knew this was the rare R.E.M song that didn't need a bridge. So I went out and bought a wah-wah pedal, and having never played one before just plugged it in and did the solo flat off – which just pushed [the song] into total absurdity.' But by the 1990s the wah-wah had recovered some of its credibility and it is no surprise to find it on a track like Haven's 'Let It Live', Verve's 'Sonnet' and 'This Time', All About Eve's 'Freeze', or Black Rebel Motorcycle Club's 'White Palms' which, with its doubled, reverbed vocals, heavily distorted bass high in the mix, and mantra-like lyrics, could be the1960s band Love in one of their darker moments.

In guitar parts its uses include:

- 'Talking' phrases – the vocalization trick carried off brilliantly by Hendrix on 'Still Raining Still Dreaming'.
- High guitar fills in a soul style, as on Sly and the Family Stone 'Family Affair', or the Supremes' 'Up The Ladder To The Roof' (played by 'Wah-Wah' Watson).
- To create a percussive click sound with strummed muted strings, as on Isaac Hayes' 'Shaft' theme.
- To 'colour' a repeat guitar lick or rapidly picked note during a solo, as done by Brian Robertson on Thin Lizzy's 'Don't Believe A Word'. This involves repeating the phrase and slowly bringing the pedal through its entire arc and back.

- To imitate the glissandos and phrasing of non-guitar instruments, as Brian May of Queen did in a pastiche trad jazz arrangement on Queen's 'Good Company'.
- To give a liquid inflection to clean guitar chords, as done by Marc Bolan on Tyrannosaurus Rex's song 'Lofty Skies'. Clean wah-wah is less common than distorted, and chordal wah less common than single note playing.
- Left switched on, but not moved with the foot, it will act as treble booster.
- Wedged half-way it can act as a weird frequency boost, as heard on the riff of Dire Straits' 'Money For Nothing'.
- To make a heavy guitar riff sound sinister – as Jimmy Page did for live performances of Led Zeppelin's 'No Quarter' and The Ocean'.

A wah-wah can also combine with other effects such as distortion or echo. It is possible to buy pedals that give you fuzz and wah. U2's 'The Fly' has The Edge doing a heavily echoed wah-wah solo. There is a remarkable echo-wah solo by Marty Willson-Piper on All About Eve's song 'Freeze'. Other instruments such as keyboards and bass can also be put through a wah-wah.

OTHER EFFECTS

Bowed guitar

Sustained notes can be generated on the electric guitar by using an actual violin or cello bow. The classic examples are Eddie Phillips with 1960s band The Creation on 'Making Time' and Jimmy Page on Led Zeppelin's 'Dazed And Confused' (especially live versions). Unless it is sticky with rosin, the bow has a tendency to slide off the string rather than gripping it, resulting in unpredictable shrieks of overtones that are part of the Gothic horror quality of this effect. The technique is also constrained by the fact that a guitar's strings are aligned in one flat dimension, unlike a violin's. On guitar only the first and the sixth strings can be individually bowed. Tremolo bowing and string-bending work well to create a dark atmosphere. So there may be rare occasions where bowed guitar might make a colourful alternative to synth strings. Since many synth patches and MIDI guitar effects will generate a bowed, sustained note, actually doing it physically is something perhaps chosen for the imperfection and unpredictability of the sound.

E-bow

The E-bow is a battery-operated device held in the picking hand which generates sustained notes when held over the strings at the pick-up. It can give a more controllable imitation of feedback. You can hear this device on Ocean Colour Scene's 'When Evil Comes', R.E.M.'s 'E-bow The Letter', and Pulp's 'The Fear'. The Raconteurs 'Broken Boy Soldier' has some nice E-bow guitar lines. On Smashing Pumpkins' 'Soma' to do one short solo three minutes in Billy Corgan claimed he E-bowed a guitar and tracked it 14 times before bouncing the result down onto two tracks!

Feedback

> ***"I love feedback because it's real musical and non-technical. 'Sweetness Follows' could have been real sappy if there wasn't the discordant cello and the feedback kind of giving it that edge."***
>
> Peter Buck

Few guitar sounds in an arrangement can match the speaker-threatening drama of feedback – the original rock rebel sound. Here's how it works.

If you have sufficient volume and are standing at the correct angle to an amplifier, the sound from the amp will cause the strings to vibrate, reinforcing the original sound you played. This creates a loop which then gets louder. Sometimes the feedback loop will be the same pitch you first played, but other times it flips onto a higher note. Why? To understand that you have to grasp upper partials and harmonics. This will give you a clue for how feedback can be worked into an arrangement's key and chord progression.

When you play the bottom E string, common sense says you're playing a single note. But in fact that single E contains within itself a range of notes of ascending pitch and volume passing beyond our hearing. They are part of the richness of the sound of a note. The note you're actually playing or fretting – the one you start with before anything groovy happens – is the *fundamental*. You can hear some of these upper partials by playing harmonics on the bottom string:

- The first harmonic: at the 12th fret you get an E one octave above the open string.
- The second harmonic: at the seventh fret you get the note an octave and a fifth above, ie, B.
- The third harmonic: at the fifth it's an E two octaves above.
- Fourth harmonic: at the fourth and nineth frets you get the note two octaves and a major third, ie, G#.

These notes are actually part of an open string E but you don't consciously hear them as audible notes. To give you an idea of what this series sounds like, imagine the bottom E string was your fundamental:

- The E on the second fret of the fourth string would be equivalent to the first harmonic.
- The open B string would be the second harmonic.
- The top E string would be the third harmonic.
- The G# on the fourth fret on the top string would be the fourth harmonic.
- Notice that these harmonics produce a major chord if they sound together.

By sustaining the root note of the chord you are playing over, or trying to create through feedback, you can build the full chord by encouraging the right harmonic.

Feedback was developed as a musical device in the mid-1960s. It's difficult to pinpoint a definitive first use but Pete Townshend's blast of feedback on the guitar solo to The Who's 'Anywhere, Anyhow, Anywhere' (1964) deserves a mention. The crown prince of feedback was of course Hendrix, who played at such high volume that getting it was easy. His live 'Star Spangled Banner' at Woodstock in August 1969 would not have had anything like the same dramatic effect without its moments of feedback. The performance has examples of open strings feeding back at the first, second, and fourth harmonics, amply assisted (pun intended) by a Univibe pedal, wah-wah, and enough Marshall wattage to bring down the walls of Jericho. Carlos Santana is another guitarist of that era who makes plentiful use of feedback to sustain notes.

Feedback can have a musical role, though this is tricky to get on tape. Andy Summers' guitar solo on The Police's 'Bring On The Night' has a high E feeding back, flipping up to an A and then dropping back to E. The late Mick Ronson made great use of controlled feedback to sustain notes on the solo of David Bowie's 'Moonage Daydream'. R.E.M numbers that use feedback include 'Bang and Blame' and 'Country Feedback', which anticipates some of the arrangements on *Monster* by combining feedback with tremolo. The tricky thing about feedback is that you can't necessarily determine which of the harmonics are going to be produced.

The main uses of feedback in an arrangement are to:

- Create 'morse code' effects by turning one pickup off, getting feedback and flicking the toggle switch so it cuts in and out. See Mick Ronson on the very end of David Bowie's 'John I'm Only Dancing' and The Who 'Anyway Anyhow Anywhere'.
- Create sustained notes, as on The Jam's 'Strange Town' and 'When You're Young'. 'Strange Town' has a triple guitar feedback where Weller gets an E feeding back, a second harmonic on G and a C first harmonic. The three notes imply a Csus2 chord.
- To get very high notes beyond the fretboard.
- As an expressive gesture to stand for rock as rebellion. Feedback crops up on The Sex Pistols' debut album to give nasty endings to tracks. In the same spirit it can be heard on Oasis' 'Be Here Now' twenty years on. Many a rock guitarist has ended a live set by setting the guitar against the speakers and walking off, leaving it to wail until the roadies save the day (and everyone's eardrums) by turning the amp off.
- A held feedback note creates drama and makes an excellent intro (see Hendrix 'Foxy Lady') or a link across sections (see Blue Oyster Cult 'Don't Fear The Reaper').
- Tremolo-arm assisted feedback is eerie – see R.E.M.'s 'OddFellows Local 151' and the intro of Elvis Costello's 'Hand In Hand'. This can also sound like a siren.
- To introduce an element of pure noise and hysteria.

CASE STUDY

LESLIE WEST

To hear controlled feedback, get hold of Mountain's 1971 *Flowers Of Evil*. Mountain were legends in their day for the volume of their concerts. Half this set is live and features Leslie West playing a Les Paul Junior through a stack. At the end of the guitar solo, which lasts for the first few minutes of the opening track, West lands on a low D (ie, fretted on the fifth string, fifth fret). He gets the note to feed back at the same pitch (ie, the fundamental). After a few seconds of the feedback developing you can hear the fundamental and all four upper harmonics, adding a D an octave above, the A above that, the D above that and the F♯ above that (the last of which being equivalent to the F♯ at the 14th fret on the top string). The note lasts about 50 seconds! Gradually you hear it 'decay' as the upper harmonics overwhelm the fundamental. Usually it's the higher harmonics that win out – in this case the note dissolves into the high F♯ and then West rips into the intro to 'Roll Over Beethoven'.

BOTTLENECK/SLIDE

> ***"Seeing Duane Allman even once before he died was enough. You'd have to put a gun to my head to get me to solo on slide after that."***
>
> Peter Buck

A bottleneck guitar can provide some telling fills. It allows for smooth glissandos, vocal-type phrases and wide vibratos. It requires a guitar with a higher-than-usual action to stop the bottleneck rattling against the frets. The handling noise is reduced if you put a finger down to touch the string behind the bottleneck. Overdrive and echo will increase the presence and sustain of the notes. Some great solos can be devised by multitracking single bottleneck lines.

Your main decision will be whether you need to put the guitar into an open tuning. If you are in standard tuning, strings one , two, and three make a minor chord and strings three, four, and five make a major. By using these triads you are able to play a major or minor chord with the slide alone, not having to worry about fretting notes. For a 12-bar in G, chords G, C, and D can be played at the 12th, fifth, and seventh frets with the slide. If there's a minor chord in the sequence just play the top three strings at the right fret.

There are non-blues lead slide guitar parts on R.E.M.'s 'Man On The Moon', Led Zeppelin's 'Tangerine', The Faces 'That's All You Need', Eric Clapton's 'Layla', George Harrison solos on 'My Sweet Lord', Coldplay's 'Don't Panic' and the chorus of 'Trouble', and Dire Straits 'You And Your Friend', where an acoustic slide part trades phrases with an electric lead. Early Pink Floyd tracks use the bottleneck with echo as a sound effect that will sound notes anywhere from the end of the fretboard to the guitar's bridge.

SECTION 6

Arranging songs with keyboards, bass, and drums

Moving on from guitars, it's time to consider some of the other instruments often used when arranging songs for a band: keyboards, bass guitar, and drums.

Having looked at the arrangement possibilities of guitars, it is time to consider the next instruments that figure in many arrangements. Keyboards can supply both melodic and harmonic elements, while bass guitar has the essential task of joining the rhythm section to the harmony. Drums and percussion provide the rhythmic power of the performance. This section offers some broad hints about putting these instruments into action.

KEYBOARDS

Keyboards are the most potent instrument there is for filling a mix. This is because of their enormous pitch range, their capacity for sustain, and the feasibility of playing up to 10 notes in a chord. A piano part can give you a bass line, melody and chords all in one. Synth/digital keyboards allow for thousands of instrumental sounds to be added, though remember that for them to sound realistic they must be played in a manner appropriate to the style of the original physical instrument. For recording purposes, you don't have to have a good piano technique to at least make a few additions. You can cheat manually by recording left hand and right hand separately and then combining them on to one track, or write the parts into a sequencing programme. The most useful keyboard ability is to be able to hold down triads. Even if you don't consider yourself competent on a keyboard, it enables you to add keyboard sounds that act as a harmonic 'pad' behind the guitars. There are hundreds of triad shapes in my book *How To Write Songs On Keyboards*, which is aimed as much at guitarists as keyboard players. Let's look at some specific types of keyboard you might put in an arrangement.

Piano

There is a long-established tradition in popular music of singer-songwriters for whom the main instrument is piano, from Carole King, Laura Nyro, Randy Newman, Jackson Browne Gilbert O'Sullivan and Elton John to Kate Bush, Jamie Callum, and Norah Jones. Even more than guitar, the piano allows a single performer to provide rhythm and a full harmony to support their voice. Many guitar bands like Queen, Coldplay (listen to 'Trouble') and Radiohead have also featured piano as a contrast to guitar-oriented numbers.

Your first decision after deciding a track needs piano is to decide whether the piano is the main instrument or whether its job is a support role. Then choose what kind of piano tone is required. In terms of symbolic identity the grand piano has classical associations (recalling the piano concerto) and with an upmarket romanticism typical of slow impassioned ballads and big productions. Think of the way the piano features in many Elton John ballads, Guns N'Roses' 'November Rain', The Beatles' 'Let It Be', and in some Meatloaf songs. Check out David Sancious' magnificent piano intro to Springsteen's 'New York City Serenade'. The nine-foot or Steinway tone will be the one to go for.

It is true that there have also been rock'n'roll artists who pounded away at the ivories, including Fats Domino, Jerry Lee Lewis, and Little Richard. The rock'n'roll piano style features accented chords struck repeatedly at fast tempos and sweeping glissandos. When Led Zeppelin wanted to evoke the spirit of the 1950s on 'Rock And Roll' they added a high piano chord part to the last verse. There are piano glissandos and high chords on T. Rex's homage to Chuck Berry, 'Get It On'. But the piano has always been in the shadow of the guitar as a rock instrument. Visuals have something to do with this: you can't move one around the stage the way you can a guitar.

A 'honky-tonk' upright piano is the dirtier bar-room equivalent to the grand, evoking bonhomie and good-times, as well as a grounded pathos in slower material. A grand piano part would never have been so moving as the upright heard on R.E.M.'s 'Perfect Circle'. You can hear the honky-tonk sound on The Beatles' 'For No-One', Bob Dylan's 'Like A Rolling Stone', The Mamas And The Papas' 'Dream A Little Dream' (where it supplies an instrumental break), The Band's 'The Weight', and Fleetwood Mac's 'Don't Stop'.

The piano has a limited role in hard rock and heavy rock styles. Bands with pianos tend to the more progressive side of things, as in groups such as Procul Harum, Supertramp, and Yes. Queen songs such as 'Bohemian Rhapsody' and 'Killer Queen' are interesting from an arrangement angle in showing how the guitar's role changes in a track with prominent piano. Since it isn't needed to play chords and fill harmonic space, the guitar is better off soloing high or playing distorted single-note bass figures. On Free's 'My Brother Jake', ousted from its normal role of supplying chords, the guitar supplies fills and the occasional wailing bend to great effect. Songs written on piano tend to have more chords (see David Bowie's 'Changes' and 'Oh You Pretty Things'), more inversions, and more complex chords, none of which are typical of heavy rock. Yet one of the most aggressive singer-songwriters at a piano is Tori Amos. A song like 'Precious Things' from her debut album *Little Earthquakes* has piano breaks of explosive intensity quite rivalling electric guitar breaks on rock songs.

If adding a piano part to an arrangement, ask yourself these questions:

- Do you want a right hand only part, or both hands – ie, treble and bass?
- Is the prime function of it to be melodic or harmonic?
- Are the chords pitched in the same octave as the guitars? If so, it may be more effective to pitch them higher.
- Do you want a grand piano or upright piano tone?
- If you use the lower range take care not to confuse any bass-line played by bass guitar or double bass. But low piano notes can effectively double a bass note on another instrument by adding a tonal edge.
- Will the track have a second or third keyboard? The Beatles' 'Let It Be' has piano, electric piano, and organ. Dire Straits and Bruce Springsteen often use piano and organ.

Here are some arrangement ideas for using a piano:

- Low, sustained piano notes are atmospheric. The Beatles used them on 'Tell Me Why', 'Any Time At All', and as a low rumble chording in 'No Reply'.
- The extreme high range has a distinctive 'tinkling' timbre which is mildly percussive and ethereal.
- The sustain pedal means the piano can provide a harmonic pad without a rhythm pattern that might collide with those generated by other instruments in the mix. Chords can be pressed once and held until the next chord change.
- The sustain pedal also allows for a chord to be struck along with other instruments at a pause. As they fade, the sound of the piano chord emerges. Felix Pappalardi did this hauntingly in the verse of Cream's 'Badge'.
- Accented octaves or double octaves (one in each hand) are a hallmark of the dramatic pop ballad typified by The Four Tops' 'Walk Away Renee' and Dusty Springfield's 'I Close My Eyes And Count To Ten', a style alluded to in Elvis Costello songs such as 'Oliver's Army' and 'Party Girl', and Abba's 'Dancing Queen'.
- Several bars of quarter-note chording makes a simple if cliched intro.
- High piano stabs can punctuate a verse dominated by guitar, as in Roy Orbison's 'Pretty Woman', where the piano breaks into a freer arpeggio figure in the bridge for contrast.
- In slow blues and soul ballads the piano often plays a vamping triplet chord figure, as in James Brown's 'It's A Man's Man's Man's World'.
- There is a very attractive piano style involving added seconds which creates tumbling decorations impossible to reproduce on guitar. It can be heard on The Who's 'Song Is Over' and Rod Stewart's 'Handbags And Gladrags'. The master of this style was Nicky Hopkins, who played with many famous bands including The Who and The Rolling Stones.
- Occasionally a song might have two piano parts. The Beatles' 'Good Day Sunshine' has two pianos, a muddy-sounding one on the right and a quieter one on the left.
- Television's 'Marquee Moon' has a high piano chord on the right in the chorus and at its climax (8:42) where the distinctive timbre of the high notes is exploited, but the track as a whole doesn't have a continuous piano part. In fact, most people would consider it a guitar track. Similarly, there is a high falling piano arpeggio figure on the chorus of their 'Torn Curtain'.
- Sometimes piano can provide the solo, as it does on Elvis Costello's 'Party Girl' and David Bowie's 'Aladdin Sane', on which Mike Garson played a solo famous for its manic invention.
- Avant-garde sounds arise from a piano when objects are placed on the strings – so-called 'treated piano'. But this involves miking up an acoustic piano.

Organ

If a piano seems too percussive a sound for your song, it could be that an organ is required. The symbolic identity of the organ for many listeners first evokes church and religious associations. A big church organ sound lends itself to Gothic horror effects and progressive rock extravaganzas, but ironically not to gospel music, where a smaller, more limited electric organ sound is more characteristic. Arthur Brown's hit 'Fire' subverts the church associations of the organ sound in an orgy of cod-baroque organ parts. The organ also has baroque/classical associations. Either of these could be the source of some nose-thumbing at classical music by rock bands. Hence the rebel value of Keith Emerson's famous concert routine which involved stabbing his Hammond with a knife. This classical association is evoked on the intro of The Doors' 'Light My Fire', the chord progression of which is noticeably different to anything that goes on in the rest of the song. The organ solo in the middle does not have this 'classical' feel. The same contrast of a classical organ approach with something self-consciously pop/blues was demonstrated by John Paul Jones on 'Your Time Is Gonna Come' from Led Zeppelin's debut.

The classic organ sounds for popular music come from the Hammond and the Farfisa. The Hammond lends itself to rock, blues, soul, and rhythm and blues songs; it was used by bands like The Animals and The Small Faces. The Farfisa evokes mid-1960s pop, an association exploited by its use on Elvis Costello's second album *This Year's Model*. Heavy rock bands like Deep Purple have been happy to distort the organ sound, as can be heard on 'Strange Kind Of Woman', 'Smoke On The Water', 'Fireball', and the intro to 'Perfect Strangers', and mess about with the pitch-bend facility. A brilliant example of distorted organ forms the intro to The Band's 'Chest Fever'.

The combination of organ and electric guitar is a signature of early 1970s progressive rock outfits like Atomic Rooster, Argent, Pink Floyd, Supertramp, and Focus, and even punk bands such as The Stranglers. ELP could only have done some of their classical arrangements with an organ – a guitar would not have been able to cover that much harmonic space. As with the piano, using an organ means the guitar has to change its role. If the organ takes chords, the guitar must find a different identity, as is demonstrated by Jimmy Page's guitar part in Led Zeppelin's organ blues 'Since I've Been Loving You', where full guitar chords are replaced by lead fills, sixths and high arpeggio figures.

If adding an organ part to an arrangement, take note:

- Do you want a right hand only part, or both hands, or bass pedal notes (traditionally played with the feet) as well?
- Is the prime function of it to be melodic or harmonic?
- Are the chords pitched where the guitars are placed? If so you may want to move them higher.
- Choose the organ tone to match the style of the song. R'n'B numbers don't require cathedral organ! Does your song need, for example, a dirty Hammond, a grainy VS organ, a D50 patch, or the thinner accordion-like reed organ?

- If you use the lower range take care not to muddy any bass part played by bass guitar or double bass. Low organ notes can effectively replace any bass-line for a short while in a pedal effect.
- Organ chords can be played as rhythmic stabs but they don't have as percussive an effect as stabbed piano chords.
- Organ complements piano very well. One on each side of a mix is a classic combination.
- Even on inexpensive and budget synths there is usually a good organ sound.

Here are some arrangement ideas for including an organ:

- Low, sustained organ notes create suspense, as on Atomic Rooster's 'The Devil's Answer'.
- The high range has a good deal of penetration.
- Organ can be used to double a guitar riff.
- Soft organ chords sit well behind guitars, as on R.E.M.'s 'The Sidewinder Sleeps Tonight' or the Arctic Monkeys' 'Riot Van'.
- A quiet organ makes an easy addition for filling out the mix in a chorus or in a bridge.
- An organ can carry a melody as a counterpoint to a vocal, as in Procul Harum's 'Whiter Shade Of Pale'. The Small Faces' 'All Or Nothing' has an instrumental half-verse where scat vocals combine with the organ playing single notes.
- High organ parts can give a celestial effect, as on the chorus of U2's 'The Fly' where it replaces the heavy guitar riff. There is a similar celestial effect on the chorus of Simon and Garfunkel's 'America'.
- The organ can supply a sanctification gesture, as at the beginning of Bob Marley's live 'No Woman No Cry', the end of Pink Floyd's live 'A Saucerful Of Secrets' and the coda of Led Zeppelin's 'Thank You'.
- Organ can take the lead role in an instrumental, such as the 1960s soul instrumental by Booker T. And The MGs', 'Green Onions'.
- Organ often fits in slow soul songs, see Percy Sledge 'When A Man Loves A Woman'.
- The organ can fill out the sound and colour it with harmony even when low in the mix and with a less treble sound. For subtle contributions listen to Coldplay 'In My Room' and Them's 'Gloria' where on the left the organ plays single notes high above the bass.

Argent's 'Hold Your Head Up' has a subtle organ intro over a steady bass line – organ left, guitar riff on right and some interplay between the two. During the instrumental break, the guitar plays a single chord repeatedly against the organ's changing chords. Curved Air's 'Back Street Luv' links organ with an early analogue synth making bubbling noises throughout. There is organ on

PJ Harvey's *To Bring You My Love* (1995), and The White Stripes added some Hammond organ to songs on *White Blood Cells*.

Other keyboards

If neither straight piano or organ sound like what you need, there are other keyboard instruments you could employ in an arrangement.

The **harpsichord** has a symbolic identity that evokes past centuries, going back to the Elizabethan period. Its sound is brittle, bright, with no sustain, and combines well with acoustic guitar. While Simon and Garfunkel retained this 'Merrie England' identity for their version of the traditional 'Scarborough Fair', as did Kate Bush for 'Oh England My Lionheart' and Queen for 'The Fairy Feller's Master-Stroke', Jimi Hendrix over-rode history by imaginatively combining harpsichord with a wah-wah guitar on 'Burning Of The Midnight Lamp'. The Beatles put a harpsichord on 'All You Need Is Love', the intro of 'Lucy In The Sky With Diamonds' and on 'Fixing A Hole'; Motown recorded one for R.Dean Taylor's 'Gotta See Jane'; and Tori Amos made spikey and sinister use of one on her album *Boys For Pele*. Mariah Carey used a harpsichord, along with a celeste and a string quartet, on her MTV *Unplugged* session in 1992. Goldfrapp included one in some of the arrangements for *Felt Mountain* (2000).

The **electric piano** (of which the Fender Rhodes is the most famous) has a less percussive, more 'rubbery' sound than its acoustic equivalent and a smaller pitch range. It features on The Beatles' 'Come Together', 'Don't Let Me Down', and 'I Am The Walrus', hits by Supertramp, 10cc's classic 'I'm Not In Love', Led Zeppelin tracks like 'Misty Mountain Hop' and 'Down By The Seaside', The Verve 'One Day', Radiohead's 'Talk Show Host' and 'Everything In Its Right Place', Air's 'All I Need', Mercury Rev's 'Holes' and Angelo Badamenti's 'Twin Peaks Theme'. You can hear it clearly on the intro to The Band's 'Long Black Veil'. The Beatles included a solo on one in 'Tell Me What You See' which comes in for four bars after the hook line and actually ends the song. In the Staple Singers 'Respect Yourself' you can hear one on the right, and on The Archies 'Sugar Sugar' an electric piano plays the main riff. On Roxy Music tracks like 'Beauty Queen' it was dramatically subjected to phasing and echo.

If you want a funky keyboard sound go for **clavinet**. This was the instrument that characterized many Stevie Wonder songs like 'Superstition', a sound Led Zeppelin appropriated for the heavy metal funk of 'Trampled Underfoot'.

The **mellotron** was an early attempt to emulate a range of instruments by having their sounds on tiny spools of tape. Heavy, unreliable, and difficult to tune, the mellotron has long been superceded by digital sampling technology. But realism isn't everything – the imperfections of early attempted synthesis and emulation sometimes have a charm of their own. The fact that the mellotron doesn't sound as close to the real instrument it copies has become irrelevant, because when bands want to evoke the hippie innocence of the 1960s they go for a mellotron. No real flutes or strings could substitute for the charm of those from the mellotron on The Beatles' 'Strawberry Fields Forever' or 'Flying', Brian Auger and Julie Driscoll's 'This Wheel's On Fire', Led Zeppelin's 'The Rain Song', Big Star's 'The India Song', or The Moody Blues 'Nights In

White Satin' and 'Tuesday Afternoon'. The Beatles' 'The Continuing Story Of Bungalow Bill' has a mellotron imitating a mandolin and a trombone. In the case of The Moody Blues, recent CD and SACD versions allow you to now hear the difference between the mellotron and the real orchestra very clearly. The Verve's 'This Time' has a mellotron in the centre from about 1:35 on a string setting.

The **accordion** is partly played on a keyboard. Its symbolic identity associates it with France (though there is an Italian version) and folk music, the latter being the reason it occurs on Dexy's Midnight Runners' 'Come On Eileen'. The **bandoneon** has a similar sound. The **celeste** is an orchestral instrument that has a magical, high-pitched tinkling sound which evokes magic and innocence, as it does beautifully on Nick Drake's 'Northern Sky'. It can be used to silver-point a melodic line in an arrangement.

Synths

When it comes to arrangements, there are two basic ways of considering the device that put the 'p' in FAT. The first is as a source of emulations of other instruments; the second – and the one that concerns us here – is the generation of its own electronic signals/sounds. There is a huge range of synth tones, not all of them easily used in a song arrangement. Some have no pitch, others are too idiosyncratic to sit with other instruments. Many synth keyboards let you combine sounds to generate a third one, or split the keyboard so that the lower half is assigned one sound and the upper half another (useful for 4-track demos where track space is at a premium). They can also automatically arpeggiate a chord, either on a designated pattern or randomly.

The symbolic identity of many synth patches revolves around concepts like inorganic, mechanistic (try a saw wave patch), technological, utopia/dystopia, altered consciousness, and the future. In some respects they are to the 1990s and the present what mellotrons, sitars and backward guitars are to the psychedelic vibe of 1966-68. Given these associations, synths can be imaginatively juxtaposed with acoustic instruments.

Some later Beatles tracks, such as 'Because' and 'Here Comes The Sun' feature the Moog synth. At the start of the 1970s a synth-dominated track like the UK hit 'Son Of My Father' by Chicory Tip was very much a novelty. Early synthesizers were monophonic – meaning you could only play one note at a time. This was good enough for David Bowie who used a toy device called a Stylophone on 'Space Oddity'. During the 1970s synths featured in progressive rock bands like Genesis, Yes, and Tangerine Dream. In a band like Yes the synth sometimes supplanted the guitar when it came to providing solos. The Who achieved the best ever integration of synths with hard rock on albums like Who's *Next* and *Quadrophenia*. Their use in soul music was pioneered by Stevie Wonder in the early 1970s. Joe Zawinul on Weather Report's *Heavy Weather* (1977) used an ARP 2600 and an Oberheim polyphonic synthesizer. They were also heard on film soundtracks like John Barry's *On Her Majesty's Secret Service* and memorably juxtaposed with a cimbalom on the theme to the TV series *The Persuaders*.

Synths entered the centre of pop music in the 1980s when they were featured by 'New

Romantic' bands such as Duran Duran, Soft Cell, Erasure, Gary Numan, and Simple Minds, where synth keyboards take up more room in the mix and the guitars are less important. As a result the guitar parts on these records often resort to 'power-chord' fifths to cut through more. It is worth listening to Blondie's 'Heart Of Glass' for the 16th-note pulse on a single note that phases in and out. Garbage's Bond theme 'The World Is Not Enough' has a synth pad that sounds like blown wooden pipes. Synths lend sinister touches to the intro of Tears For Fears' 'Shout' and Marilyn Manson's *Antichrist Superstar*. Vintage synths are heard on *The Love Below by OutKast*. Air's *Moon Safari* (1998) has many vintage synths such as Mini Moog.

Here are tips for their use:

- A smooth sustained synth tone makes an effective unobstrusive background for acoustic guitars.
- 'Fizzier' synth tones lend themselves to lead fills and solos, and riffs.
- Striding octave figures can be powerful, as in Tubeway Army's 'Are Friends Electric' and Kraftwerk's 'Autobahn'.
- Synth tones are often subject to EQ manipulation so that the pitch stays the same but the timbre changes. This effect became a cliché of 1990s dance music and can be heard frequently on Madonna's *Ray Of Light* album.
- They can form a strong contrast with the main instrumentation of a song if central to an intro or instrumental bridge. Synths dominate the intro of Dire Straits' 'Brothers In Arms' (1985) despite the track being essentially a guitar song.
- Any synth part that pulses regularly has the potential to establish the rhythm before the drums come in. Most of these sounds can be set in tempo.
- Synth parts can often be arpeggios. 'Crystal Lake' by Grandaddy has a rippling synth figure on the verse based on the chord, which changes pitch direction after a verse. It fits the lyric (rippling water) but is over-used so that different sections of the song sound the same.
- Many synth sounds will occupy a lot of frequencies in a mix, so you may not need many of them.
- Synths are a good source of windswept, sinister or other-worldly atmospheres.
- Synths can supply their own version of acoustic strings.

BASS GUITAR

The four-string electric bass guitar is tuned (low-to-high) E A D G, each note being one octave below the guitar's lowest four strings. This means that all the notes are in the same positions on the fretboard as on a guitar. If you know your way around a guitar you can have a go at putting a bass-line on your demos. But to play authentic bass you need to think like a bassist, not a guitarist. One of the hallmarks of guitarists who play bass is that they play too many notes and aren't strict enough about the rhythm of what they're doing, often falling 'out of the pocket'. A bassist has reserves of patience and discipline, and will hang onto a note, a rhythm or a figure for as long as is needed.

Even if there are no drums, adding a bass guitar to a guitar demo deepens the sound of the chords and could add an element of groove even if the track does not have any percussion.

Fingerstyle bass

Bass sound and style are influenced by how the strings are played. Fingerstyle bass gives the notes a softer edge and is closer to double-bass style. This suits anything with a jazz or traditional soul character. This particular sound is strengthened by:

- Turning the tone down on the pickup.
- Playing closer to the fingerboard.
- Using a mute.
- Putting foam under the strings near the tail-piece.
- Using flatwound strings.

These will give the bass less of a guitar and more of a double-bass tone. Reducing treble frequencies and sustain also has the important result of keeping the bottom end of the music uncluttered, allowing space between the percussive thump of bass notes and kick drum hits. If bass guitar notes are sustained they can partly mask the rhythmic pulse coming from the kick drum. This is one of the secrets to getting more of a groove from the rhythm section, as heard from many late 1960s/early 1970s bands. The drive for bass sustain has made its rhythmic role harder to make clear.

Plectrum bass

Once the electric bass guitar was designed it was understandable that some players would approach it more as a guitar than as a descendant of the upright bass, especially if they had no prior experience of playing the upright. Since guitars were played with a plectrum, they figured why not bass? Playing bass with a pick gives a harder edge to the notes and suits new-wave, punk, and rock styles, especially quicker tempos and riff material. The sound of the pick hitting the string adds a percussive quality. The guitar aspect of electric bass reached its fulfilment with the invention of eight- and 12-string basses, which create a very distinctive sound, as can be heard on John Paul Jones' solo albums *Zooma* and *The Thunderthief*.

Click bass is another style using a pick. The difference with click bass is that the notes have little sustain and thus foreground their rhythmic content. Approaching the bass as a guitar also affected musical thinking. In click-bass the line tends not to be quite as 'locked' into the bass-drum as in most bass styles. The other important trait of click bass is a fascinating example of trans-Atlantic musical influence. In the mid-1960s many bassists in the UK were trying to figure out what James Jamerson was doing on the Motown records. They adapted his melodic approach and syncopated eighth- and 16th-note rhythms – but played them underneath pop tunes with a pick. Click bass is a response to the example set by the Motown hits. Alan Taylor's bass line on The Casuals' 'Jesamine' demonstrates this influence. Other great click bass tracks are on Gainsbourg and Birkin's 'Je T'Aime', John Barry's 'Diamonds Are Forever', The Marmalade's 'Reflections Of My Life', and The Congregation's 'Softly Whispering I Love You'.

CASE STUDY

JAMES JAMERSON

Your concept of what a bass guitar can do in an arrangement will be revolutionized if you listen to 1960s Motown hits, on which many bass-lines were invented by James Jamerson. The strong beat of most Motown songs gave Jamerson the freedom to pull and push against it. The time-keeping role was covered by other instruments in the arrangement; Jamerson's bass supports the overall beat, but sets up a counter-pulse. The real Motown groove is not four-to-the-bar snare hits on two and four – it's the tension between a strong 4/4 beat and a bass-line full of bubbling syncopation. Examples would include 'Reach Out I'll Be There', 'Standing In The Shadows Of Love', 'Ain't Nothing Like The Real Thing', and 'I Was Made To Love Her'.

Here are some Jamerson-inspired ideas to make your bass-lines more interesting:

- **Look for moments when the bass line could reinforce the lead vocal or a significant upper melodic part.**
- **Add melodic interest by sprinkling the bass line with unexpected drops or leaps.**
- **Develop root-fifth bass parts by syncopation and turn them into eighth-note figures that fill a whole bar.**
- **Avoid playing many continuous bars of unbroken eighth root notes.**
- **Develop bass figures that feature an open string with a fretted phrase above it. The greater thickness of a bass string allows the electric bass considerable powers of sustain – very handy if you don't have a keyboard to hold notes on. If your song is in the keys of E, A, D, or G there may be a chance to play two-note figures on the bass, with the lower note being an open string.**
- **Include a few 16th-notes. For example, hold a note longer than expected and then squeeze several 16th-notes in at the very last minute.**
- **Syncopation is created by moving off the root note half a beat earlier than expected or tieing a note across a bar-line.**
- **Add chromatic passing notes and chromatic open strings – ie, playing the open E, A, and D strings as offbeat passing notes in a song whose key has those notes flattened.**

Bass guitar and M-H-R

In an arrangement a bass guitar part has three functions:

- Its *harmonic* function is to anchor the chords. It does this by playing the root note of each chord, occasionally the third of the chord (to create a first inversion) and very occasionally the fifth of the chord (to create a second inversion).
- Its *rhythmic* function is to emphasize the beat and pulse of the music by locking with the drums or other percussion, especially the kick drum. To stress the harmonic and rhythmic element of bass cut back on the treble and shorten the notes. The style known as 'slap' bass is a bass style in which the rhythmic function is stressed.
- Its *melodic* function is to play riffs, short phrases and fills, or passing notes and scales that join up the root notes in pleasing ways. Players like Paul McCartney, Jack Bruce and John Entwistle developed a melodic rock bass style. To stress the melodic function of the bass use an unmuted bass tone with plenty of treble and let the notes sustain. The extreme form of treating the bass as a melody instrument is represented by Jaco Pastorius' fretless bass work in the 1970s with Weather Report and on albums like Joni Mitchell's *Hejira*.

A really good bass-line manages to perform all three functions, and in a band where there are only three instruments it may have to.

Here are some ways to use a bass in an arrangement:

- A sudden minimising of the mix down to just bass and drums accentuates the rhythm.
- Solo bass, or bass and drums, make an effective intro. Carly Simon's 'You're So Vain' intro has a fast arpeggio on bass guitar. Green Day's 'J.A.R.' comes in on a bass solo only. Listen also to 'Cuyahoga' by REM, 'Town Called Malice' by the Jam, Martha Reeves and the Vandellas' 'Nowhere To Run', and many songs by The Zutons for prominent bass on intros.
- Instead of playing bars and bars of eighth-note roots, try omitting some of those eighths to give the music more of a pulse
- Quick ascending scales under a chord sequence provide drive and urgency. Listen to Bruce Foxton's bass on tracks like 'Down In The Tube Station At Midnight' by The Jam. On The Beatles' 'I'm A Loser' the change of style into the chorus from quarter-note bass to eighth-note 'walking' bass means a release of energy.
- Bass harmonics are effective decorations because the heavier string means a stronger note than on guitar. Use chorus and a short echo to increase the sustain. Listen to the intro and coda of The Icicle Works' 'Love Is A Wonderful Colour'.

- The bass part could be a riff, even if that riff is not doubled on guitar.
- Pedal notes on bass are a great way of making a chord progression sound different to when the bass is playing its root notes. Experiment by playing the key note or the fifth of the scale through a verse and hear the tension and new harmonic colour that results. Motown hits 'What Becomes Of The Broken-Hearted' (Jimmy Ruffin), 'You're All I Need To Get By' (Gaye/Terrell) ,and 'I'm Gonna Make You Love Me' (Temptations/Supremes) all make great use of pedal notes.
- As mentioned above, the electric bass can take on a melodic role. Its ability to play cello-like phrases is brought out on fretless models, heard on many Kate Bush albums and on the intro of Buggles' 'Video Killed The Radio Star'.
- Occasionally the bass comes right to the front of the arrangement, either as a designated bass solo (as on The Who's 'My Generation') or playing a link riff (as on Fleetwood Mac's 'The Chain').
- Sometimes you can omit the bass from a song's opening section. Elton John's 'Saturday Night's Alright For Fighting' intro has guitar riff and drums but no bass – bass comes in on the upbeat before the verse. This is a good tactic on a couple of songs if you're a power trio.
- Feature the bass in high register initially so it supports the guitar and only drops into true bass register for the chorus. Make sure the bass drum pattern is emphatic to compensate for the missing low end.
- Bass can imply a chord change when there isn't one. The combination of guitar riff and bass notes colouring it in different ways is heard in U2's 'Pride (In The Name Of Love)'. There are two guitar figures in the main riff but four bass notes make it sound as though there are four. A similar thing happens in The Jam's 'Strange Town' and The Pretenders' 'Don't Get Me Wrong'.
- Play a tone and half below the root note of a straight major chord and you automatically turn it into something that sounds like a minor seventh. Play a tone and a half below a minor chord root note and it will sound like a major seventh.

Bass guitar and chord inversions

The band Muse often put notes other than the root in the bass. At times their progressions sound almost baroque, as a result of the first and second inversions formed by bass lines moving in ascending or descending semitones (half-steps). You can hear this in 'Falling Down', 'Micro Cuts', and the guitar break at the end of 'Cave' which is played over the progression B minor-Bb-D/A-E/G#-G7. The '/' means that the root note of the chord is not the lowest, either because the chord is not in root position on the guitar, or because the bass guitar is playing one of the other two notes of the chord. For another example, listen to the opening of The Kings Of Leon's 'Slow Night, So Long', from their album, *Aha Shake Heartbreak*. Under the opening chords the bass is initially on A and then moves to D and F# – so there is a strong impression of the chords being inversions. A first inversion D means having an F# in the bass; a second inversion D means an A in the bass.

DOUBLE BASS

> ***"I wrote it ['The Love Cats'] that night. We did loads of jazzy stuff to get into the feel. Bill Thornley had never played double bass before but just took to it instantly, chalkmarked where he should be playing".***
>
> Robert Smith of The Cure

In some circumstances you might want to put the electric bass down and get a double bass player, or play a fingerstyle double bass sound from a keyboard. Properly a member of the orchestra string section (see **Section Seven**), especially when bowed, the double bass also moonlights in jazz trios. In pop the the symbolic identity of upright bass is jazz, sophistication, and 'old-time', therefore they lend sophistication. 'Stand By Me'. Like many rock'n'roll hits 'Rock Around The Clock' has a double bass line, and it can also be heard prominently on Ben E. King's 'Stand By Me' and early Motown hits like Mary Wells' 'My Guy'. It provides the left channel slow glissando on Nancy Sinatra's 'These Boots Were Made For Walking', intro and after he chorus; on the right side of the mix there is an electric bass.

DRUMS

The invention of drum machines, and later drum loops and samples, has made adding drums on a demo much easier than recording an acoustic kit. To give your song demos an effective drum track it is useful to understand a few basics about a drum-kit. A standard kit has four basic elements:

- The snare drum – which supplies the 'crack' noise on beats two and four in rock tracks.
- The kick/bass drum – which gives a muffled low thump on beats one and three.
- Side drums/tom-toms – which add fills or reinforce the snare or bass drum.
- Hi-hat/cymbals – the hi-hat, which can be open or closed, marks the beat or smaller divisions of it, supplemented by the ride cymbal. Crash cymbals are hit to accent bar changes, chord changes, or moments of drama.

Obviously in most songs that feature drums neither the snare nor the kick-drum is locked onto the beat all the time. Rhythmic groove comes from the interplay between kick-drum and snare and their placing on and off the main beats. The sound of any part of the kit is affected by the type of stick a drummer uses. Brushes applied to the snare, for example, is a very different sound to a snare played by sticks. To get familiar with the sound of these individual parts, drum solos can be helpful, such as Dave Brubeck's 'Take Five', The Edgar Winter Band, 'Frankenstein', Cream's 'Toad', Led Zeppelin's 'Moby Dick', and Cozy Powell's 'Run With The Devil'. Electronic drum kits offer another set of sounds, as do 1980s pre-sampling drum machines (like the Roland TR505) now regarded not as a poor man's imitation of real drums but a set of interesting sounds in their own right.

For less conventional rock drumming it is worth listening to tracks where the emphasis is less on the snare drum, such as the subtle accompaniment by Mick Fleetwood on Fleetwood Mac's 'Albatross' or the torrent of tom-toms by Ginger Baker on Cream's 'Sunshine Of Your Love'. The African Burundi drumming featured on a hit single in 1971, 'Burundi Black', was later used by Joni Mitchell on *The Hissing Of Summer Lawns* and was an influence on Adam and The Ants. If Ginger Baker had a successor in this field it was Budgie, the drummer with Siouxsie and the Banshees. Budgie's drumming is unmistakeable, with its African influence, frequent use of toms, and sparing reliance on conventional rock patterns. His interest in non-standard rhythm found further expression on what might be termed drums'n'vocals albums recorded with Siouxsie Sioux under the name of The Creatures. Peter Gabriel was another songwriter who decided to re-think the role of drums when he embarked on a solo career after Genesis. He famously dispensed with hi-hats and cymbals and developed a 'gated' snare sound which compressed the natural decay of the snare, increasing its explosive force, as can be heard on *Peter Gabriel 3*. This in turn formed a cornerstone of some of Phil Collins's sound.

Click tracks and tempo

If you record a demo with a drum machine it functions by default as a click track. In other words, the tempo is set and does not deviate. While this has the advantage of keeping the main parts in time it also means that other important musical means of expression such as increases in speed over the whole track, or localized rallentandos (slowing up momentarily) are lost. The regimentation of rhythm in popular music is one of the unrecognized tragedies of its development over the past 30 years. If you are recording a basic guitar/vocal demo, don't be afraid to do without it occasionally, if you can keep basic time yourself.

Tips on using a drum machine

Many songwriters who make demos will do so using a drum machine or drum loop. There are two ways of approaching this. The first is to forget about realism and use the drum sounds any way you want to generate rhythm – as would happen in dance music. The second is to treat the sounds as a substitute for a real drummer, in which case you want to make them sound as human as possible. This is the course you will take in much songwriting.

Here are some tips on the drum sounds:

- Balance the volume of individual parts of the kit so they are in realistic relation to each other
- If your drum machine allows it, get more from one snare-drum sound by fractionally altering its tuning and volume. This will also make snare-drum rolls sound less 'machine-gun' like.
- Avoid preset sounds that were sampled with reverb if you have a reverb unit to supply that effect at mix-down.

- Don't mix-up 'wet' sounds with 'dry' sounds when building a kit. This causes problems during mix-down.
- Try to separate the sounds onto more than one recording track so you can, for example, put more reverb on cymbals than on the bass drum. Cymbals don't sound realistic unless they die away over more than a few seconds.
- Have two crash cymbals at different pitches.

Here are some tips on writing drum tracks:

- Don't rely on preset rhythms – everyone else may be using them.
- Write plenty of patterns and write small variations on them. This takes patience, but the results can be worthwhile. See below for a drum pattern map.
- Refresh the snare sound by having a pattern where it isn't used, or where it is omitted from the fourth beat and replaced by a tom-tom fill.
- Have a good selection of drum fills for the transitions between one section and another.
- Contrast closed hi-hat on a verse with open hi-hat on a chorus where you want more noise.
- Write patterns based on rhythms heard on recordings.
- Don't quantize everything if you are tapping rhythms in. Quantization is a means by which imprecise tapped rhythms are moved to the nearest quaver or semi-quaver. Too much of this will make the rhythm patterns seem stiff.
- To write a more complex roll or rhythm temporarily slow down the tempo. Play the rhythm at this slower speed and then return to your original tempo to hear the result.
- Save time by writing two-bar patterns as single units, bearing in mind that you will need some single patterns if your song sections feature an odd number of bars.

Two drum pattern 'maps'

You can map out the drum patterns for a song when you have the song structure. There are many ways to do this.

Drum map one, over the page, is one I've used for my own demos. Our example song has a four-bar intro, 16-bar verse, eight-bar chorus, four-bar link, and a middle eight. Following the system used on the Alesis SR16, the numbers indicate a drum pattern, letters 'a' and 'b' indicate variations on the basic rhythm, 'f' is a fill or part fill with cymbal crash.

Each number/letter is a bar of 4/4. You would need a four-beat click as a lead-in unless the song were starting with solo drums. The first drum map is very simple and might do as the foundation for a quick demo. There are no fills and only six patterns for the complete song. These help to distinguish one section from another.

DRUM MAP ONE (SIMPLE)

Intro:	1a	1a	1a	1b
Verse:	1a	1a	1a	1a
	1a	1a	1a	1b
	1a	1a	1a	1b
	1a	1b	1a	1b
Chorus:	2a	2a	2a	2b
	2a	2a	2a	2b
Link:	1a	1a	1a	1b
[Repeat verse and chorus]				
Middle eight	3a	3a	1b	1b
	3a	3a	3b	3b
Chorus	2a	2a	2a	2b
	2a	2a	2a	2b
[Repeat chorus]				
Coda	2a	2a	2b	2b
	2a	2a	2b	2b

DRUM MAP 2 (COMPLEX)

Here is a more complex map based on a slightly extended version of the same song. This uses fills and a total of 22 patterns.

Intro:	1a	1a	1a	1b
Verse:	2a	2a	2a	2b
	2a	2af	2a	2bf
	2a	2a	2af	2b
	2af	2a	2a	2bf
Chorus:	3a	3b	3a	3b
	3a	3af	3b	3bf

Link:	4a	4a	4a	4b
[Repeat verse and chorus]				
Verse:	2a	2a	2a	2b
	2a	2af	2a	2bf
	2a	2a	2af	2b
	2af	2a	2a	2bf
Chorus:	3a	3b	3a	3b
	3a	3af	3b	3bf
Middle eight	5a	5a	5b	5a
	5a	5af	5b	5bf
Half verse:	2a	2a	2af	2b
	2af	2a	6af	6bf
[Chorus]				
Last chorus	7a	7b	7a	7b
	7a	7af	7b	7bf
Coda	4a	4a	4a	4b
	4a	4a	6af	6bf

Notes on the drum maps

- The 1 group uses part of the kit, possibly avoiding the snare and saving it for later.
- The 2af rhythm doesn't always appear at the same point in the four-bar verse phrases.
- The 2bf fill comes at the mid-point of the verse and immediately before the chorus.
- By the time the chorus is reached we need a new rhythm – so in comes the 3 group, complete with fill 3af in the last bar or chorus 1 and 3bf in the last bar of chorus 2.
- The 4 group is a stronger or partial version of the '1' group. There might, for example, be no snare on the latter. This means the link to verse 2 sounds similar to the intro but is stronger, otherwise too much momentum would be lost.
- The middle eight has its own group, 5. This could feature a new percussion instrument like congas, or switch from hi-hat to ride cymbal.
- The final half verse has two bars of previously unheard fills to take it to the choruses.

- The last chorus has a new pattern, a small variation on the 3 group, to differentiate it from the previous chorus. The variation might be adding handclaps to the snare, or doubling a tambourine to eighth-notes which was earlier playing quarter-notes.
- The coda combines patterns from the link with the fills at the end of the half verse.On a cautionary note, although drum pattern variations are good, beware of making the kick-drum pattern too complicated and shifting, partly because when you come to put a bass-line on the track it will be difficult to remember exactly where the kick-drum is hit. This can be a problem if you want your bass note to coincide with it.

'Dual layer' drums/percussion

Since the advent of drum machines, and with the perceived need in the rock field for bands to look up-to-date, there has been some emulation of dance music. This takes the form of an arrangement approach that involves starting a track with a drum loop, sample or drum machine pattern and then adding the acoustic drum kit later. Robert Plant's 'Tie Dye The Highway' and U2's 'Beautiful Day' and 'Elevation' do this, reserving the full kit for later in the song. Note how in the U2 song the drums are pulled out at 2:15 for the bridge with voice. Wheatus's 'Teenage Dirtbag' has an intro drum loop with acoustic guitar and bass over it. Teenage Fanclub's 'Sparky's Dream' does the same thing with distant guitars on its intro. A drum machine provides the beat for most of R.E.M's 'Everybody Hurts'. Electric Soft Parade's 'Silent To The Dark' uses a slowed down drum loop on its bridge. Radiohead's 'Sit Down. Stand Up' has a drum machine pattern.

Effective use of the snare-drum:

- Use your snare drum sound thoughtfully. It is the most squandered instrument in rock by virtue of being played all the time.
- 'Pounding' by Doves delays its snare drum until the verse, the chorus of the song using a pounding four-to-the-bar Motown beat. Four-to-the-bar snare rhythms are very difficult to produce on a drum machine because the sample is always triggered at the same tone and volume which sounds artificial.
- There are powerful snare fills in the middle of Blondie's 'Heart of Glass'. The explosive force of a drumkit is in the snare – so taking it out then bringing it back in is very powerful. See Kate Bush 'Leave It Open' for a much-delayed snare-drum entry.
- On a song that doesn't require much percussion try reserving the snare drum for a few special moments as Hal Blaine did on The Beach Boys' 'God Only Knows', an effect imitated by R.E.M. on 'At My Most Beautiful'. Try adding reverb and pulling this to the back of the mix.
- Military march-like snare figures can be expressive even when the lyric subject is not war, as in R.E.M.'s 'King Of Birds', Kate Bush's 'Cloudbusting', Wishbone Ash's 'The King Will Come', Jefferson Airplane's 'White Rabbit', and Television's 'Venus'.

- Quiet repeated snare-taps create tension and drama.
- When the snare is hit with both sticks a fraction of a second apart a 'flam' is created. This is powerful and a great way from the drums to re-enter. You can hear flams on the intro of The Knack's 'My Sharona'.
- The snare beat alone makes an intro, as with The Beatles 'I Want To Tell You'.
- Experiment placing the snare anywhere but the second beat. The Marbles' 'Only One Woman' has a delayed second snare hit to the fourth beat.
- A crescendo snare-roll is a powerful approach to a new section. Television have one at the start of 'Friction' (and on another type of drum for the intro of 'Torn Curtain').

Arrangement points for the rest of the kit:

- A drum entrance is potentially one of the most powerful moments in a song. See The Beatles' 'Lucy In The Sky With Diamonds', Phil Collins's 'In The Air Tonight', Simple Minds' 'Alive and Kicking' and 'Come A Long Way', the snare-roll after the guitar solo in Led Zeppelin's 'Whole Lotta Love' and into the final section of 'What Is And What Could Never Be'.
- A temporary drop out of the drums, even if only for a few beats, can be effective, as on the bridge of 'Eight Days A Week', the choruses of Television's 'Prove It' and American Hi-Fi's 'Flavour Of The Week', Ash's 'Goldfinger', or the bridge of U2's 'Beautiful Day'. Hole's 'Doll Parts' has repeated drum stops and re-entries – more so than any other recent song I know. These entries and exits become the trademark of the song. Only in the latter stages do the drums stay in.
- To get a contrasted verse/chorus with drums, carry the verse with a side-stick, snare-rim, brushes ,or wood-block. Bill Haley's 'Rock Around The Clock' is carried by sticks with the occasional snare hit. The Arctic Monkeys' 'Mardy Bum' also features a side-stick contrasting with snare.
- A simple rhythm on the kick-drum alone makes an effective intro or bridge. Listen to The Supremes' 'My World Is Empty Without You'.
- Listen to The Isley Brothers' 'This Old Heart Of Mine' for an example of a thumping kick pattern, with the bass-drum more frequent than usual.
- Cymbal crashes don't always have to go on the first beat. Try the second beat, or the first and second with two crash cymbals of different sizes.
- For a 'jugband' feel, try bass drum and cymbal but no snare, plus tambourine, and possibly maracas.
- Drums can be added to a song progressively, piece by piece. Fleetwood Mac's 'Man Of The World' has drums missing from its intro and first verse. Its second verse has kick-drum and hi-hat, with cymbal crashes for accents. The drums finally enter at 1:40 to give the bridge an exhilarating punch.

- Drums are sensitive to reverb. The distant snare explosions in Simon and Garfunkel's 'The Boxer' are caused by heavy reverb. There are fine examples of drum-fills with EQ and reverb treatments in Madonna's 'Frozen'.
- Put a drum machine through echo to get a more interesting rhythm from a simple pattern.
- Toms are handy for fills at the end of a song section, allowing you to momentarily rest the snare and bass drum.
- See The Beatles 'Ticket To Ride' for a verse carried by rhythm beaten on toms, which contrasts with the standard rock rhythm on the bridge.
- A second drum kit can add accents to particular sections of a song while the first drum kit keeps the beat – the former is a core instrument, the latter secondary. The Who's 'I Can See For Miles' has two separate drum performances, one on the left keeping time and fills on the right.
- Echo and distant miking give depth to drums, as on Led Zeppelin's 'When The Levee Breaks'.
- The first of a last run of choruses can be sung over just a drum beat. This arrangement was featured in The Spin Doctors' 'Two Princes'.
- Drum fills often go in the gaps between vocal lines, as on The Move's 'I Can Hear The Grass Grow'.

Tricky rhythms

A song's rhythm can be spiced up by including the odd bar that does not have four beats, or by including a rhythm pattern with a pattern of accents that go counter to the beat. In Blondie's 'Heart Of Glass', during the middle eight, some phrases drop a beat so you get bars of four and three beats alternating (1:51-2:02), then the same music is repeated in straight 4/4. Current band The Fratellis include interesting rhythms in some of the tracks on *Costello Music*, notably 'Flathead', 'Country Boys And City Girls', and the last bar of the verse phrase in 'Chelsea Dagger'.

PERCUSSION

Percussion is used to support the drums in a song, to stand in for them, or to accent particular bits. Percussion can be increased as the track progresses to refresh and strengthen the beat. Almost anything can be percussion, from tapping the guitar body (Cat Stevens 'Lady D'Arbanville'), stomping on a recording studio floor (The Supremes 'Where Did Our Love Go', T.Rex 'Jeepster'), slapping thighs (Buddy Holly 'Peggy Sue'), or making maracas out of a close-miked box of matches. Songs like Simon and Garfunkel's 'Cecilia', Hot Legs' 'Neanderthal Man', The Beach Boys' 'Barbara Ann', and John Lennon's 'Give Peace A Chance' take a campfire approach with minimal percussion and possibly a kick-drum to hold it all together. Other songs such as John Kongos's 'He's Gonna Step On You Again' have noticeably greater amounts of percussion that usual.

Timpani

The grand-daddy of additional percussion, timpani (also known as 'kettle' drums) are a standard piece in an orchestra. They add big-scale drama (sometimes pretension) to large production romantic ballads, but can be used with subtlety to avoid being bombastic. In Springtseen's 'Stolen Car' or The Temptations 'Just My Imagination' there are some subtle moments of timpani, like the roll into the second verse and during the bridge. Bob and Earl's 'Harlem Shuffle' certainly wouldn't be the same without that evocative timp "barrooomm!" every now and then.

Congas and bongos

Congas are tall drums you stand up to play, **bongos** are a higher-pitched version held between the knees. Both lend arrangements a funky, unbuttoned Latin warmth, hence their deployment in rock bands that stray into soul/funk territory. It is sometimes forgotten that Hendrix took the stage at Woodstock with a conga player. Congas can be heard on many tracks by Santana and on Beatles songs like 'You're Gonna Lose That Girl' and 'And I Love Her'. Congas are heard on the intro of The Supremes' 'In And Out Of Love', the drums delayed finally coming in at about 0:25.

If you want to work acoustically, without a drum-kit, they can form your rhythm section. Played fast bongos give a feeling of rising hysteria, as on the Dr No soundtrack. Marvin Gaye got a new sound from them by adding reverb to them for the *What's Going On* album. Marc Bolan recorded four albums as Tyrannosaurus Rex with bongos as the main percussion instrument. Later, Micky Finn's congas gave T.Rex's glam rock a certain funky feel, even if he wasn't prominent in the mixes. Bolan's rhythm guitar style partly evolved from having spent so long playing to bongos. You may find you play rhythm guitar differently if you record with bongos or congas rather than a drum-kit.

Tambourine

A tambourine combines something of the sound of a snare-drum with a ringing cymbal. It gives what Dave Marsh described as the rattlesnake touch on Marvin Gaye's 'I Heard It Through The Grapevine', and the 16th-note patter on Smokey Robinson and the Miracles' 'I Second That Emotion'. Sparing use of it keeps the beat on The Beatles' 'You've Got To Hide Your Love Away'. On 'Ticket To Ride' the tambourine is initially on beats two and four but in the bridge goes to 16ths. Tambourine goes well with strummed acoustic guitar. A 16th-note shake will fit on top of an eighth-note hi-hat. It is a good idea to save it to an up-tempo bridge to give the bridge extra lift. For an example of minimal use listen to The Smiths' 'Please Please Please Let Me Get What I Want'.

Other percussion

Since instruments that are made to be struck and beaten do not involve pitch they are relatively easy to make. Therefore there are vast numbers of percussion items from across the world and samples and emulations of some are now standard on many synth keyboards.

Additional percussion can:

- Amplify the main parts of the beat already established by drums.
- Accentuate precise moments in the lyric like a word or phrase.
- Accentuate musical features like a chord change or key change.
- Create interesting cross-rhythms and fill higher frequencies.
- Invite audience participation.
- Keep the rhythm going if the drums are temporarily pulled out.
- Help contrast one song section with another.
- Give a track an identity by virtue of 'world music' associations.

The **gong** is the grandaddy of cymbals. Its symbolic identity is exotic – it stands for mystery and the Far East. It can produce a dramatic shimmer or an explosive crash that takes a long time to die away.

Tablas are a distinctive sounding Indian drum, normally heard with sitar. They feature on The Beatles' 'Within You Without You', Kula Shaker's 'Temple Of Everlasting Light', and Led Zeppelin's 'Black Mountainside'. The Page/Plant track 'Most High' has a variety of exotic percussion, as do Plant's 'Down To The Sea', and The Mission's 'Tower Of Strength'. They were popularized in the mid-1960s because of the vogue for Indian music and mysticism, for which they, along with the sitar, became the expressive signature. From another continent, African talking drums vary in pitch when you squeeze them.

A **washboard** gives the 'zip' sound in Mungo Jerry's 'In The Summertime' and The Beatles 'Tell Me What You See', and is also heard in the verse of Blue Oyster Cult's 'Don't Fear The Reaper' (which also has a **cowbell**). Ever since The Beatles 'You Can't Do That', The Rolling Stones' 'Honky Tonk Women' with its classic drum/cowbell intro, and Mountain's 'Mississippi Queen', nothing evokes good-time rock'n'roll better than a cowbell. For an incongruously prominent use listen to the bridge of The Beatles' 'I Need You' bridge where it is louder than the drums on the left.

The **triangle** has an unpitched hard bright metallic ring good for accents. Ben E. King's 'Stand By Me' intro features double bass, triangle and a washboard-type instrument whose signal is panned via reverb to the right.

Maracas make a continuous shuffling sound, which, like the sound of cymbals, is a good space filler. They provide rain noise in R.Dean Taylor's 'Gotta See Jane' and the intro to Tyrannosaurus Rex's 'Seal Of Seasons', the bridge of The Beatles' 'The Night Before' and the chorus of 'You've Got To Hide Your Love Away', and The Archies's 'Sugar Sugar'.

Sleigh bells feature in Christmas songs, and are associated with The Beach Boys' *Pet Sounds* album. **Claves** are heard on Jethro Tull's 'Living In The Past' and The Beatles' 'And I Love Her'. **Finger cymbals** are heard on 1960s band Nirvana's 'Tiny Goddess' toward the last verse and Siouxsie and the Banshees' 'Arabian Knights'.

Handclaps and finger-snaps

The most basic musical resource of all is the human body itself, which can create pitched sound through singing, and percussive noise by hand-claps. The symbolism becomes one of community (think of a gospel service and the pejorative 'happy-clappy') and the expression of physical energy. The simplest form of joining in with music is to clap your hands. Handclaps are symbolically related to applause, celebration.

The high frequency snap of a handclap fits well with a snare drum and/or tambourine, so the obvious place to put them on a recording is on beats two and four. They are often reserved for choruses and the last chorus and coda in particular, as at the end of David Bowie's 'Starman', and the end of Suede's 'Animal Nitrate'. This use makes the handclap symbolize the presence of a larger group of people, which in turn implies the audience and the listener being pulled in. The unwritten implication is: they're joining in so why don't you?

Handclaps feature on many Motown hits – think of the way they are heard on the start of The Supremes' 'Baby Love' and 'Where Did Our Love Go'. They are used to contrast bridge from verse in The Beatles' 'No Reply'. They contribute a wild pop atmosphere to the Queens Of The Stone Age's 'Quick And To The Pointless'.

Another use for handclaps is to introduce a separate rhythmic figure between vocal phrases. Think of the hand-claps on The Beatles 'Eight Days A Week', where they come between vocal phrases in the chorus.

Handclaps sound good panned left and right rather than in the middle of the stereo.

Rhythmic stops

It can be a very good arrangement touch to refresh the rhythm section on a track by pausing for several seconds. This could mean stripping back to just a hi-hat or tambourine, or silence. Arthur Conley's 'Sweet Soul Music' stops for a moment at 1:30; until then the rhythm has been constant. Tori Amos's 'Caught A Lite Sneeze' has a break from its drum loop. 'Soul Man' drops down to lighter percussion before the last choruses. The drums are taken out of Aretha Franklin's 'Respect' where she spells out the word toward the end. There is an important pause in Nashville Teens' 'Tobacco Road' where everything stops for the chorus hook which refreshes the riff. Queens Of The Stone Age's 'Better Living Through Chemistry' pulls the amazing arrangement stunt of stopping the song at 1:35, letting a chord drift in low-level feedback for almost 40 seconds, re-entering with a guitar solo which in turn is pushed aside at the three-minute mark by vocal harmonies, as though CSN&Y had gate-crashed a Soundgarden session.

PRIMARY INSTRUMENTS AND THE BACKING TRACK

We have now looked at the basic instruments musicians use in laying down a backing track to which secondary instruments and parts are added. Here's Izzy Stradlin, ex-Guns N'Roses, on recording his solo album *River*: "We did four tracks in LA a few weeks back. It's just acoustic, bass, drums, and electric piano; it just sounds so natural. You play less, and it counts more because you don't have the amp to resonate the notes. One note on the acoustic is all you get and then it fades. You play less on some bits, more on others, but when you hear it back it sounds wonderful.

"I'll come in with the idea on cassette, me on acoustic guitar, and I play it. Once they've got the idea we go out in the room, everything's already miked up, we all stand in front of the drums, go through it, get the arrangement down, and then work on it for a while – get the feel and timing. But we track everything live. Then you overdub mistakes, add solos, go back and fix vocals." River was recorded on 24-track tape through an old Neve console, half of it in Seattle and half in LA, and with manual mixing.

Another insight into the recording process comes from Ocean Colour Scene's guitarist Steve Craddock, around the time of *North Atlantic Drift*. "Simon [Fowler] writes the songs and he turns up with an acoustic guitar and plays them to us. We just exchange it for electrics and then, in the studio, as soon as we've got a strong guitar-bass-drums track down that's the backing track. It just unfolds as we make it. We recorded it at the Townhouse on Goldhawk Road in just over two months. We played mostly to a click because we wanted to keep it steady but powerful all the same. Over the first month we had most of the tracks recorded. We'd then overdub the other stuff – guitars, backing vocals, percussion."

Now we can range further in the quest for instrumental colour.

SECTION 7

Secondary instruments for arranging

Moving beyond standard rock instrumentation is a great way of making your arrangements stand out. And these days, thanks to synthesizers, that's more of a practical possibility than ever.

If guitars, keyboards, bass guitar and drums are the core instruments of popular music, many other instruments play a crucial supporting role. In years past, recording with these meant either learning to play them yourself or hiring someone who could – which could be time-consuming and/or expensive. Now, you don't have to worry so much, as most of these instruments are available on sound-cards, hardware synths, sound modules, and sample libraries. It may not be the real thing, but in the background of an arrangement it doesn't always matter. One way of making your band and arrangements stand out is to have an additional non-rock standard instrument.

Remember the following when selecting some additional instruments:

- The rarer the instrument the greater the chance that it might be hard to find a musical use for it in a song. The most-recorded secondary instruments are the ones that fit easily in a range of styles.
- If a rare instrument has been used it may be associated with one or two famous songs. That might make it hard to use it in your recording, unless you want to make an allusion to that song. For example, the cimbalom's eerie silvery rattle is strongly associated with some of John Barry's 1960s soundtracks, an association Portishead were presumably happy to evoke on their trip-hop album Dummy. The bass harmonica wheezing on Simon and Garfunkel's 'The Boxer', The Beatles' 'Being For The Benefit of Mr Kite', and Pet Sounds was included by R.E.M. in their Brian Wilson homage 'At My Most Beautiful' precisely for its Beach Boys connection.
- Choice of instruments may be dictated by style if you are doing a pastiche, as with the woodwind on The Beatles 'When I'm Sixty-Four'. If you want to evoke the ghost of George Formby, get a ukulele.
- There are pleasing arrangement touches to be had by adding non-rock instruments such as flute, oboe, clarinet, French horn, or viola to a sparse acoustic guitar number. It is down to how you use them, not how exotic the instrument is.
- Some instruments are non-specific in terms of time period. Others carry strong connotations of a past era – such as the early drum machines of the 1980s and analogue synths like the Moog. Traditional instruments aren't tied to a single era in the same way. Using modern gear makes you sound up-to-date today but possibly dated in the future – you have to decide if this matters.
- Samples of instruments can often be played beyond the pitch range of the real instrument. For realism, be idiomatic and keep to the authentic pitch-ranges. If you

want to experiment with what instruments sound like outside their pitch range, samples open up a world of new virtual sound. To check pitch ranges of instruments, refer to a manual of orchestration.

- Likewise, the level of sustain on a sampled horn note could go beyond what a player could manage without turning blue.
- Mike Oldfield's Tubular Bells, Benjamin Britten's Young Person's Guide To The Orchestra, and the Naxos label's multi-CD Instruments of the Orchestra are all good in their respective ways for hearing the sound of a range of instruments, if you want to do some aural research.
- Secondary instruments do not play all the time in an arrangement. They make their presence felt here and there, supporting the harmony from back in the mix, or coming forward to add moments of melodic interest.

Some secondary instruments have even had songs named after them, witness Kate Bush's 'Violin', Nick Drake's 'Cello Song', The Who's 'Squeeze Box', Freddie and the Dreamers' 'Susan's Tuba', and Gomez's 'Love Is Better Than A Warm Trombone'.

FULL ORCHESTRAL ARRANGEMENTS

Although the following pages describe the use of individual orchestral instruments, it is not anticipated that you will be creating full orchestral arrangements. There are several reasons why you don't have to score for all the instruments and why just a few may give the same impression:

- Although strings, woodwind, or brass are occasionally added to mainstream songs (though not as often as in the 1960s when there was no sampling), a full arrangement of them, such as would be satisfactory if they were heard on their own, is rare.
- The foreground position of a lead vocal, strummed guitars, keyboard washes, and drum-kit, can contribute to obscuring detail in background orchestral parts. Soaring high-pitched violins and flutes are one thing, but there is no point in writing the complex parts found in a 'classical' composition, as they won't be heard.
- Similarly, electric bass guitar and the orchestra's double bass and low cello parts will clash unless they closely duplicate each other. If they aren't clashing there's a real chance the end result will be a mix that is too bass heavy.
- Pitch-wise, strummed guitar chords cover most of the cello range and the lower half of the viola. So cello and viola parts could easily be masked by guitars.
- Most synths include a couple of patches called 'orchestra hits', a cheap and quick way of accenting a chord change or moment of drama, and something of a mid-1980s cliché. Few could resist triggering an 'orchestral bang' at any pitch with one finger.

If you do like orchestral features in a song, one possibility is to have a dedicated orchestral section, such as the intro and bridge. An example would be the way orchestral instruments contribute to The Beatles' 'A Day In The Life'. To give a song an orchestral flavour try adding parts for flute, clarinet, two horns or two trombones, trumpet, two or three violin lines and cello. Full orchestra arrangements feature on Elvis Costello and Burt Bacharach's *Painted From Memory*. To give you an idea of the number of musicians involved, the session for The Beatles' 'Hey Jude' used a total of 36 musicians: ten violins, three violas, three cellos, two double-basses, two flutes, two clarinets, one bass clarinet, one bassoon, one contra-bassoon, four trumpets, two horns, four trombones, and one percussion player. These joined in on the coda 'na-na' section. But their effect is to add weight to the sound but not clearly distinguishable lines.

WOODWIND

This family of instruments primarily comprises flute, oboe, clarinet, bassoon, and French horn, but I have also included other blown instruments such as the recorder and harmonica. For woodwind parts to sound realistic remember that notes should not sustain longer than a player could hold a single breath. Occasionally a woodwind section might be booked onto a recording session. The Beatles' 'Here Comes The Sun' features the unusual woodwind line-up of two piccolos, two flutes, two alto flutes, and two clarinets, a choice that lends itself to high-pitched lines and a smooth timbre, fitting in with the song's airy character.

Flute/Piccolo

Both instruments are metal with a high, bright, and smooth tone. The piccolo operates about an octave above the flute's usual range and can be piercing. In an arrangement:

- These are useful for doubling a vocal line an octave up, or a high string part at the same pitch.
- The association of flute and piccolo with the high register connotes freedom and flight; both have imitated bird-song in music. Listen to The Association's 'Windy'.
- The breathy wind sound gives a cool, carefree or lyrical ambience.
- The flute's low range can have a sultry, erotic quality, but is easily masked. This can be compensated for in the mix.
- They are good for short melodic fills in between vocal phrases, or longer link melodies.
- Both are associated with innocence and the countryside. Listen to Van Morrison's Astral Weeks album, The Beatles' 'Fool On The Hill', Traffic's 'Paper Sun', Nick Drake's 'Bryter Layter' and Canned Heat's 'Goin' Up The Country' where, supported by strummed acoustic and electric guitars, the flute comes in as a solo instrument after about a minute and intermittently throughout.
- Combined with a martial snare-drum rhythm, the piccolo can evoke a military air.
- The flute was a lead instrument in some progressive rock groups such as Jethro Tull ('Living In The Past') and Focus ('House Of The King').

- The flute can supply a solo for a song, as with The Moody Blues' 'Nights In White Satin', in the middle or at the end, as with The Beatles 'You've Got To Hide Your Love Away', or the hook – as on Manfred Mann's 'Mighty Quinn'.

Along with mandolin and violin, flute embellishes some of the tracks on Nick Cave's recent album *The Lyre Of Orpheus*.

Recorder

The recorder is not usually part of the orchestral woodwind section. Wooden or plastic, easy to play and cheap to produce, it has long associations with amateur music-making in schools. Therefore it evokes childhood and children, innocence, the pastoral and rural, the old and antique, and folk music. It can be heard on Manfred Mann's 'Ha Ha Said The Clown', and 'My Name Is Jack', a song about a children's home.

- Rural, organic symbolism is strong with the recorder, hence the decision to include an arrangement of recorders on the intro of Led Zeppelin's 'Stairway To Heaven'.
- The simplicity of playing associates the recorder with childhood – hence the use of the instrument on psychedelic songs of 1967-68 such as The Herd's 'I Don't Want Our Loving To Die', The Troggs' 'Wild Thing', and The Move's 'Fire Brigade'.

Oboe

The oboe has a plaintive, reedy quality which is often used to add pathos to music. You can hear the instrument on Sony and Cher's 'I Got You Babe' and Neil Young's 'A Man Needs A Maid'. It loses this plaintive quality in its highest range and can become shrill. It does not go as low as the clarinet and does not have the clarinet's jazz ambience as part of its symbolic identity.

- Coupled with strings the oboe can give music an English character, as on The Casuals' 'Jesamine'.
- Its tone is best heard on exposed solo melodies of held and slow-moving notes.
- A related instrument is the English horn (cor anglais) which has a slightly lower range but a similar plaintive, mellow timbre. If you have a song which might need this tone and you have access to both sounds contrast them and see which you prefer.

Clarinet

The clarinet is brighter and smoother than oboe. As a lead instrument it is associated with traditional Dixieland jazz and the city more than the country (partly because of the unforgettable glissando that opens George Gershwin's *Rhapsody In Blue*, which Woody Allen assigned to the soundtrack of his film *Manhattan*). Its first octave (the so-called 'chalumeau' range) has a dark, velvet quality all of its own which suits slow melodies. (There is also a bass clarinet with an even lower range). Two clarinets support the jazz pastiche of The Beatles' 'Honey Pie'.

- A low clarinet line could double a clean guitar riff or a slow descending bass line.
- A medium to high clarinet could supply melodic fills or double a vocal, or harmonize a vocal.

Bassoon

The bassoon is the bass member of the woodwind family. It has a fruity tone that is reedy and 'smoky'. It is rarely heard in popular music outside of orchestral arrangements, where it would not be heard separately. Producer Tony Visconti used a bassoon to double descending bass lines on the chorus of T.Rex's 'Jeepster'. There is also a bass version of the bassoon, the contra-bassoon, for even lower notes. But this is unlikely to be of use on a song, since the pitch range would be covered by bass guitar or double bass. In an arrangement the bassoon:

- Will give a double bass note at the same pitch a wiry edge.
- Will amplify the wiry quality of a bass piano note at the same pitch.
- Is heard on novelty records for comic purposes. There is one on Sandie Shaw's Eurovision hit 'Puppet On A String' and on Sony and Cher's 'I Got You Babe'.

HARMONICA/BASS HARMONICA

The harmonica or 'mouth organ' is a blown instrument with a long history in folk music. Its associations are campfire sincerity, mournful tunes, blues, and folk song. Highly portable, it was a significant weapon of the early 1960s protest singer, mostly now because of Bob Dylan's early protest songs, although Dylan carried it with him into his mid-1960s electric period. It was also used by other singer-songwriters such as Donovan and Neil Young. A special wire support was invented to hold the harmonica so that a guitarist could play it and strum chords simultaneously. With its quasi-vocal pitch glides, vibrato, variable volume, and unpredictable switches from single notes to thirds, the harmonica is a tough instrument to emulate from samples and keyboards. If you want this sound, it would be best to play it or get someone who can. The harmonica:

- Gives a bright and cheerful sound to an upbeat song, as on Van Morrison's 'Bright Side Of The Road' and The Rolling Stones' 'Not Fade Away'.
- Can be piercing and supply raucous solo passages, as on Stevie Wonder songs like 'Fingertips'.
- Its mournful swoops and elegiac vibrato suits blues and slow ballads such as Bruce Springsteen's 'The River'.
- The larger bass harmonica has a small but distinguished place in pop history for its asthmatic contributions to Simon and Garfunkel's 'The Boxer', The Beatles 'Fool On The Hill', The Beach Boys Pet Sounds, and R.E.M.'s 'At My Most Beautiful'.
- Listen to Led Zeppelin's 'When The Levee Breaks' for some epic harmonica given a widescreen treatment with reverb and echo, and 'Bring It On Home' for a harmonica note that imitates a blast of feedback as a link to a guitar riff.

BRASS

Brass instruments lend great weight, volume and drama to a song when deployed in pairs or trios. The brass section in an orchestra will comprise French horns, trumpets, trombones, and tuba, collectively capable of being a bass-line, harmony, and melody all in one. So in a song you may only need a couple of these instruments. Blown hard, brass instruments can sound raw; they can also be muted for a softer effect. Muted brass is associated with erotic jazz songs, something evoked by the brass sample on Pulp's 'This Is Hardcore'. Controlled by the breath, they can imitate vocal phrases through pitch-bending and smooth volume fluctuation. There is also the marching brass band evoked on Dylan's 'Rainy Day Women # 12 & 35'.

Brass parts are often heard in jazz, in film scores/songs, musicals, and in larger rhythm and blues outfits. Many 1960s pop hits, like Cat Stevens' 'Matthew And Son', or James Bond theme songs like Shirley Bassey's 'Goldfinger' and Tom Jones' 'Thunderball', have prominent brass fills. They were crucial to large outfits like Blood, Sweat and Tears (who had an international hit with the brass-dominated 'Spinning Wheel' in 1968) and, in the 1970s, Chicago. The brass-band parts on Brian and Michael's 'Matchstick Men', Roy Harper's 'When An Old Cricketer Leaves The Crease', and The Who's 'Red, Blue And Grey' evoke the era of the Salvation Army band and working-class life in the North of England. The Who also used brass sounds on *Quadrophenia*, where on songs like '5.15' they took the riff for themselves. This Who-like brass was copied on Dodgy's 'In A Room'. A mad brass ensemble brings Radiohead's 'The National Anthem' to a chaotic conclusion.

Some typical uses of brass include:

- Driving low-pitched riffs, as on Amen Corner's 'Bend Me, Shape Me'.
- Sudden stabs and short interjections, like the brass on the fourth offbeat in Sam and Dave's 'Soul Man' in the second and third verse. Al Green's 'Tired Of Being Alone' has brass on the right side, with sharp accentuated chords plus upward glisses. These parts can be minimal.
- Sustained brass notes that increase in volume to lead into a chorus (see The Hollies 'Air That I Breathe').
- In soul, brass often links with organ, freeing the guitar from sustaining chords and giving it a more rhythmic role, as on Al Green's 'Take Me To The River'.
- Distant brass on the left of the stereo versions of Nancy Sinatra's 'These Boots Were Made For Walking' adds subtle colour.
- Several brass parts can occupy one side of a stereo mix. In Fontella Bass's 'Rescue Me' there is strong brass presence occupying the right channel with backing vocals, whereas piano, guitar, drums and bass are squeezed into the left.
- Hold back brass toward the end of a song to give a real lift, as happens in Percy Sledge's 'When A Man Loves A Woman' where the brass enters only for the last two times through the chord progression.

- Write parts that start as single note figures, then go to octaves and then bloom into chords, as on The Beatles' 'Got To Get You Into My Life'.
- Experiment writing three-note brass chords in first or second inversion, not root position. So make an E chord G#-B-E or B-E-G# in the brass.

Many synth keyboards carry patches and samples that combine brass sounds for you. As with woodwind, keyboard brass sounds must not sustain longer than a player could hold their breath if you want them to sound realistic. Use the pitch-bend wheel to add a touch of glissando to them.

French horn

A standard orchestra normally has four horns – the number that can provide self-contained four-part harmony or double up if matched against other brass. Horns have an airy, smoother sound compared to trombone or trumpet.

- They are associated with the countryside, because of hunting calls.
- They can evoke open spaces, aspiration, drama – good for romantic ballads.
- They can provide a harmonic pad that binds other parts together.
- They can play effective pedal notes.
- In popular music, the French horn's greatest moment is the swooping melodic motif on the intro to The Beach Boys' 'God Only Knows'. The French horn is also featured on The Beatles' 'For No One'.
- The chorus of The Marbles' 'Only One Woman' has two high horns on the end. The Temptations' ballad 'Just My Imagination' has soft horn parts.
- They can add snatches of counter-melody, as in The Beatles' 'I Am The Walrus'.

The Who's bass player John Entwistle could play horn and therefore they are heard on The Who's *Tommy* and *Quadrophenia* albums, and even solo on the single 'I'm A Boy'. There are four horns on The Beatles' 'Sgt.Pepper's Lonely Hearts Club Band'. An obscure member of the horn family, the flugelhorn, turned up as a lead instrument on T.Rex's 'Girl' (from *Electric Warrior*).

Trumpet

Arguably, trumpet is to jazz what lead guitar is to rock. Players such as Miles Davis occupy a position in jazz comparable to venerated electric guitar players. As such, a single trumpet can easily be used as a lead instrument for a solo passage. The trumpet's tone is bright, piercing and will cut through even a full arrangement. They are often employed in pairs or threes. The main uses of a trumpet in an arrangement are:

- A trumpet solo easily gives track a jazz vibe, and in symbolic terms implies a sophistication which an electric guitar solo doesn't.
- This effect is magnified if a jazz instrumentation (piano, double bass, drums with

brushes) is used for a song, such as Bruce Springsteen's 'Meeting Across The River' and Elvis Costello's 'Shipbuilding'.

- The Four Tops' 'Walk Away Renee' has a muted trumpet solo doubled by cello (1:20) during its second half. Manic Street Preacher's 'Ocean Spray' features a trumpet with echo, and there's one on Mercury Rev 'Holes'.
- Trumpets traditionally have a fanfare function – they announce the entrance of something, so they make good intros and links, or anywhere where you feel the arrangement requires an element of declaration, as in The Beatles 'Magical Mystery Tour' or at the start of 'All You Need Is Love'. Trumpets can be heard punctuating 'Strawberry Fields Forever' as well as sustained chords.
- One particular strand to the trumpet's symbolic associations is with the mariachi bands of Mexico and Latin American music. This is brilliantly evoked on the track 'Maybe The People Would Be The Times Or Between Clark And Hilldale' on Love's *Forever Changes* album. M.I.A's album Arular features Brazilian trumpets on 'Bucky Done Gun'.

There are different models of trumpet, of which the most common is the Bb trumpet. To reach extra high notes The Beatles hired a piccolo trumpet for 'Penny Lane'.

Saxophone

The saxophone comes in various sizes and pitch-ranges, so there are soprano, alto, tenor, and bass saxophones. Although associated with jazz outfits, the saxophone has always had a role in rock music because it was present on many 1950s rock'n'roll records. The sight of a player puffing his cheeks as he leant back and pointed his sax at the sky was as common a sight as rock'n'roll double bassists climbing onto the sides of their instruments. The raw honk of a saxophone suggested dirt and danger, and is perhaps the brass family's closest approximation to a distorted electric guitar.

The saxophone contributed to many 1960s soul outfits and rhythm and blues bands. Low sax plays the riff with the bass on Wilson Pickett's 'In The Midnight Hour'. You can hear it on The Beatles' Lady Madonna' (two tenor saxes, two baritone), on Nick Drake's 'At The Chime Of A City Clock' (alto sax), and Rolling Stones tracks like 'Brown Sugar', where it solos on the coda. On T.Rex's 'Telegram Sam', the sax is there to recall the rock'n'roll era. It led a more unconventional life in bands like 1970s progressive-rockers King Crimson and Hawkwind, art-glamsters Roxy Music, and later the ska-influenced music of 1980s nutty boys Madness. Wayne Shorter added sax to Steely Dan's *Aja* (1977). Currently, the first thing you notice about The Zutons' sound is the presence of Abi Harding's saxophone on songs like 'Zuton Fever' and 'Valerie'.

The uses of a saxophone in an arrangement:

- To play short 'burps' and chord stabs, as with other brass. Bill Haley's 'Rock Around The Clock' has saxophone and guitar playing stab chords, with the saxophone shifting into its higher register later on.

- Saxophone plays a single note low line after the first chorus of 'Echo Beach' by Martha and the Muffins, then shifts to a higher register before taking a solo.
- Saxophone can make a great featured solo instrument, as Gerry Rafferty's 'Baker Street' shows, where the sound dominates the intro, Tears For Fears' 'The Working Hour', and at the end of T'Pau's 'China In Your Hand'. Clarence Clemons with Springsteen plays lots of significant sax solos (see 'Jungleland'). You can hear another on Etta James' 'I Just Want To Make Love To You'. The sax solo on Aretha Franklin's 'Respect' is recorded over a pad of other brass but accentuated by the fact that the track has just jumped key.
- Generally, the saxophone's expressive function is to be bright, cheerful, optimistic, a party instrument suited to arrangements that are big celebratory rave-ups, and like other jazz instruments it evokes the bright lights of the big city.
- Played quietly, it can be sensual and reflective, as on Dave Brubeck's jazz classic 'Take Five'.
- On early Roxy Music and King Crimson albums the saxophone is used in an unconventional way. On the latter's '21st Century Schizoid Man' it doubles the guitar riff.

Trombone/tuba

Trombones often work in pairs or threes. At moments of musical tension and excitement they can add bite and drama, but can also supply medium-pitched smooth sustained harmony. As with other brass instruments, if you are adding triads on them, don't always put these in root position. The **tuba** is the bass member of the brass family. Ponderous, low-pitched, and slow to phrase and articulate notes, it is unsuited to the fast rhythms of rock and soul music, and unlikely to occur on a song unless for comic or satirical purposes, as Bruce Springsteen used it on the acoustic 'Wild Billy's Circus Story'. There, its idiosyncratic puffing is an effective symbol for the motley crowd of circus performers described by the lyric. There may be a tuba on Dylan's 'Rainy Day Women # 12 & 35', doubling the bass line, and The Band's 'Long Black Veil', and one is listed in the sleeve notes of their eponymous second album.

STRINGS

Strings are probably the most popular secondary group of instruments to add to an arrangement. Strings have a versatile sound and many applications in an arrangement, especially in pop and ballad songwriting. Strings make an arrangement appealing to a wide audience and are powerful emotion generators. It is hard to remain unmoved by strings even when you know your feelings are being crassly manipulated. To take one recent example, consider the contribution strings make to The Verve's emotive 'The Drugs Don't Work'. In terms of symbolic identity, they add classical elegance.

The string group comprises four distinct instruments: violin, viola, cello, and double bass. An orchestra's string section has two groups of violins, 'first violins' and 'second violins'. This means such a section, including also violas, cellos, and double-basses, is written on at least five staves of music. A sizeable orchestra string section might include 14 first violins, 12 second violins, ten violas, eight cellos, six double basses – that's 50 players! So you can see that to have a real string section on a record isn't cheap. However, the division into first, second violins and violas is not essential in popular songs, unless the strings are exposed in a minimal arrangement, or featured as a quartet. Cellos and basses would work together. In popular music arrangements you can operate more in three or even two lines than five. The Beatles' 'Hello Goodbye' is unusual in featuring only two viola players and no other strings, whereas the string orchestra for 'Something' comprised 12 violins, four violas, four cellos and a double-bass.

Fortunately, songwriters now have access to sampled string sounds. At their best these can be surprisingly realistic if handled by a skilful programmer, and many TV and film soundtracks are in part, if not wholly, based on orchestral samples in order to save money. Inexpensive synth keyboards will have not so realistic string sounds, but if they are at the back of a mix where the foreground is dominated by a band, it won't matter so much. Many string samples and patches have octaves built in that widen the pitch range, and there are settings just called 'strings' that emulate the sound of an entire section. These can be handy as quick solutions when recording a demo if you want strings but not the time and trouble of working out the parts.

To plan realistic-sounding parts it is helpful to know about the pitch range of the string instruments. The G-string on a guitar is at the same pitch as the lowest string on a violin. The top string on a violin is the E at the 12th fret on a guitar. Here is a table of open string to guitar pitches for violin, viola, and cello (open string double bass pitches are the same as those on an electric bass guitar).

Violin: G Guitar: string three (open)	D string two, fret three	A string one, fret five	E string one, fret 12
Viola: C Guitar: string five, fret three	G string three (open)	D string two, fret three	A string one, fret five
Cello: C Guitar : n/a	G string six, fret three	D string four (open)	A string three, fret two

Solo violin

There are some situations where you might want a single string line. This is likely to be a violin. Few instruments can match the violin's capacity for expression, from subdued poignancy and introverted mourning to extraverted passion. This is a central lead instrument for folk songs, since the fiddle traditionally plays dance tunes, jigs, and reels, a character exploited on

Van Morrison's 'Bright Side Of The Road', 'Come On Eileen' by Dexys Midnight Runners, and by bands like The Pogues and The Waterboys. The Dixie Chicks' *Wide Open Spaces* has the typical country fiddle sound. The violin sound was extended through the electric violin, as featured by Curved Air, Steeleye Span, Fairport Convention, Alan Stivell, and outside the folk realm, The Velvet Underground (see 'Venus In Furs'). 1970s glam-rock band Slade owed the individuality of their breakthrough hit 'Coz I Luv You' to the violin part, including a solo, during which the electric guitar plays lead on the right channel with plenty of reverb giving depth to simple phrases.

The solo violin has also distinguished itself on recordings such as Rod Stewart's 'Reason To Believe', Cockney Rebel's 'Sling It' (where the violin plays a rock'n'roll shuffle idea normally heard on guitar), Kate Bush's 'The Fog' and Talk Talk's *Spirit Of Eden* (both played by Nigel Kennedy), the coda of Robert Plant's 'Calling To You', and in an unearthly way to the coda of The Who's 'Baba O'Reilly'. Violinist Scarlet Rivera made a memorable contribution to Bob Dylan's Desire (1976). John Cale played a viola on Nick Drake's 'Fly'.

Cello

A solo string part could also be provided by cello, with its mellow passion and deep, often mournful quality. Cello is useful because it doesn't collide with the electric bass as much as double basses. It is famed for its ability to simulate the phrasing of the human voice. The cello is good for creating a bass-line before the bass guitar enters. The Beatles included cello parts on 'I Am The Walrus', 'Blue Jay Way', and 'Strawberry Fields Forever'. The prize for the first significant cello part on a pop recording tends to go to The Beach Boys' 'Good Vibrations', where choppy, up-and-down bowing gives the part real edge. The first verse of R. Dean Taylor's 'Gotta See Jane' is carried by bass, cello, and voice only. The other instruments enter suddenly at 1:00. A cello adds suitably mournful notes to James Taylor's 'Fire And Rain'. Violin and cello were added to some of the quieter tracks on The Smashing Pumpkins' *Siamese Dream*.

String quartet

If you write and record singer-songwriter material, an orchestra's string section might overwhelm your material, quite apart from the challenge of building one up through a synth or samples. The full string section works better with piano/vocal than it does with acoustic guitar/vocal songs (see some of Elton John's early albums, such as *Madman Across The Water*), partly because the piano holds its own better with an orchestra – there are vastly more piano concertos than there are concertos for acoustic guitar. If so, consider adding a string quartet. For this you need sampled solo string sounds, not ensemble sounds.

A string quartet comprises first violin, second violin, viola, and cello.

Note there is no double bass, which solves the problem of it colliding with an electric bass guitar part. The two violin lines can sit happily above the pitch of most guitar chords, and the viola can be pushed up there too, with the cello doubling some of the guitar chord root notes. If you want the quartet to supply sustained harmony simply give each one a note of the chord. Remember:

- For a simple major or minor (three notes), one of the notes will be doubled.
- It is preferable to double the root or fifth (in C or C minor the C or the G), rather than the third.
- If the chord has four notes, such as a C7, Cmaj7, Cm7, C6, or Cadd9 (all common chords), assign one to each instrument.
- There is an art to proper string writing which makes the lines markedly different to keyboard shapes. As a general rule, pitch the notes wider than you could play in one hand.
- Individual string instruments can play more than one note. Two notes are mostly not a problem, and even three or four are possible (though arpeggiated at speed with a single stroke of the bow). The question of which combinations are physically possible can be ignored if you are working with samples, since samples don't complain about fingering or fingering impossibilities!
- To improve your string parts, even when they are primarily chordal, try to get some individual rhythm and movement into each line with passing notes (especially when going to the next chord/bar), or having one instrument re-sound a note. But don't make them fussy and over-complicated – after all, they are meant to be an accompanying figure, not the main focus of interest.
- Authentic string quartet parts need even more care than orchestral strings because the instruments are likely to be more exposed in the arrangement and there is no compensating weight of string tone. You are more likely to use a quartet configuration when there aren't that many other instruments in the arrangement.
- String quartets do not sound 'lush'. If you want a lush string sound go for a larger string ensemble.

As there are only four musicians you might be able to find a real quartet to record with you, though this will involve learning how to write out their parts – a task beyond the scope of this book.

Finally, if you make it that far, playing with a string quartet on video or TV visually sends the message "I am a sincere and serious performer".

In some contexts strings lend an English sound to an arrangement, as in the case of Nick Drake's *Five Leaves Left* (1969) and T.Rex's *T.Rex* album (1970). Green Day probably have a quartet on 'Good Riddance (Time Of Your Life)'. The Beatles made strings a feature on 'Eleanor Rigby' (a string octet), 'Yesterday', and 'She's Leaving Home'. Colin Blunstone's 'Say You Don't Mind' is vocal and strings only. Strings are vital to The Stones' 'Moonlight Mile', R.E.M's 'Everybody Hurts', The Turtles' 'You Showed Me', Metallica's 'Nothing Else Matters', Oasis's 'Cast No Shadow', Madonna's 'Frozen', ELO's '10538 Overture', The Verve's 'Bitter Sweet Symphony'; and

David McSpencer's 'Days Of Pearly Spencer' has fast string arpeggios on the chorus. The verse of James Brown's 'It's A Man's Man's Man's World' has pizzicato strings; the strings answer the lyric in verse two. Pulp's 'The Trees' commences with a rhythmic string figure, and on Jeff Buckley's 'Last Goodbye' the strings have a Middle Eastern quality with lots of slides.

General string tips for arrangements:

- Think carefully about when you bring strings into an arrangement. Precisely because they do create emotion so easily, save this for a moment when it will have more impact. This could be a particular song section or it might be cued to something in the lyric. Strings enter on the bridge of Al Green's 'Take Me To The River', which hitherto is driven by organ and brass.
- The entrance of strings toward the end of Simon and Garfunkel's 'The Boxer' greatly increases the emotion of the song.
- Strings can provide a harmonic pad of chords. Unlike guitar, being bowed means their notes can carry on almost indefinitely.
- Strings offer a variety of other sounds than lush sustain. Fast or accented up and down bowing can make string lines more percussive and forceful
- Tremolo strings – created by rapid bowing – are a staple horror film effect
- Pizzicato (plucked) strings give percussive notes with almost no sustain that drop nicely into an arrangement. In pop there is a long-standing connection between high violin pizzicato and images of tears and rain, as in Buddy Holly's 'Raining In My Heart'.
- A single-note, sustained, high string line is a good way of creating tension and suspense, especially if the arrangement is fairly empty at that moment. Listen to the high string line on Air's 'All I Need'.
- Strings can double the vocal melody, adding support, often at the octave above.
- Strings can play a counter-point melody to the vocal, as they do in R.E.M.'s 'The Sidewinder Sleeps Tonight' (with pizzicato touches on the bridge section).
- Muted strings and harmonics are sounds you are unlikely to find on most string sample libraries.

HARP

If they struck a medal for the least rock'n'roll instrument ever, the harp would beat even strings into second place. The epitome of romanticism, and traditionally the instrument of choice in heaven, what could the purveyors of the devil's music possibly want with a harp? The harp's symbolic identity is love, romance, heaven (literal or figurative), dreams, and a soft and gentle passion.

The typical use of the harp in popular music is in easy listening, MOR ballads, and other songs where a full orchestra is heard. The harp supplies big chords, rippling arpeggios, fast two-note alternations, eerie harmonics, and swooping gales of glissandos. So popular is this last effect that many a harp-player has been heard to lament that he/she might as well be playing the thing with a broomstick rather than ten fingers. Many a romantic ballad has ended swooning into unconsciousness in clouds of harp glissandos. If the part is dissonant enough it can do sinister, especially against sustained strings. Harp bass notes have a mysterious quality but the lower register of the arrangement has to be clear for them to be effective. On the intro and bridge of The Beach Boys' 'Wouldn't It Be Nice', the reverb brings out the crystalline quality of single high harp notes.

The Four Tops' 'Walk Away Renee' has harp glissandos, as there are all over the first 25 seconds of 'The World Is Not Enough' by Garbage; there are harp touches on the left channel of The Temptations 'Just My Imagination' (matched nicely with tremolo guitar), and The Beatles 'She's Leaving Home' has a prominent harp part.

In folk music you can hear the Celtic harp, a smaller instrument than the orchestral version. This smaller harp suits folk ballads and has been played to great effect with an electric folk band by Alan Stivell, who made a guest appearance on Kate Bush's 'Between A Man And A Woman'.

PITCHED PERCUSSION

The pitched percussion family is a group of instruments that you may occasionally want to add to an arrangement. They generate a percussive noise but also a note, though the note may not last very long. The important members include the soft-sounding **vibraphone** (**'vibes'**) a mainstay of lounge and jazz outfits that can supply a bloom of muted, reverberating chords, or play a melody line. The **marimba** is more percussive in sound and to most ears will suggest Africa; it has featured on *Peter Gabriel 3* and kd lang's *Ingenue*. If you want a harder version of that sound try the **xylophone**, which has no sustain and is suited to rhythm roles; The Isley Brothers' 'This Old Heart Of Mine' has a xylophone part. The **glockenspiel** has bars that are struck but is high-pitched and adds a stellar sparkle to arrangements, famously on Bruce Springsteen productions like 'Born To Run', and on many Christmas songs produced by Phil Spector. Its musical-box connotations give it the role of battered innocent on Radiohead's 'No Surprises', or something more sinister on 'Sit Down. Stand Up'. Finally, when its time for those church bells to ring (or is it merely someone at the front door?), reach for the **tubular bells**, as on the Association's 'Cherish' or Mike Oldfield's album.

Now it's time to look at arrangement details in relation to building songs, and how.

SECTION 8

Arrangements, song sections and mixing

Arrangement is not just a matter of choosing and using instruments. It also involves organising the various sections of your songs and bringing out their qualities in the mix.

So far we have looked at the relationship between the choice of instruments and tones in an arrangement. In this section arrangement is viewed from two new angles, first by song section and then at the connection between arranging and mixing.

Before recording there are a number of final checks and adjustments that can be made to your song, any one of which could improve it. These do not involve any major re-composing, though they may require the transposing or editing of ideas.

On sophisticated computer programmes like Pro-Tools, recordings become very malleable, and this kind of editing very easy. Butch Vig of Garbage once said, "Most of our songs come from simply improvising while we're running our 48-track Pro Tools … We compile bits and pieces, cut them up, and edit them together, and keep working on them until eventually it sounds like a song that was written on an acoustic guitar."

If you're working with more limited means, it is a matter of reviewing the song before you record it to pick up changes that will affect the whole arrangement (like dropping a bar). Some of these changes can be made even after recording has begun, though that may result in re-recording an instrumental part, or a section of it.

LAST-MINUTE CHECKLIST

Length of intro

How quickly is the song reaching the verse and the start of the vocal? It is easy to lose objectivity here. As the song is yours, you know what's coming. The glow from the satisfaction of having written it can make a mundane and over-long intro seem an appropriately long approach. This can also be caused by enjoying whatever you're playing, like a guitar riff. But the listener doesn't know the song, and may find a long intro merely dull.

Length of second verse

If your song has a long verse a handy songwriting trick is to abbreviate the second verse (the one after the first chorus). This puts the second chorus earlier than expected. As this also brings forward the next performance of the hook, this is a tactic favoured on commercial-oriented songs. Where you make the cut in the verse will partly depend on the lyric – which lines can be omitted with the verse still making sense?

The chorus

The chorus is the heart of the song, so take care with it. Songwriters tend to stop thinking about a chorus once they have one they're happy with. Try these perspectives on it:

- What if the second chorus was twice the length of the first?
- What if the first chorus was actually an abbrieviated version of the full chorus?
- How would the song sound if the second chorus was omitted and the song went straight to the bridge? This is a ploy that can work provided the song is not too long and/or it doesn't take too much time to reach the next or last chorus. Boston cut the second verse and second chorus from their 'More Than A Feeling' track when they edited it for a single. The single version plunges straight from the first chorus into the guitar solo.
- What happens if you put the first chorus before the first verse?
- What happens if you delay the chorus past several verses? This happens on Tracy Chapman's 'Fast Car', of which producer David Kershenbaum said, "It took a little while to get to the chorus, which worried some people. It broke rules of great song construction, and I wouldn't advise people to try it, but for some reason, it milked it so much that when it hit the release of the large chorus, it blew you over."

Length and character of solo

If you include an instrumental solo, check it over once more. Ask:

- Does it fit in character with the rest of the song?
- Is it the right length?
- Is it on the right instrument for the arrangement as a whole?
- Does the backing provide the right harmonic and rhythmic backing?
- How might you intensify its best points?

Harmony

If your song has a regular structure, there will be several verses and choruses. Instead of having these retain identical chord progressions each time they appear, why not re-harmonize part of one of them when it is repeated. By then the original pattern is established in the listener's mind. This gives extra spice to a later verse or chorus.

There are many ways in which part of a melody can be thus re-harmonized. The simplest technique is to listen for what happens when a major chord is converted into its relative minor, the chord whose root note is three semi-tones lower.

Imagine a song in the key of G major where your verse has a chord sequence of G-D-C-D-C-F-C-D, one chord to a bar of 4/4 (notice there are no minor chords). On its third and last appearance this progression could be partially re-harmonized to E minor-B minor-C-D-C-F-[C-A minor]-D, where the C-A minor change puts two chords into bar seven.

The substitution of E minor for G at the beginning also has the effect of removing the only use of the key chord from this verse, making its next appearance (presumably in the chorus) substantially more potent.

Arrangements and inversions

Another way of putting variety into the harmony is to try inverting some chords. This might mean only changing a bass guitar or bass keyboard note. This can be done by:

- The bass playing the third or the fifth of the chord (E or G under a C chord). This inverts the chords even if none of the harmony instruments have inversions
- Using a pedal note – where the bass stays on a single note while the chords move. This works well on intros and last verses. The third verse of James Taylor's 'Fire And Rain' has a pedal technique that re-colours the verse harmony. Listen to the verse of Tears For Fears' 'Everybody Wants To Rule The World'.
- The bass playing a root/minor third/ minor seventh figure (the notes C-Eb-Bb) under a major chord (C major). This has a tough sound because the flattened bass notes sound tense against the upper chord.
- Playing fast-moving scale ideas in the occasional bar.
- Removing all bass notes for a section to let it 'float'.

The fragile atmosphere of the verse of Razorlight's 'America' or The Kings of Leon's 'Milk' is created by delicate finger-picked first inversions. Root chords in those parts of the songs would not have had the same effect. The 'muddy' quality of second inversions can be exploited if you want part of a chord progression to sound slightly sinister – see the B minor/F♯ chord in The Beatles' 'Help', the verse of Hendrix's 'Spanish Castle Magic', and Nirvana's 'On A Plain'.

Check the key

Unless you are attached to the sound of a song in a certain key, or know that you couldn't sing it higher, checking the key is a pre-recording step I would always advocate. It is easy to demo a song at the wrong pitch, by which I mean a pitch that prevents you using your voice (or your vocalist's voice) to its best. If a melody is pitched too low you may find it hard to project and to put expression into; if too high you may strain for the upper notes. To change key of a guitar song refer back to **Section Three** and the discussion of how to use the capo.

Would the song benefit from a change of key? A good key-change:

- Adds to the musical content of a song.
- Enhances the contrast between one section and another.
- Refreshes a section already heard.
- Makes repetition less obvious
- Has the potential for enhancing instrumental resonance. This would be apparent if a guitar song were played in a key that required barre chords but after a key-change had switched to a key full of open string chords.

Lifting the final chorus(es) of a song by a semi-tone (half-step) or tone is a traditional songwriting device to add sparkle to the end of a song. The other song section to which key-changing could be easily applied is the bridge. Whether it can simply jump into the new key without preparing with a suitable lead-up will need to be thought about. Similarly, coming out of the bridge and returning to the original key may need careful planning.

Tempo

Many songwriters record a song, as a demo or even something for release, only to find later that the song now sounds too slow to them. Ruefully, they reflect that it would have been better quicker. There is a natural, human reason why demos in particular often turn out too slow. They are generally recorded when the composer is still learning the song, still getting to grips with it. As a result, it's not surprising that this should affect the tempo by keeping it a little below what it could be. This change in perception also happens after a song is played during the excitement of a live performance. Many bands like to road-test songs in concert for this reason.

So, before recording, check if the song is at the right tempo. The 'wrong' tempo is usually one which is too slow for the character and intention of a song. It is always a good idea to experiment by playing a song gradually faster, noting the speed with a metronome, to discover how much faster it could go before sounding silly or clumsy. Often songs that are meant to be up-tempo lose some energy through not being recorded fast enough. This will also make sure that songs intended to be slow aren't too slow (an easy trap). A slow ballad shouldn't sound lethargic just because it has a slow tempo.

In the case of a song built on a riff, for a medium-to-up-tempo song, speed it up gradually until the riff loses its character and potency (or your fingers fall off). What you're looking for is not the fastest tempo at which the riff could be played, but the fastest tempo the riff can be played without losing its identity. Riffs are tempo sensitive. Take any famous riff and play it faster or slower than the original. Quickly a point is reached where it doesn't sound as good; the riff loses something. The change in tempo eventually robs the riff of its character. To test the tempo of a slow riff make it slower. At a certain point it becomes ineffective because there isn't enough forward momentum. An audience will get bored ... and so may the band!

This relation of riffs and tempo was demonstrated dramatically to me when I heard an early bootleg of Led Zeppelin's 1979 Knebworth concerts. The vinyl pressing was cut at the wrong speed, with the consequence that the songs were faster than they should have been, and the guitar pitch was at least a semi-tone sharp! This made upbeat riff numbers like 'Black Dog' sound silly, but the slower riff songs sometimes gained. 'Kashmir' became relentless, and 'Ten Years Gone' was spectacular when played with more drive.

Odd time signatures

It may also not be too late to consider changing the number of beats in the odd bar, where such a change might make a phrase more memorable or effective. Deep Purple's 'Strange Kind Of Woman' has a striking change of rhythm at 1:25 to half-time. Led Zeppelin's 'Fool In The Rain' has a drastic double time/half time change. The Beatles' 'Don't Let Me Down' has occasional bars of 5/4, while 'Happiness Is A Warm Gun' has many weird time features. Some of the songs on Snow Patrol's Final Straw feature irregular numbers of bars – see 'Gleaming Auction' – to make it less easy to predict when sections are going to begin and end. In the verse of The Raconteurs' 'Blue Vein' there is a clever time signature change. The first bar is 12/8 (four beats counting 1-2-3 on each) with a D minor chord. The second bar is countable as 13/8, ie, count 123, 123, 123, 1234. An extra quaver is added to the bar. Try adding or subtracting a quaver from a 4/4 or 12/8 bar occasionally when writing a song.

Repetition

As a general point, check the level of repetition in the song, for example the number of repeats of sections, or the number of times a riff is repeated. Sometimes a song has hidden repetition, where a section only occurs a couple of times but is itself made up of a one-bar figure that is repeated many more times. Ask how much of this do you need?

ARRANGING BY SECTION

Arrangement is often concerned with song structure. Arrangement features are often intended to make song structure explicit. Each of the recognized song sections – intro, verse, pre-chorus, chorus, bridge/middle eight, solo and the outro/coda – needs careful consideration.

So you will find yourself pondering such questions as:

- Which instruments go in which section?
- How will each section be distinctive without making the song discontinuous?
- How will the arrangement build to an exciting end?
- When is the right moment for an instrument to enter?
- When does a part need to become fuller or busier, and when pared back?
- When do some instruments come out of the mix?

It is important to stress that there cannot be only one way of building an arrangement. Otherwise, all songs would sound the same. Obviously in any era of popular music a good many chart songs do sound the same, because they conform to the formulas of that era, including arrangement. There are formulas of rebellion as well as conformity. The songs are intended to sound the same on the basis that this will make them sell. Many of the ideas and suggestions in this book derives from commercial songwriting.

Look at how many instruments you want to use and plan how they appear in relation to structures like the intro, verse one, verse two, chorus, bridge, solo, final verse, final chorus, coda/outro. Each of these will have its own character/colour within the overall scheme of the song. Your instrumental choices may be constrained by the number of instruments you have available – for example an acoustic duo or a rock three-piece – in which case it will be dynamics and the parts that make the difference. Think of the way Nirvana's 'Smells Like Teen Spirit' carries its verse on bass and drums but minimal guitar, whereas the chorus has huge guitar sounds on it.

To these sections must also be applied the basic arrangement strategy, as outlined in **Section Two**. Ensure the arrangement doesn't take attention away from the melody and the lyric. Music in which the lyric narrative is paramount is often sparse, as with early Bob Dylan, or Bruce Springsteen's *Nebraska* and *The Ghost Of Tom Joad* albums. The dynamic contour of a song has to relate and illustrate its emotional contour. More instruments may well enter when the feeling intensifies, many could drop out for a sense of desolation. If a song has a pre-chorus, that is a good place to bring in a new instrument to suggest a build-up to something (ie, the chorus).

It is useful to make a map of your arrangement. Here's one such map, structured with an cumulative approach. Instruments appear in bold on their first appearance:

Intro	**Acoustic guitar**, **bass**
Verse one	**Vocal**, acoustic guitar, **acoustic guitar two**, bass, **side-stick drums**
Chorus one	Vocal, acoustic guitar, acoustic guitar two, bass, **full drums**
Verse two	Vocal, acoustic guitar, acoustic guitar two, **electric guitar lead fills**, bass, side-stick drums
Chorus two	Vocal, acoustic guitar, acoustic guitar two, **electric guitar chords**, bass, full drums
Bridge	Vocal, acoustic guitar, **organ**, partial drums
Solo	Acoustic guitar, acoustic guitar two, **electric guitar solo**, bass, full drums
Last verse	Vocal, organ, **tambourine**
Last chorus	Vocal, **backing vocals**, acoustic guitar, acoustic guitar two, electric guitar chords, organ, **strings**, bass, full drums, tambourine
Coda/outro	Vocal ad lib, backing vocals, acoustic guitar, acoustic guitar two, electric guitar lead, organ, strings, bass, full drums, tambourine

Notice that:

- There are more instruments in toward the end.
- The drums are not always full.
- The full complement of guitars is not brought in right at the start.
- The arrangement builds in intensity, so chorus two is more full than one but not as much as the last chorus.
- The way the mix thins out after chorus two, steps up for the solo, thins out again for the last verse.
- The acoustic guitar drops out in the last verse, having been present since the beginning, and tambourine keeps the rhythm going instead of drums.

As a listening exercise, take The Rolling Stones' 'Angie' and follow the way the instruments grow from a single acoustic guitar to multiple guitars, piano, bass, drums, and strings.

ARRANGING AN INTRO

A song's introduction is critical in setting the scene for what is coming and grabbing people's attention. Consider these questions:

- How will you get people's attention?
- What's the first sound they will hear?
- Which of your instruments will they hear first?
- How many will they hear of what you've got?
- Will you go for a big bang beginning or something subtle?

Here are some possible approaches to arranging an intro:

Unaccompanied vocal: Elvis Costello started 'No Action' with just a line of vocal. Queen's 'Bohemian Rhapsody' opens with unaccompanied vocal harmony.
Percussion: Simon and Garfunkel, 'Cecilia'.
Drums only: David Bowie, 'Five Years'; The Shadows, 'Apache'; Led Zeppelin, 'Rock And Roll', 'When The Levee Breaks'; T.Rex, 'Raw Ramp'; Spin Doctors, 'Two Princes'; Coldplay, 'In My Place'; Pulp, 'This Is Hardcore'.
Drums and bass: Dexy's Midnight Runners' 'Come On Eileen' intro is bass guitar and bass drum for the first few seconds. Bjork's 'Army Of Me' comes in on rumbling synth bass line and heavy drums.
Drums and guitar: Roy Orbison, 'Pretty Woman' (snare drum plus 12-string acoustic guitar).
Drums plus sound effects: The Sex Pistols, 'Holidays In The Sun' (marching feet); Led Zeppelin, 'In The Evening'.

Bass guitar: The Jam, 'A Town Called Malice' and 'Going Underground'; R.E.M. 'Cuyahoga'.
Bass guitar and acoustic guitar: Otis Redding, 'Dock of The Bay'.
Strummed/picked acoustic guitar. Dodgy, 'In A Room'; The Who, 'Pinball Wizard', 'Substitute', 'Behind Blue Eyes'; Joni Mitchell, 'Big Yellow Taxi'; The Kinks, 'Lola' (a dobro?); Rod Stewart, 'Every Picture Tells A Story'.
Electric guitar riff: Golden Earring, 'Radar Love'; Blue Oyster Cult, '(Don't Fear) The Reaper'; Status Quo, 'Caroline'; Jimi Hendrix, 'Voodoo Chile (Slight Return)'; The Faces, 'Miss Judy's Farm'; Blondie, 'One Way Or Another'; The Beatles, 'Ticket To Ride'; The La's, 'There She Goes'; The Seahorses, 'Love Is The Law'; The Cult, 'Wild Flower'.
Keyboards: Led Zeppelin, 'Trampled Underfoot'; Dire Straits' 'Tunnel Of Love' starts with a snatch of 'The Carousel Waltz' to evoke a fairground; Bruce Springsteen, 'New York City Serenade' (piano); The Who, 'Baba O'Reilly' (sequencer).
Other instruments: Gerry Rafferty, 'Baker Street' (saxophone); Madonna, 'Frozen' (strings); Siouxsie and the Banshees, 'Fireworks' (strings); Arthur Conley 'Sweet Soul Music'; Bob and Earl, 'Harlem Shuffle' (brass); The Beach Boys, 'Wouldn't It Be Nice' (harp).

To this list can be added some conceptual, rather than instrumental, options:

Brevity: The Small Faces' 'Itchycoo Park' takes only eight seconds to get to the first verse. The Beatles' 'Things We Said Today' has two bars only on a single chord, while 'You've Got To Hide Your Love Away' has only a bar of strumming the key chord to introduce the vocal. The Stereophonics' 'Have A Nice Day' comes in immediately with the song's hook.
Extended: Rolls Royce's 'Car Wash' has a one minute intro featuring handclaps, wah-wah guitar, bass drum, rhythm guitar, off-beat hi-hat, low piano, then strings and flute. See also the atmospheric 'Breaking Into Heaven' by The Stone Roses.
Fragments of melody: Catatonia, 'Londinium' (the guitar plays some of the verse melody); Bruce Springsteen, 'Thunder Road' (harmonica plays some of the melody).
Recording accidents/talk: Led Zeppelin, 'Black Country Woman' (an aeroplane flew over); The Police, 'Roxanne' (Sting sat on a piano he thought was closed); David Bowie, 'Andy Warhol' (Bowie talking to producer Tony Visconti); The Faces, 'Too Bad' (engineer talking); Radiohead, '2+2=5', and Oasis, 'Cigarettes And Alcohol' (both ambient band recording noise).
Sound effects: Catatonia, 'I Am The Mob' (voices from a film); The Move, 'Fire Brigade' (siren); Madness, 'Night Boat To Cairo' (ship's foghorn); Madonna, 'Erotica' and Marshall Crenshaw, 'Starless Summer Sky' (sampled vinyl crackle).

Crescendo: Ash, 'Goldfinger' (starting from a sound effect); The Beatles, 'Twist And Shout'; David Bowie, 'Let's Dance'; The Smiths, 'What Difference Does It Make?'.
Fade-in: Boston, 'More Than A Feeling'; Wishbone Ash, 'The King Will Come'; The Beatles, 'Eight Days A Week'.
Spoken voice: Smokey Robinson And The Miracles, 'Shop Around'.
Spoken count-ins: The Beatles, 'Taxman' (along with background noise).
Free-time: The Beatles' 'I'm A Loser' (comes in on a vocal harmony plus acoustic guitar chorus) and 'Here There And Everywhere'; Thin Lizzy, 'Soldier Of Fortune'; The Isley Brothers, 'Behind A Painted Smile'.
An arresting chord: The Beatles, 'Hard Day's Night'; Thin Lizzy, 'Jailbreak'.
Feedback: Jimi Hendrix, 'Foxy Lady'; The Beatles 'I Feel Fine'.
Establishing a dominant rhythm: Queens Of The Stone Age, 'Feel Good Hit Of The Summer'.

The single-note intro

Starting a song on a single held note is a great tactic for messing with the listener's expectations. When we hear a single note we tend to interpret it as the key-note and will anticipate the harmony entering on the key-chord for which the single note is the root. However, when a chord enters over or under it the note will be heard against the chord and it may turn out not to be the key note. The horn A note at the start of Wings' 'My Love' turns out to be the seventh of Bbmaj7 (Bb-D-F-A), not the key note of the song. Likewise, The Hollies 'Air That I Breathe' comes in on a single bent guitar note. 'Echo Beach' by Martha and the Muffins starts with a single-note synth pulse going left and right which fades in over eight seconds and then is joined by a guitar riff, then drums and bass. Coldplay's 'Spies' has a single high sustained note which turns out to be the root of the minor chord played by the acoustic guitar on its entry.

The 'false' intro

The deceptive single note intro is a particular version of the type of intro that teases the listener. The 'false' intro does something – in terms of tempo, time signature, chords, instruments, key or arrangement style – that is actually not representative of the track as a whole. To create a 'false' intro means looking carefully at how your song currently begins and seeing if there is some element you can change or twist to make the intro deceptive.

The Beatles' 'I'll Be Back' enters on two bars of a major chord, which then goes to the tonic minor, a change which is repeated in the verse so is an integral part of the song. 'I've Just Seen A Face' has an intro which is in compound time and slower than the actual song. U2's 'The Fly' comes in with what sounds like a messy edit before the drum and riff settles into place. Television's 'Marquee Moon' disguises where the beat is on the intro. Only when the drums are fully in are you sure where the downbeat is (at 0:24). Bebop Deluxe's 'Maid In Heaven' has an intro which suggest F major but the song is really in D major. The Who's 'Pinball Wizard' enters in the key of B minor but the main part of the song is in B major.

ARRANGING CHORUSES AND PRE-CHORUSES

A pre-chorus is a short section that leads in to a chorus. This is a good place to add an instrument, change the parts that the primary instruments are already playing to create a feeling that something is about to happen. A classic way to do this on guitar is to play constant eighth-note fifths or chords gradually increasing the volume. You could add one item of percussion like a tambourine, or change a hi-hat or cymbal rhythm to be more frequent (quarter-notes to eighth-notes.) The end of the pre-chorus can be marked by a drum-fill.

Arriving at a chorus usually means an increase in the depth of sound and increased intensity, so this is a section where extra instruments might come in, such as strings, piano, organ, extra percussion, or where instruments might change register. Aerosmith's 'Crying' brings organ in for its first chorus. Badly Drawn Boy's 'Something To Talk About' adds an organ part to its second chorus and a high piano line following the melody. Electric Soft Parade's 'Empty At The End' adds organ to its chorus. You could take the example of Lisa Loeb's 'Stay (I Missed You)' or James Taylor's 'Fire And Rain' and delay the drums until the chorus. Lenny Kravitz brings in much-delayed guitar for the chorus of 'Fly Away'. Check the new instruments don't swamp the lead vocal. Also, don't overdo it on the first chorus, otherwise the remaining ones might sound like an anti-climax. Other relevant techniques include double-tracking the vocal or adding a vocal harmony.

ARRANGING A BRIDGE/SOLO

By the time a song reaches the end of its second chorus it generally feels like a good time to have something new happen.

For a bridge you may want to rest some instruments to create a different texture and musical space, reinforced by things like new chords, new melody, or even a new key. The solo is a means by which the lead vocal can be rested. If a solo happens, think about what instrument you want to take it – what is right for the song and/or the genre. Make sure the arrangement at this point doesn't detract from the solo instrument. Refer back to **Section Four** for information on lead guitar scales.

Here are some tips on approaching a bridge/solo:

- In any track with prominent drums, this section is an ideal opportunity to pull them out, or thin them (say by omitting the snare in the pattern), so as to refresh them for the remaining verses and choruses. In hard rock/heavy metal this may not be possible'. An example is Blink 182's 'All The Small Things', which also adds organ at this point.
- In any track where drums have not been a big feature, the reverse applies. They can be brought in to play a steady beat for this short section.
- This section is also a place for a temporarily ambient mix. The Jam's 'When You're Young' momentarily turns to a texture closer to dub reggae than rock, and there are similar changes of texture and rhythm in 'Strange Town' and 'Going Underground'.

- Duran Duran's 'Hungry Like The Wolf' and Whitesnake's 'Still Of The Night' both have drums reined back, sustained notes, and a sense of space in the texture. Dodgy's 'In A Room' has voice over strings for its quiet middle bit just before the guitar solo.
- In Led Zeppelin's 'Whole Lotta Love', The Doors' 'Light My Fire' and Queen's 'Bohemian Rhapsody', this middle section becomes far more than a mere transition and takes on a life of its own.

ARRANGING AN OUTRO/CODA

The outro/coda of the song often reuses an earlier section. The intro and the chorus are probably the two most frequently recycled sections. If the song has used a cumulative arrangement everything will be going full tilt and supporting vocal ad libs on the hook phrase. Alternatively, the arrangement could be pulled down a few dynamic notches, giving more of a glide to the end than a charge. If the coda/outro consists of a short progression – say of four bars – work out how many times it needs to repeat. Then decide whether you want the track to fade, to fade to an almost inaudible stop, or to have a definite end chord/bar. 1960s fade-outs can be very short, as with The Beatles' 'Things We Said Today' and 'The Night Before', which ends a few beats after the last sung title. (Proper fades also often fall victim to the engineers who edit and compile 'Greatest Hits' collections.) If the track ends on a chord does it require a sudden cut-off or a held chord? Golden Earring's 'Radar Love' and David Bowie's 'Jean Genie' both have a sudden loud ending after an instrumental crescendo.

Here are some suggestions for endings:

- Repeat your intro and adapt it to give the song a circular structure. Led Zeppelin's 'Bring It On Home' repeats part of its intro 12-bar to finish.
- To give the song an emphatic finish, end on the key chord. Give this chord some extra colour by turning it into a decorated chord like a sixth or add9, etc.
- To leave the song hanging on more of a question mark, end on chord IV or V (F or G in C major).
- A fade-out can be magnified by increasing the reverb or going to a wet signal as the volume of the dry signal is faded out during mixing.
- A 'false' ending is one where the song seems to have finished and then re-starts. This could be after a few moments silence, or it could be a fade-out followed by a fade back in, as with Led Zeppelin's 'Thank You'. The grandest 'false ending' is represented by the ending of the album version of Eric Clapton's 'Layla'. This coda actually turns out not to be an ending at all, but almost a second half to the entire song, dominated by slide guitar and piano.
- Try fading on a single instrument playing a repeated figure, like the guitar arpeggio on the end of The Beatles' 'Hard Day's Night. 'You Can't Do That' ends with a few bars of electric 12-string and bass. 'Another Girl' ends with a solo lead guitar phrase.

- The Manic Street Preachers' 'There By The Grace Of God' and David Bowie's 'Five Years' both end with a lone drum pattern. Blur's 'The Universal' fades all but the strings. Roxy Music's 'More Than This' fades out on a synth two-chord loop. Otis Redding's 'Dock Of The Bay' ends with the singer's nonchalant whistling.
- It became a cliché of 1990s dance records to end with a solo lead vocal phrase. 'Doll Parts' by Hole ends with a solo vocal phrase.
- If you want an ending which is less certain, try using unrelated chords or going from major to minor on the same root note. David Bowie's 'The Bewley Brothers' goes from B minor to F in its coda, and Love's 'The Red Telephone' goes from A to A minor and back.
- Bring in a new instrument on the coda. On The Beatles' 'You've Got To Hide Your Love Away', the coda has a short solo of four phrases played by flutes an octave apart.
- The informal ending is deliberately ragged. Some of the parts stop before others, and some instruments deviate from what they are strictly supposed to be playing. Informal endings draw attention to the process of music-making. They are heard on unedited fades, which frequently show that musicians don't always repeat their part the same number of times on the coda of a track they know will be faded. David Bowie's 'Life On Mars' has an informal ending, the piano part left isolated in a spacious rehearsal-hall reverb after the orchestra has stopped, with snatches of control-room voices. Tracks by punk bands like The Sex Pistols often feature informal endings ragged with feedback and out-of-time guitar stabs.

ARRANGEMENT AND MIXING

Questions to do with arrangement come into play twice during the process of recording a song. The more the recording departs from the basic notion that it is a recording of all the musicians playing together and there will be no overdubs, the more arrangement becomes something that also happens at the stage of mixing. For readers unfamiliar with the term, mixing is the stage when a multitrack recording is copied and reduced down to 2-track stereo – the master mix which forms the template for the reproduction and distribution of the music through vinyl, tape, CD, download, etc. Mixing involves such decisions as:

- Establishing the frequency and special effects that apply to each instrumental and vocal part.
- Deciding when and for how long a part is audible in the mix.
- Setting its volume in relation to all the other parts.
- Choosing how much of an effect like reverb a part has applied.
- Positioning a part in the stereo image.

So within the recording process there are two levels of arranging: the first is the original selection of instruments; the second, during mixing, is a selection of how the first level of the arrangement will finally appear. There are many technical aspects in mixing, which are the province of the engineer and producer rather than the songwriter. Some arise in relation to specific pieces of sound equipment. This book is concerned with broader issues that a songwriter needs to understand to successfully combine instruments.

The difference between a mix and an arrangement is that you can do different mixes of the same instrument selection. But the basic selection of instruments you have recorded – which were the product of the original arrangement decisions – is not supposed to be changed at the mixing stage. That means re-recording, which will cost you.

Having said that, it does sometimes happen that a mix is abandoned because it is felt the track needs more work and different instruments; or, less drastically, one or two new parts might be added, and then the mix resumed.

One way to grasp what mixing can do is to listen to different mixes of the same track. There are several such on the CD that accompanies this book. The availability of mixes of the same song has always had a strong stimulus, for reasons that include commercial considerations by record companies, artistic laziness on the part of the band, and then artistic pretension (or creativity). The earliest alternate mixes date to the late 1960s/early 1970s when the B-sides of singles sometimes merely featured the A-side without the lead vocal. It saved having to write and record another song. The increased vinyl acreage of the 12-inch single in the 1980s and the requirements of the dance-floor also encouraged re-mixes. Digital technology made the process of copying, editing, and re-shuffling parts much easier.

The 'heritage' re-issuing of back catalogue music since the 1990s has meant the release of the same material in mono/stereo mixes, radio edits, and alternate mixes, as well as demos. Also helpful are live concert recordings, unplugged versions, radio/single edits.

All of this can be highly educational if you want to learn about arrangement and mixing decisions. You hear something of the same process every time a band records acoustic versions of its rock material. Back in 1979 Elvis Costello released his third album *Armed Forces*, which opened with an up-tempo band performance of 'Accidents Will Happen'. But on a free EP that came with the album he also released a slower live version, featuring only piano and voice, which turned the song into more of a ballad.

Some excellent examples to listen to would be Marvin Gaye's *What's Going On* double-CD reissue, The Beatles *Anthology* CDs, *The Yellow Submarine Songtrack* and *Let It Be Naked*, The Jam's *All Mod Cons* double-CD version, and best of all the 4-CD box-set *The Pet Sounds Sessions*. It gives us the album in the most amazing detail. The compilers went back to the original instrumental masters (which Brian Wilson usually bounced onto another tape-machine), made a digital copy and synchronized the vocals with it. This means we hear the instrumental tracks closer to source than the 'bounced' ones that were always part of the finished version before. The box includes a wealth of information about the sessions, the first ever true stereo version, a new mono version, backing tracks, vocal only tracks, alternate mixes, etc, etc. It is an astonishing revelation of the quality of the Beach Boys' vocal harmonies, and of the intricacy and texture of Wilson's arrangements.

Stereo image/position

In **Section Two** it was explained that an instrumental or vocal part is given a position, somewhere in the 180-degree stereo image stretching from left through centre to right. This placing influences how it blends with or stands out from the other parts. The stereo position of a part can help contrast its rhythm, pitch, and timbre with others. Most mixes you hear follow these basic guidelines:

- Drums, bass lines, and lead vocals tend to go in the centre of the mix. We turn to face things that interest us, so parts of greater interest should be straight in front.
- Pitch hierarchy will to some extent differentiate parts that are in the same middle area of the stereo image. Vocals usually don't occupy the same pitch area as bass, and drums don't have pitch in that sense either.
- Lead solo parts can be centre, when there is no vocal, or just off-centre.
- Harmonic parts – the ones that supply chords can be left and right, although a lower-pitched or lower-volume harmonic part can also be placed centrally.
- Melodic parts can also go left and right for balance, but ideally not in exactly the same position as the harmonic ones.

The modern view is that a stereo mix should not be lop-sided for very long, if at all. But for contrasting ideas listen to recordings made prior to 1970.

As stereo became the norm instead of mono, record companies sought to re-mix mono albums into stereo. With older 2-, 3-, and 4-track recordings this was a problem because whole sections of parts were bunched onto a single track and could not be broken up and distributed around the 180 degrees of stereo. This causes many 1960s recordings to have what many would consider eccentric stereo balances. The drums are on the right of Dylan's 'One Of Us Must Know (Sooner Or Later)'. On Cream's 'I Feel Free' the rhythm section and chordal guitar part are crammed into one speaker, vocals and lead guitar in the other. Similar things happen on their song 'Badge', on The Beach Boys 'Don't Worry, Baby', and many early Beatles tracks. On Simon and Garfunkel's 'Sounds Of Silence' the drums and bass on the second verse are squeezed into the left-hand speaker; 'I Am A Rock' also starts with nothing on the right channel. Jefferson Airplane's 'Somebody To Love' has the drums on the left channel, and 'Today' has nothing in the left channel initially. The Beatles' 'Yesterday' starts with acoustic guitar on the right and nothing else. In 'A Day In The Life' John Lennon's vocal is off to the right intitially, and the first verse has nothing in the middle, which is an appropriately disorientated stereo image for a psychedelic song. If your hi-fi has a balance control you can flick it hard left or hard right and remove great chunks of some of these songs' instrumentation.

Stereo positioning is also a statement about what you consider important in the music. It says much about the importance of drums and the rhythmic element in popular music that a drummer usually sits stage centre facing the audience (sometimes on a raised platform) at a gig, and on recordings is bang in the middle. In styles of music where the drums are less important there is no reason they couldn't be shunted to one side and lowered in volume as befitting an accompanying role.

The invention of 5.1 multi-channel music complicates the issues of part placement in a mix because it means contending with potentially 360 degrees of sound. This raises complex aesthetic questions about where the listener is supposed to be in relation to the performers. In a rock context, the listener can be placed right in the middle of the band, instead of facing the group as in conventional stereo. If there aren't many instruments playing 5.1 mixes can have the effect of localizing instruments so that there is no longer a feeling of cohesion to the music. But since no-one makes demos in 5.1, you can stick with placing instruments in the 180 degrees of traditional stereo.

Mixing in mono

One excellent method for testing your arrangement for part cohesion, timbre, dynamics, rhythm and pitch hierarchy is to deliberately pan everything into the centre and mix in mono. What this does is create a lump of focused sound coming at you in one direction, from dead in front. The parts are not distinguished from each other by the spatial means of stereo. Instead they are distinguished (if at all) by how well they fit with each other, whether they get in each other's way, whether the instrumental timbres are sufficiently different, whether they are bunched up at the same pitches and frequencies. A temporary mono mix can reveal some useful insights into the arrangement. It will be very obvious if all your chords are in the same pitch range, or if there is too much happening in the same range as the vocal.

A mono mix is also an excellent opportunity to learn about the art of EQ – the manipulation of frequency after a part is recorded – what the layman knows as 'treble and bass'. Sophisticated equalisation allows the frequency spectrum to be cut up into smaller and smaller slices. So if two instrumental parts are too alike and getting in each other's way, EQ can assist in separating them. The guidelines are:

- EQ can be cut as well as added. Don't just go for the one thing
- If parts have been well-recorded, EQ. should need only minimal tweaks, so try to get the frequencies on an instrument right before recording.
- How much difference an EQ cut or boost makes depends on how much of an instrument's sound occupies that part of the bandwidth you are altering. Bass guitars don't have much in the higher frequency range, so cutting or boosting at that point won't make a huge difference.
- Low frequency cuts can diminish the 'boominess' of acoustic guitars if they were recorded with the microphone too near the soundhole.
- Small high frequency boosts can add sparkle to vocals, strummed guitars, and other parts that need a touch of brightness. Don't do this on everything, otherwise nothing will stand out.

- Small EQ adjustments can emphasize a contrast of timbre between one instrument and another if you find the frequency range where the character of the instrument is most felt.
- An EQ boost can remove the necessity for pushing up the volume fader on a part. Volume isn't the only way to make something stand out, and if you use it across the board – the 'everything louder than everything else' paradox – no part gains.
- Check you don't accidentally replicate EQ changes across the desk, adding or cutting in the same band, otherwise the mix will sound lop-sided frequency-wise.
- EQ on a voice can give the impression of someone talking down a telephone, as on the tight, dry vocal sound for The Strokes *Is This It* album.

When you feel that your mono mix is working and everything is clear and balanced, then pan the parts left and right into stereo and it should sound even better, because spatial division left and right will give additional distinction to the parts.

Refreshing instruments

The principle of 'refreshing' instruments in a mix arises from the psychology of listening. After awhile a listener gets accustomed to the sound of an instrument on a track. We begin with a sense of novelty (you're newly aware of it) then familiarity (you're enjoying it) to indifference (it's just there) and then in the worst case to boredom (you don't want to hear it anymore). In a rock song on which the snare drum is hit on beats two and four, that sound, though still heard, after awhile does not necessarily register as an individual sound – it is part of the overall effect. The attention wanders to the vocal/lyric, or possibly the solo. However, if the drums stop playing for a stretch, and then re-enter with a fill in which the snare is dominant, that sound will really make an impact.

Arranging, and to an extent mixing, is about juggling. You need an instrument present to play an important role in the sound, but you are also looking for opportunsities to remove it to refresh it. This is easy to do with secondary instruments, because they will not be missed when absent; but it may be less important because they are not used so much. Core instruments have an important task most of the time. Pulling them out of a mix may risk losing energy or cohesion. The importance of refreshing a sound varies from one instrument to another. In my view, the most sensitive instrument to this effect is the drum-kit, and an understanding of how to refresh drums is essential to making great, explosive rock arrangements. It is obvious that drums and rock music go together. But think about the way the drums are pulled out of Who tracks like 'Baba O'Reilly', 'Won't Get Fooled Again', 'Who Are You', and 'Bargain', or Led Zeppelin's 'Heartbreaker' and 'Ramble On'. This principle also applies to temporarily suspending percussion loops to create a moment of silence, as in Tori Amos's 'Caught A Lite Sneeze'.

Using reverb

Reverb (short for 'reverberation') is the effect applied to the whole of a mix to make it sound as though the music was played in a certain physical space. Reverb programmes go from small, medium and large rooms to halls, churches, and cathedrals. They often emulate the differing characteristics of reverb technology, such as plate reverb. Generally when recording a monitor mix has some reverb to make the sound going to tape more pleasing to the performer. Monitor reverb makes a big difference to singers and soloists alike, who change their phrasing accordingly. Even though this reverb does not go on to the tape it will affect the performance. Another reverb setting is applied at mix-down and that does go on the 2-track master mix.

Reverb has gone in and out of fashion throughout the past 50 years of popular music. Large amounts of it suit some genres more than others. Music intended to be spacious, ambient, reflective, and slow in tempo, will take more reverb than energetic, fast and rhythmic music. Different amounts suit different instruments. Higher-pitched instruments and phrases are better suited to big reverb. Instruments such as bass guitar are traditionally given very little at all, since reverb can make low frequency parts muddy. Reverb creates distance – the notes appear to come from somewhere behind the speaker – whereas 'dry' sounds seem as though they are at the speaker's surface.

Reverb can be very effective for an atmospheric outro, where the fade is itself a moving into the aural distance. The conclusion of Simon and Garfunkel's 'The Boxer' goes into greater and greater reverb as instruments are added and the emotional intensity increases, before coming back to a dry sound for the last bit of finger-picked guitar. Jefferson Airplane's ballad 'Today' has reverb-soaked drums in the distance on the left channel. Big reverb, especially where there is no dry signal, blurs drum sound and takes away its rhythmic energy, but it massively increases atmosphere and emotional expressiveness of even a simple pattern. Marshall Crenshaw's magnificent 'Laughter' shows how melodic electric guitar phrases take on added expression through the reverb and sustain.

Many songs on an album like The Verve's *Urban Hymns* depend on reverb. The Stone Roses' 'I Wanna Be Adored' would never have generated the atmosphere it does without the reverb. It is what the reverb does to those notes. In The Smiths' 'Back To The Old House', notes from the two finger-picked acoustics hang in the reverb, helping to fill out the sound and smooth the chord changes. On Robert Plant's 'The Greatest Gift', reverb makes the notes float away into the ether, an effect especially good on clean notes. Led Zeppelin famously could not get their arrangement of 'When The Levee Breaks' to work until they got a drum sound that was inspiring. That finally happened when the natural reverb in the hall at Headley Grange, in which they were recording, came together via distance miking and a Binson echo unit.

Sound effects

In a mix, sound effects fall into two basic categories – those which imitate or reproduce a real life sound and those used for their own sake. Imitative sound effects are the introduction of a non-musical sound to evoke an object or place. Whereas once people had recourse to vinyl albums of sound effects, samplers have made it an easier and more precise task. The most common sections for this to be used are the intro, bridge, links, or on a coda. If sound effects occur in a verse or chorus it is probably to illustrate the lyric. Two major areas of sound effect come from manipulating the speed of a sound to make it unfamiliar, as when a band like Gomez samples drums from a vinyl record playing at the wrong speed, or when on *Murmur* R.E.M. recorded billiard balls colliding and slowed that down, or when The Beatles speeded up Paul McCartney laughing to get a 'seagull' effect on 'Tomorrow Never Knows'.

Here are examples of sound effects that have appeared on record:

Car noises: as a consequence of the many songs written about travel and worshipping the automobile. See the intro of R.Dean Taylor's 'Gotta See Jane', Rod Stewart's 'True Blue' (revving), Mungo Jerry's 'In The Summertime', and the motorcycle on The Shangri-Las' 'Leader Of The Pack'.

Trains: passing at the end of *Pet Sounds*, a London underground tube train at the start of The Jam's 'Down In The Tube Station At Midnight'.

Weather: a howling wind on The Troggs' 'Night Of The Long Grass', rain on The Smiths' 'Well I Wonder' and The Who's *Quadrophenia*. The sea and waves on The Who's 'Sea and Sand', (Pete Townshend walking along a beach singing to himself just before 'Bell Boy'), Otis Redding's 'Dock Of The Bay', someone diving into water on the intro of Wings' 'I Lie Around'.

Nautical noises: down in the engine room for The Beatles' 'Yellow Submarine'.

Party noises: The Temptations' 'I Can't Get Next To You', Marvin Gaye's 'What's Going On'.

Birds and animals: the water bird taking off from the lake on Pink Floyd's 'Grantchester Meadows'; a cock crowing on the intro and coda of The Beatles' 'Good Morning, Good Morning' along with dogs, various farmyard animals, the hunt that gallops across from right to left; birds on All About Eve's 'Paradise'.

Human speech and impresario voices: The Beatles' 'Magical Mystery Tour'; military barked orders, Kate Bush's 'Army Dreamers', R.E.M.'s 'Orange Crush'; astronauts, Kate Bush's 'Hello Earth'; film soundtrack voices, Siouxsie And The Banshees' '92 Degrees', Marshall Crenshaw's 'Soundbite', Catatonia's 'I Am The Mob'; political speech, Living Colour's 'Personality Crisis'; actors speaking Shakespeare, The Beatles' 'I Am The Walrus'; people speaking on the telephone, Super Furry Animals' 'Rings Around The Moon'.Tuning a radio: Dexys Midnight Runners' 'Searching For The Young Soul Rebels', Kraftwerk's 'Autobahn'; a radio in the background, Pink Floyd's 'Wish You Were Here'.

Mechanical devices: a cash register on Pink Floyd's 'Money', a typewriter on R.E.M.'s 'Exhuming McCarthy'.

Applause, crowd noise: The Beatles' 'Sgt.Pepper's Lonely Hearts Club Band'.

Backward effects

One of the most dramatic sound-effects that can be added to a song is a backward noise. These are extraordinary because they represent an acoustic phenomenon we never hear in real life; they are an aural version of time running backwards. Voices running backwards speak nonsense syllables, though the brain strives to interpret what is being said as real words. Reverse a musical phrase and its pitch curve changes direction: a descending scale becomes an ascending one, and *vice versa*. A backward guitar note gets louder, not softer, and ends suddenly.

Backward guitar is a great effect, discovered in the 1960s by bands reversing tapes, recording guitar on them, and then playing the tape back the right way. It was a means of expressing the disorientation of the psychedelic vision. There are backward guitars on T.Rex's 'Cosmic Dancer' and 'Woodland Rock', The Clash's 'London Calling', The Beatles' 'I'm Only Sleeping' (two on the solo and on the coda to fade-out), The Jam's 'Start' and 'The In-Crowd', and a backward solo on R.E.M's 'What's The Frequency, Kenneth?'. Backward guitars can be heard on several tracks from Ocean Colour Scene's *North Atlantic Drift*: 'I Just Need Myself' (along with backward drums), 'Oh Collector', 'Second Hand Car', and 'For Every Corner'. Backward, strummed 12-string acoustics have a nice brush-like sound (listen to the intro of The Icicle Works 'Chop The Trees'). There are many sequences with backward music on the soundtrack of the film *Eternal Sunshine Of The Spotless Mind*.

Any echo or reverb recorded along with the guitar notes will also be reversed. There is backward echo or reverb on Led Zeppelin's cover of 'You Shook Me', the solo in the middle of 'Trampled Underfoot', and the guitar overdub high on The Smiths' 'How Soon Is Now' and the two high guitar parts on the coda of 'That Joke Isn't Funny Anymore'. Backward reverb is a favourite of horror film soundtracks when applied to voices.

Backward sounds can make a striking intro, as can be heard on Jimi Hendrix's 'Are You Experienced', Tomorrow's 'My White Bicycle', and The Darkness's 'One Way Ticket'. Queen's 'Ogre Battle' begins with the ending of the song running backwards. There is backward percussion in The Beatles' 'Strawberry Fields Forever'. Tyrannosaurus Rex's 'Debora' exists as an album version in a different key in which the entire song is reversed back to its beginning, titled 'Deboraarobed'. The Stone Roses created an entire backward track in 'Waterfall'. The Raconteurs 'Blue Veins' has a 'false' intro created by 30 seconds of entirely backward music which rights itself into a minor key blues in A minor. It features lovely echoed tremolo guitar and spooky piano, with another backward section in the middle instead of a guitar solo.

Lead vocals

In some ways lead vocals are the easiest part of an arrangement to deal with. Writing a song, the presumption is you need a voice to deliver the melody and the lyric. The structure of the song dictates where the vocal happens, so you don't have to think about which section it will be in. Always take care with the first attempt at a lead vocal. A first vocal take often has a spontaneity and unselfconsciousness that can't be recaptured – so don't be half-hearted on it. This is the most noticeable facet of a frustrating phenomenon encountered by many songwriters and bands, which is that when they demo a song they can never reproduce its feeling in the studio. Some bands even avoid recording demos for this reason. So if you are recording a demo, make it the best technical quality you can and sing as well as you are able. Don't be afraid to use hand gestures and other physical movements, even though you're not in front of an audience, if that helps with expression.

Vocal effects

At the mixing stage the lead vocal can be subject to a variety of tweaks that might make it sound better, from echo and reverb to EQ and even pitch-shifting if the vocalist's pitch is wayward. A very short echo thickens without being audible as a separate echo. Use slapback echo for a 1950s sound, like John Lennon on The Beatles cover of 'Rock And Roll Music' or Led Zeppelin on 'Rock And Roll' – where the echo is long enough to almost hear the word distinctively after the end of the line. As an extreme example of vocal effects, listen to the production of Brett Anderson's voice on early Suede records, giving it a borderline-hysterical androgyny. Echo can also be applied with more drama to a single word or phrase if you want that to stand out, as at the very end of Lenny Kravitz's 'Fly Away' or Robert Plant's 'Anniversary'. Extreme EQ can give the effect of a voice speaking down a telephone or from a radio, as in parts of the lead vocal in Buggles' 'Video Killed The Radio Star'. Phasing was applied to George Harrison's voice on The Beatles' 'Blue Jay Way'.

Consider the style in which you sing a particular song. Sometimes it can work if you sing a song with a different voice to the one that would have been expected for the musical style. The Foo Fighters' *One By One* has many of the band's traits: grunge guitar, saturated distortion, detuning. But it also has a laid-back vocal sound, whose melodies are far from the usual high-pitched wailing of HM and the bronchial bellowing of other hardcore alternative bands. The idea of putting restrained 'singerly' vocals over a heavy rock backing was pioneered by Cream in the 1960s on songs such as 'I Feel Free'. In U2's early records, Bono had established himself as a vocalist in the Roger Daltrey mode, barking and wailing. But on the band's recent 'Beautiful Day' the forceful vocals are put into the background on the right, and Bono's lead vocal is generally sung in a more restrained manner. In other words, the arrangement effectively reverses a trademark of the band.

To give a voice more weight, it can be double-tracked. One method would be to use automatic double tracking (ADT) which does it for you. Otherwise, you sing the melody twice on separate tracks, attempting to match them as close as possible. Depending on how much of a perfectionist you are, you can leave small deviations in the melody. A double-tracked vocal was sometimes panned left and right. On The Beatles' 'And Your Bird Can Sing' and 'Doctor Robert', Lennon's lead vocal is panned left and right. The stereo version of 'It's Only Love' has extreme left/right panning of the double-tracked vocal and gives one of them echo. On Deep Purple's 'Strange Kind Of Woman', the vocal is double-tracked and in the last verse panned to extreme left and right. The lead vocal on Mungo Jerry's 'In The Summertime' is on the left, with the second half of each line sung on the right in answer.

Sometimes the two vocals don't match perfectly, as in The vocals Lennon's performance on The Beatles' 'No Reply', Steve Marriott's on the chorus of The Small Faces' 'Itchycoo Park', Brian Wilson's on The Beach Boys' 'Don't Worry Baby', and on several tracks on Love's *Forever Changes*. If you feel the voice needs more support a vocal can be backed up by an instrument, such as guitar, flute, clarinet, piano, or strings, playing the melody line.

Beyond one lead vocal

A song can also have more than one main melody. Marvin Gaye's 'What's Going On' has several lead vocals that don't match up with each other, which are different takes of the lead vocal left in the mix. Some Michael Stipe melodies and double vocals on R.E.M tracks sound like they originated with him trying different melody ideas, which were then mixed together. When alternate melodies are formally worked out so they will fit together, what would have been a backing vocal is raised to the level of counterpoint. Thus in The Beatles 'Help' and 'She's Leaving Home', John Lennon sings one melody and Paul McCartney sings another. Often this will involve two different voices, and it is part of the identity of some bands to have more than one voice.

In the case of R.E.M., Mike Mills' vocal contributions are crucial to the band's sound and to the multi-hooked nature of some of their best choruses like 'Fall On Me' or 'Near Wild Heaven'. The contrasted character of two people's voices can become part of the music at a deeper level. In R.E.M. the contrast between Stipe's mumbled early vocals and obscure lyrics was offset by Mike Mills' higher-pitched vocal. In some bands, two different voices share the lead vocals. The Who had two voices (heard to good effect on 'Bargain' and 'The Song Is Over'); The Band, Jefferson Airplane, The Faces, R.E.M., Jefferson Airplane, Fleetwood Mac, and Queen had three singers available for lead vocals; The Beatles and The Four Tops had four; The Temptations had five (!). The Temptations' 'Ball Of Confusion' relies on individual lyric lines being passed round the five voices in order for the arrangement to work. Contrasting voices can articulate different parts in the song if the lyric has more than one aspect or character. With a duet like the Everly Brothers their voices were so akin in tone that they almost functioned as one, but in other bands there is more of a contrast. A hit like the Association's 'Windy' has an extraordinary amount going on in the vocals.

This contrast is especially potent in a duet between a male and female voice, and writing and arranging a song for this is a challenge. Good examples include Led Zeppelin's 'Battle of Evermore'; the many love duets of Marvin Gaye and Tammi Terrell; Sonny and Cher's 'I Got You Babe'; Tom Petty and Stevie Nicks' 'Stop Draggin My Heart Around'; Elton John and Kiki Dee's 'Don't Go Breaking My Heart'; Clannad's 'In A Lifetime'; Kirsty MacColl and The Pogues' 'Fairytale Of New York'; and Peter Gabriel and Kate Bush's 'Games Without Frontiers' and 'Don't Give Up'. Love duets need to be written into the lyric itself to work at their best. The same contrast can be potent even when the female voice is in a clearly supportive role, as with Marie Brennan's singing on Robert Plant's 'Come Into My Life' or Julianne Regan's singing on The Mission's 'Severina'. It is quite a shock to hear a female voice enter toward the end of Prince's 'Little Red Corvette', after so much masculine lust. Wheatus's 'Teenage Dirtbag' has a female voice on its last verse, offering those tickets to see Iron Maiden. In Sly And The Family Stone's 'Family Affair' a single female answers the male lead vocal. Kristin Hersh's 'Your Ghost' (on which Michael Stipe sings) and R.E.M.'s 'E-Bow The Letter' (where Patti Smith sings) are also effective in this respect.

Backing vocals

In terms of symbolic identity, backing vocals are about more than voice, ie, other people. When disciplined into harmony singing they begin to evoke communal feelings. This reaches its apotheosis when the number of singers reaches the proportions of a choir. Then you have a symbolic congregation on your hands. A variant on the choir is the massed bank of children. This was originally deployed on horribly sentimental records. Risk this only if you have a great song with a theme of innocence, or a subversive, funny, or satirical intent, as with Pink Floyd's 'Another Brick In The Wall', The Smiths' 'Panic', The Darkness' 'Christmas (Don't Let The Bells End)', Wizzard's 'I Wish It Could Be Christmas Everyday', and Alice Cooper's 'School's Out' and 'Department Of Youth'. On the latter, Alice asks the kids "Who's got the power?" several times, to which they reply "We do!" Then he asks, "And who gave it to you?" To which the answer is expected to be "You did." Instead, they reply "Donny Osmond!" "Whaat!?" shouts Alice, horrified.

Backing vocals are less in fashion than they once were, but they remain an effective resource on an arrangement. Remember that:

- In four-part harmony singing four voices create a melody, chords and a bass-line.
- There is always the option of an a cappella (unaccompanied) song or song section.
- Backing vocals can be provided by one, two, three, or four voices. For a bigger sound double-track each line.
- Try to be as tight and precise with timing as you can when doing block vocals, otherwise they sound ragged. You need to be obsessive about the timing of the first note of each phrase and when the last ends.
- Backing vocals cease to be so when their melodic lines are of the same weight as the lead – as with the multiple lead vocals on the end of The Beach Boys 'God Only Knows'.

Vocal harmonies are usually sung a third or sixth above or below the lead vocal and can move in parallel with it. As passing notes they can move by other intervals to land on the notes of a chord at the end of a vocal phrase.

- Backing vocals can contribute to an arrangement in the following ways:
- To provide a single interjection, echoing part of a line. Usually there isn't time for a whole line to be repeated before the next one begins in the lead, which is why you will be used to hearing a line like "I keep searching down every street" answered by the backing vocals as "every street".
- Wordless backing vocals – using "ooh" or "ah" sounds – can add smooth, sustained notes, sometimes chords, as a pad idea instead of (or as well as) a keyboard or strings.
- A backing vocal might echo the hook-line, or sing it unison, or an octave higher, or an octave lower. On Blondie's 'Heart of Glass' the backing vocal on some of the choruses is Debbie Harry singing a low octave to her own lead vocal.
- A backing vocal might carry a nonsense refrain for people to join in with.

- A backing vocal might emphasize an important line in the lyric.
- In between lines of lead vocal you can sing the song title, as on The Beatles' 'The Night Before'. This doesn't work so well in a song that has a chorus.
- High voices can be brought in to the middle and end of a song to increase emotional intensity and aspiration. High voices are brought in for the bridge of Percy Sledge's 'When A Man Loves A Woman'.
- A backing vocal can be a counter-pointed melody rather than a harmony. From early in their career R.E.M. had a trademark of sustained wordless notes that overlapped. This is vocal harmonising without the usual parallel thirds.
- Backing vocals will tend to punctuate a song rather than continuing all the way through.
- Backing vocals can contradict the lead lyric. Note the ironic effect of the backing vocals in The Beatles' 'Getting Better', where they contradict the lead vocal by saying things can't get worse. See also the idea of having a contradictory voice, as in songs like 'Old Man' on Love's Forever Changes.

Mixing checklist

The contents of a mix fall into four groups: the main focus (usually lead vocal and/or solo instrument), instruments meant to be noticed for brief spells, instruments that are present but not consciously listened to, and parts that contribute to the sound without your noticing.

Here are some general points about arrangement that you could usefully remember when you are mixing a track:

- Decide where the listener's focus is supposed to be at any moment. Make sure that other instrumental parts do not get in the way. (Many late 1960s rock records have a habit of allowing lead guitar all through, which can be very distracting.)
- Check the stereo image for balance, and make sure this remains satisfactory even during passages where certain instruments are pulled out. Check there is one instrument left on each side, even if it isn't very full or loud.
- Listen for low, mid, and high frequencies, in case any are over-emphasized.
- Listen for how much space a sound takes up when balancing volume.
- Check the effect of any or all harmonic chord-playing instruments by listening to the mix with them all removed. This exposes how many melodic parts there are and how effectively they alone imply the chords. It may be that you don't need as many chord-generating instruments, or that a more spacious mix suits the song. On the album *Yankee Hotel Foxtrot*, Wilco first recorded with standard band arrangements, then broke them down to see how sturdy the melody was, and then rebuilt them.
- Are the accompanying parts as interesting as they could be? Could parts that are chordal be arpeggiated? Could they be more rhythmic and tied closer to the percussion and drums?

- Keep instruments in reserve if the arrangement strategy is intended to be cumulative.
- Be ready to drop instruments out to contrast sections with each other.
- Bring instruments in that might illuminate the imagery or emotion of the lyric, even if momentarily.
- Occasionally bypass reverb that is applied to the whole mix and see what the mix sounds like without.
- Use headphones to check for unwanted noises and playing glitches; speakers for the main mixing.
- Mix at low volumes – this saves your ears, and fits the volume at which many people will hear the music. This is especially important with rock, where the temptation is to listen loud because that is how it is meant to be heard. If it sounds dynamic and exciting at low volume then you know the mix will sound great louder.
- Don't forget the time-honoured tricks of checking rough mixes by playing them in the car, on other hi-fis than your own, or by standing just outside the room with the door open.

STUDYING ARRANGEMENTS

Much can be learned about arrangement and mixing by carefully listening to your favourite tracks, especially on headphones. Hearing what is done in practice helps you to create more effective arrangements and to find templates for the type of music you write. A great arrangement alone can even inspire a song. To appreciate the art of arrangement, all you have to do is listen carefully to tracks that have been well thought-out. Some tracks I think are exceptional for their arrangements are 'Being For The Benefit Of Mr Kite' (The Beatles), 'You're All I Need To Get By' (Marvin Gaye/Tammi Terrell'), 'Theme From Shaft' (Isaac Hayes), 'I'm Not In Love' (10cc). For a crash course in arranging songs, try these albums: anything by The Beatles or The Beach Boys from the 1964-67 era, *Motown Chartbusters volumes 1-5*, Led Zeppelin's *Houses Of The Holy*, Kate Bush's *Hounds Of Love*, Jeff Buckley's *Grace*, Radiohead's *OK Computer*, and Goldfrapp's *Felt Mountain*.

With this intention, let's look at four arrangements in detail:

CASE STUDY

THE RACONTEURS 'STEADY, AS SHE GOES'

The Raconteurs are Jack Lawrence (bass), Patrick Keeler (drums and percussion), Jack White (vocals, guitars and synthesizers), and Brendan Benson (vocals, guitar and keys). Their debut album *Broken Boy Soldiers* (May 2006) was nominated for a Best Rock Album Grammy and 'Steady, As She Goes' as Best Band Performance. Many of the tracks have interesting arrangement details.

From a songwriting perspective, 'Steady, As She Goes' demonstrates how little music is needed to make a song. It comprises a two-bar phrase which lasts roughly four seconds, repeated about 38 times, a link bar, and a middle eight made up of four different bars (G to A to B and G to A to E). That makes a total of 15 seconds of music. The repetition of those bits stretches the song to 3:35.

The basic progression is a four-bar turnaround, using chords I-V-bVII-IV in B (B-F♯-A-E), with the bridge using a bVI (G). The verse/chorus progression is a three-chord trick with an additional bVII chord. Talking about the arrangement, it is worth observing that instruments often disguise the number of actual repetitions in the music. The track starts with a drum part minus the bass drum for four bars. Then the bass guitar enters with the bass drum (at 0:9 seconds), followed by a guitar on single notes (0:17), guitar chords on the second and fourth beats (0:25). At about 0:34 the second chord in the progression moves to the third offbeat – ie, half a beat earlier than it had been. Many of the tracks have shifted rhythmic accents, which happens early on.

During this intro the progression is ambiguous because it isn't clear whether the 'chopped' B is a major or a minor. Playing the sequence in fifths retains this ambiguity. So here's a second tip for maximising a progression – play it first in fifths and therefore neither major nor minor – and then play full chords.

Dynamically, 'Steady, As She Goes' contrasts a quiet verse and a loud chorus where both use the same progression. Notice also how the bass guitar fits in between the guitar chords and the lead guitar parts, which are very 'dry' (no reverb) and to the front of the mix.

CASE STUDY

SNOW PATROL *EYES WIDE OPEN*

Final Straw sold two million and won an Ivor Novello award for Best Album of 2005. Eyes Wide Open went to Number One in the UK album chart in May 2005. Snow Patrol's arrangements are guitar-based but with touches of electronica to add spice. They are not afraid to work with reverb, space, and distance, in contrast to the currently favoured dry productions on many indie rock records. The coda to 'Spitting Games' is a case in point, with a vocal and guide guitar part picked up by a distant mic.

Snow Patrol make expressive use of inversions. These are an effective way of getting more mileage out of a small number of chords. Write a three-chord trick and you have three chords – use all the inversions available and you increase it to nine (three times three). 'How To Be Dead' has F going to F/A then Bb and then G or G minor (it is difficult to hear). The same F/A crops up in 'Same', the closing track, along with G/B and G minor/Bb. The change F-F/A-Bb can be heard in 'Grazed Knees'.

One signature, a way of increasing the tension and expression in a chord sequence, is to have a note, or possibly a one-bar phrase of a couple of notes, which remains the same while

the chords change. These notes will fit with some chords but be tense with another even though the notes themselves don't change. This is a function of part-playing, or it can be put into the chords or added on secondary instruments. A high one-note phrase is heard on The Supremes' 'You Keep Me Hanging On'. Snow Patrol use this:

- **During the first sequence of 'How To Be Dead' (the chords F-F/A-B♭-G or G minor), a high guitar plays an Fsus2 arpeggio (the notes F G C). Over the F and F/A chords, these notes are heard as the root, second, and fifth of the scale. But over the B♭ chord the 'value' of the notes changes to fifth, sixth, and ninth. And over the G chord it changes to flattened seventh, root, and fourth.**
- **During the verse of 'Wow', the chord changes go G♯-A-E and the note E is played across all three. The note E sits happily in A and E (as fifth and root respectively) but forms a tense sixth against the G♯.**
- **In the opening sequence of 'Run', the note C is common to A minor, F, and Gsus4 (as third, fifth, and fourth).**
- **In 'Spitting Games' there is a descending sequence of D-C-B minor (or B)-G. The note F♯ is heard against all four chords. It functions as a third, sharpened fourth, fifth and major seventh. The third and fifth blend, the sharpened fourth is very tense, and the major seventh is mildly tense but expressive.**
- **'Somewhere A Clock Is Ticking' has the chord sequence C minor-B♭-F with a four note keyboard phrase over the top, made of the notes B♭ A E♭ F. Over those chords this motif is heard three ways: major seventh, sixth, third, fourth; root, major seventh, fourth, fifth; and fourth, third, minor seventh, root. Same notes, different qualities.**

CASE STUDY

RADIOHEAD 'THERE THERE'

This song from *Hail To The Thief* (2003) is a lament about the perils of romantic temptation. It has a slow-burn arrangement that perfectly acts out the message of danger described in the lyric. You know from the tension that it is heading towards an explosion of sorts. It begins with a mostly drum and bass intro, with a feedback-type note on the right lending an air of danger. With a drum pattern dominated by tom-tom, the initial absence of a snare rock beat gives a mildly exotic sound to the opening. Guitars play in stereo at 0:31. Things are harmonically static, with about 28 bars of Bm7. The chord changes after the vocals enter at 0:46.

There's an effective sudden snare fill at 1:53, preceded by a crash cymbal. The song has no obvious chorus; it is more that verse and chorus flow together. After the second verse at 2:55, there's a new sequence which uses a 'woody' guitar tone on some late-Beatles-type barre minor seventh chords. There's a powerful arpeggiated guitar entry on the left at 3:16. The remainder of

the song is built on an asymmetrical 11-bar sequence which features a Dm6 chord. The minor sixth combines the sadness of the straight minor with an edgier, spikier feeling. On 'There There' the effect of these chords is accentuated because they are played arpeggio-style, not strummed. The climax of the arrangement takes place at 3:58, where the drum steps up into a more intense snare-beat with fills, and where Jonny Greenwood plays a typically idiosyncratic and deranged guitar solo. The song ends with a fog of feedback and a couple of brutally final snare fills.

CASE STUDY

LED ZEPPELIN 'NO QUARTER'

This snowbound masterpiece has an epic sweep despite clocking in at only 6:57. The attention to detail in the arrangement is brilliant. Originally, it was rehearsed at about twice the speed, the basic chords having a jazz feel. But the song got its identity when it was slowed down.

It begins with electric piano and a burbling synth, a deep bass root note, and the simple tune sketched out. At 0:47, led by Bonham's snare-fill, the bands enter with two augmented fourth chords and then hits the fuzzy riff for the first time. After four riffs the arrangement thins out again. The cymbals leave the burbling synth for Plant to sing over, his voice smoking with a flange effect. Note the echo applied to the word 'cold'. The band demonstrates its sense of dynamics, punching in on the riff and then dropping out.

Heralded by a single piano flourish at 3:07, the instrumental section starts. Jones plays a chordal piano break, deliberately tentative. At 3:52 Bonham is back in and Page takes his solo. Things here get intricate. Page's first guitar is a clean, jazzy-sounding lead break full of tumbling runs. At the back of it is a fuzzy lead, rising into the ether from time to time. Eventually the two run parallel before the fuzzy one takes over altogether. Notice Bonham's off-beat open hi-hat pattern, which punctuates the playing. The instrumental break winds up at 4:46 with a synth glissando and then progresses to the last verse. For the "dogs of doom" mentioned in the lyrics, Page brings in an echoed theremin to provide a far-off wail. Plant overdubs a second vocal on the coda, and at 6:16 climbs into his higher register as the track fades.

CASE STUDY

BLACK REBEL MOTORCYCLE CLUB 'LOVE BURNS'

The challenge for bands playing this type of material is to find new variations on an old theme. BRMC manage to do this both through their approach to recording and sounds, and in the important area of harmony, in terms of what chords they use. 'Love Burns' commences with a

38-second atmospheric texture of voices and sounds over a looped minor chord, a 'false' intro. The intro proper brings in an acoustic guitar and two electrics panned left and right. These guitars play a descending E-C♯-C riff over an E pedal. Since the key is E major, the C♯ implies a C♯ minor chord but the C that follows is unexpected. This progression's brooding air of menace is largely responsible for the power of the verse.

The chorus uses a standard blues-derived E-G-A-G sequence. Verse two is preceded by a higher guitar playing single notes. At 1.57 a fuzzy guitar playing an E octave appears high in the mix. This fuzz guitar sends great washes of distortion over the second chorus and the bridge. The bridge uses the E-G-A idea but there's a subtle touch in that the bass puts a D under the G in some of the bars. Again, with arrangement in mind, it's interesting that the song's coda features acoustic guitar playing E-D-A in 5/4. So although the core musical elements are standard rock harmony, BRMC put enough unexpected extras in to lift 'Love Burns' into the must-hear-that-again category.

COVER VERSIONS

There is an awful lot to be learned about arrangements from comparing versions of the same song by different artists. When you decide to do a cover version you have no compositional decisions to make, but you are immediately plunged into questions about arrangement. If you decide to copy the original version then you have to figure out how the original arrangement works. If you decide to do something new with the song then you have to decide on how to go about the arranging. If the versions you are comparing have been recorded a long time apart they will reveal something of the difference in their eras. You can compare

- Are they in the same key?
- Are the chord sequences intact or have they been simplified?
- What instruments have been changed and if so why?
- What is the overall musical intent of a given change?
- Has the song changed from one style to another?
- Has new material been added, or have things got cut?
- Is the artist male or female? Consider Tori Amos turning 'Smells Like Teen Spirit' into a torch song; Marilyn Manson covering The Eurythmics' 'Sweet Dreams Are Made Of This'; Kate Bush covering Marvin Gaye's 'Sexual Healing'. Such interpretations can often make very different artistic statements.

Thus some arrangements can set out to parody or destroy the original, some pay homage to it, some copy it, some try to re-imagine it. When you understand these options you can apply them to your own new song or even to re-arranging some of your old songs to find a better arrangement for them. Here are some revealing cover versions (the original artist is given first): Badfinger/Harry Nilsson, 'Without You'; Bob Dylan/Jimi Hendrix, 'All Along The Watchtower';

Bob Dylan/The Byrds, 'Mr Tambourine Man'; Bob Dylan/Manfred Mann, 'Mighty Quinn'; The Beatles/Joe Cocker, 'With a Little Help From My Friends'; Martha Reeves and the Vandellas/The Who, 'Heatwave'; Wings/Guns N' Roses, 'Live and Let Die'; The Association/The Casuals, 'Never My Love'; Slade/Oasis, 'Cum On Feel The Noize'; Bob And Earl/The Rolling Stones, 'Harlem Shuffle'; Pink Floyd/Scissor Sisters, 'Comfortably Numb'; Frank Sinatra/Sid Vicious, 'My Way'; The Band/Joan Baez, 'The Night They Drove Old Dixie Down'.

I do not imply that these are necessarily great covers: sometimes inept covers are just as revealing about arrangement as great ones.

Arrangement strategies for a cover version

Here are some ways you might stamp your identity on a song and give your cover version character:

- Change the tempo.
- Change the time signature. Go from straight 4/4 to a swinging 12/8.
- Lengthen one or two bars in important moments.
- Change some of the chords.
- Turn a rock number with fifth chords into majors and minors.
- Invert the genre – re-interpret a ballad as a rocker, or a rocker as a ballad.
- Change the instrumentation – replace guitars with piano. Changing the instruments makes a big difference. If you use the same arrangement instruments as the original you run the risk that it will sound the same.
- Add or take away the drums.
- Put a section over a bass pedal note.
- Re-interpret the song by re-reading the lyric carefully and finding a new angle.
- Bluesify the song by flattening some of the melody notes.
- Change the timing of some phrases in the melody, especially the hook.
- Change the solo instrument, so that what was a guitar solo becomes a saxophone solo.

Finally, let's turn to the audio CD to hear examples of many of the instruments and topics discussed through the book.

SECTION 9

On the CD

The CD that accompanies this book illustrates many of the techniques and sounds featured in the text. The notes here explain what to listen for in each case.

The 50-track CD which comes with this book is designed to illustrate some of the instrumental sounds and arrangement techniques mentioned in the text. This section gives a brief guide to what's on each track. But because the tracks provide examples of more than one technique there is a separate index, grouped according to theme or instrument. That offers another way of navigating through the audio examples.

The notes to each CD track are organized by the primary and secondary instrument division featured in the book. This will enable you to find comments on specific instruments faster. The leading category of 'arrangement' refers to a variety of musical elements such as answering phrases, key-changes, or tempo changes, etc. The abbreviations 'L', 'R' and 'C' refer to left, right and centre of the stereo image.

Note: remember that with the majority of these tracks there would be a vocal (possibly backing vocals) to go on top. Make sure there is still space for it. If the instrumental version of an arrangement gets too interesting in itself, you may have problems getting the vocals to 'sit' in it. The issue is usually not how many instruments are playing but how much they're playing.

Some of these tracks are featured in more than one mix so you can hear how various arrangement and mixing decisions affect the same musical material.

CD TRACK 1

Guitar: the riff is first heard on guitar one (L), then guitar two (R) is added. Guitars one and two play slight rhythmic variations on the riff and the chords. In the chorus sequence, guitar one sustains chords, guitar two plays more in the second half of the bar. The chorus ends with no chords; instead, the guitars play a single-note descending line. This thinner texture contrasts with what has preceded it and refreshes the guitar sound for the re-entry of the riff.

Drums: the intro riff is supported by bass drum, delaying the snare.

Bass: notice how the bass guitar's entry is delayed until after guitar two.

Secondary: the chorus is decorated by a high synth string line which provides a moving melodic part in contrast to the more static guitar chords.

CD TRACK 2

Guitar: the guitar chord shapes used during the first verse section are not the same as each other, which creates a richer harmony. Guitar two (R) plays chord stabs in contrast to guitar one (L) with its continuous rhythm. Guitar two's chord shapes pitch higher in the later part.

Percussion: on the chorus section the drum beat is thickened by handclaps and eighth-note tambourine.

Secondary: saxophones provide sustained notes and brief, accented chords.

CD TRACK 3

Arrangement: this is the first track to feature two different arrangements. This bridge section from a song is heard here with guitars and a rhythm section.

Bass: the bass guitar stays close to the bass-drum pattern, leaving a conspicuous space on the off-beat of beats two and four.
Drums: quarter-note open hi-hat on the beat.
Percussion: congas supplement the drums.

CD TRACK 4

Arrangement: this arrangement of CD track 3 removes the guitars. The harmony is carried now by other instruments.
Keyboard: notice the contrast between the brittle harpsichord chords (L) and the fatter rising synth figure (R). The harpsichord figure is static, not true moving chords, and this heightens the tension.
Secondary: strings are also featured on this part (L).

CD TRACK 5

Arrangement: this track features answering phrases, and a double ending, where the majority of the instruments stop on a single beat and chord, leaving one to continue through a fade.
Guitar: the guitar chords (R) on the chorus have rests and thus are not continuously chording in the manner of the piano.
Keyboard: the piano (L) answers the guitar /sax phrase on the verse, and supplies eighth-note staccato chords on the chorus.
Percussion: congas are used with the drums and handclaps thicken the snare beats in the chorus.
Secondary: sustained low saxophone (L) notes contrast with the higher-pitched, staccato piano; the sax also doubles with the guitar on the riff. A sequencing effect is created by a music box patch triggered by a random arpeggiator. This provides the outro with a single sound.

CD TRACK 6

Guitar: this piece is in the key of C♯ minor and the featured chords of this extract are B, G♯ minor and C♯ minor. Acoustic guitar one (L) has a capo at the fourth fret and plays the open-string shapes G, E minor and A minor. Acoustic guitar two (R) is detuned by a semi-tone (D♯ G♯ C♯ F♯ A♯ D♯) and plays the open-string shapes C, A minor and D minor. This enhances the sound of the chords. Since there is no percussion, rhythm comes from the guitar strumming.
Secondary: flute/recorder adds an extra part, first as a single line, then as three-part harmony.

CD TRACK 7

Arrangement: this track is heard first in a mix without reverb ('dry'). It features three short sections. The first is up-tempo and dominated by guitar; the second drops into half-time, and then the fullest sound is reserved for a third coda/outro. The harmony is extensively coloured by inversions, especially in the last two bars before the bandoneon's solo link.
Guitar: guitar one (L) plays an eighth-note riff; guitar two (R) plays chord stabs on the second and fourth beats.
Keyboard: piano/music box (R) enters in section two, chording on the beat. Bandoneon (L) links to the final section and provides grainy chords.
Bass: the bass guitar part has echo added and is played with a pick in a medium register. It is doubled by an upright bass.

Drums: this track does not use a conventional drum pattern. The hi-hat keeps the beat, the bass-drum does most of the work, with occasional snare on the outro.
Percussion: timpani add drama, with sleigh bells, tambourine, and wind chimes.
Secondary: horns (L) supply chords and a rising motif in the last section.

CD TRACK 8

Arrangement: CD track 7 is now heard with reverb ('wet'). Notice the difference in the spaciousness of the mix.

CD TRACK 9

Arrangement: this arrangement with guitars only, and then without, provides a chance to see how an arrangement can have the same chord progression stated in many different ways.

CD TRACK 10

Arrangement: this version of CD track 9 removes the guitars. Other instruments articulate the chord progression. It shows how the same progression can be presented in different ways. Notice the rallentando – the slowing down to the end – and the mixture of choppy versus sustained sounds.
Keyboard: harpsichord (L), low-pitched organ (L).
Drums: kick drum, hi-hat, no snare.
Percussion: congas, tambourine.
Secondary: there is a banjo (R), whose sound goes well with harpsichord. Trumpet (L) plays a repeated melodic phrase (and a jokey conclusion), high woodwind (R) plays a rising line. There is a solo low violin and cello line (R).

CD TRACK 11

Arrangement: on this track a sparse verse arrangement contrasts with a bouncier chorus. The first mix features guitars with the rhythm section.
Guitar: guitar one (R) plays standard open chords. Guitar two has a capo at the seventh fret.

CD TRACK 12

Arrangement: in this version of CD track 11, the guitars are replaced by other instruments, except for guitar one, which is present as a reverb-only ('wet') signal to balance the organ.
Keyboard: organ (R) colours the verse, with quarter-note chords from piano (R) on the chorus. Vibraphone (L) and electric piano (L) enter to add chords to the second half of the verse.
Bass: plectrum bass guitar with echo has an active role, playing melodic high arpeggios, not its usual bass function. It reverts to type on the chorus, playing deep root notes.
Drums: reserved for the chorus.
Percussion: sleighbells and hi-hat in the second half of the verse.
Secondary: cello (L) enters to introduce the second half of the verse. A small string section plays sustained chords on the chorus (L).

CD TRACK 13

Arrangement: this track features answering phrases, and a transition from 12/8 time, with its distinctive 'swing', to a straight 4/4 link section. The 4/4 section sounds as though it is slower, but the pulse of the music has remained the same.

Guitar: these comprise a guitar playing a standard rock'n'roll shuffle figure, a low-pitched electric, and an acoustic playing chords.

Keyboard: full organ with bandoneon provides the shuffle accompaniment rhythm figure. There is a honky-tonk piano fill (R) at the end of each section that announces the beginning of the next.

Drums: this track does not have a standard continuous beat. Instead, notice the use of toms to carry most of the beat until the delayed snare drum fill.

Percussion: tambourine during the main sections. Timpani make a dramatic appearance in the link section.

Secondary: some high-pitched sparkle is added by the glockenspiel (R). Saxophone (R) octaves provide fills. Brass, flute, and horns play a melodic phrase in the link.

CD TRACK 14

Keyboard: harpsichord plays chords, piano supplies low bass notes, which are enhanced by low-pitched organ (L).

Drums: the beat is marked by hi-hat and a conga hit.

Percussion: triangle.

Secondary: flutes provide a high melody over a string quartet (R), which carries the chords. Brass is heard toward the end. A music box is also featured.

CD TRACK 15

Arrangement: this includes a static 'telegraph' note during the chorus section, which creates tension against the chords. It also has a chord progression where the bass guitar has two roles.

Guitar: picked 12-string (R) on the chorus section.

Keyboard: accordion (R) and harpsichord (L).

Bass: minimal playing in the verse section. In the chorus it plays a steady pedal note first time through and then moves with the root notes of the chords. Listen for the contrast.

Percussion: tambourine and conga.

Secondary: cello (L) supplies rich, sustained low-pitched notes, with strings (R).

CD TRACK 16

Arrangement: this track illustrates contrary motion – the piano bass notes rise and the higher notes fall. Notice the shift to a high register at the end.

Keyboard: piano (L).

Bass: bass guitar, doubled by upright bass, plays a steady rhythm on root notes.

Percussion: timpani roll.

Secondary: music box and harp (R) sounds combined provide an answering phrase after the piano. Strings (R) play low sustained chords.

CD TRACK 17

Arrangement: this track has an example of a 'false' intro with contrasting instrumental timbre. Inversions occur in the descending passage.

Keyboard: piano adds some bass notes. Organ provides subdued pad, with harpsichord (R) and vibraphone (R).

Bass: double-bass sound.

Drums: ride cymbal.

Percussion: conga slap, tambourine reinforces the beat.
Secondary: tubular bells used on intro over synth pad. Brass, banjo, and clarinet lines (L).

CD TRACK 18

Arrangement: this progression is first heard with three guitars and a rhythm part.
Guitar: guitar one (L) and guitar two (R) are acoustic. Guitar three is a high arpeggiated electric.
Bass: bass guitar with echo and double bass.
Drums: occasional tom-tom.
Percussion: timpani, tambourine, hi-hat.

CD TRACK 19

Arrangement: this version of CD track 18 removes the guitars and arranges the sequence for other instruments.
Keyboard: organ (L), harpsichord (L).
Secondary: bandoneon (R), glockenspiel/music box (R), flutes (L), cello (L).

CD TRACK 20

Arrangement: this track features guitar harmonics.
Guitar: guitars one and two, guitar harmonics, tremolo-effect guitar in the centre.
Bass: double bass sound.
Drums: hi-hat, ride cymbal.
Percussion: tambourine.
Secondary: horn call motif (L), string quartet (R) sustained chords, harp (L) arpeggio, bandoneon (L).

CD TRACK 21

Arrangement: this is a 1960s soul ballad arrangement, with a nod to Marv Tarplin (guitarist with Smokey Robinson and The Miracles), intro and verse.
Guitar: three guitar parts feature in intro. Guitar three, muted electric playing a melody, guitar one, strummed acoustic with capo, strummed electric.
Drums: fills before steady beat.
Secondary: synth string line (R), single notes.

CD TRACK 22

Arrangement: this features a chorus to the previous track. The arrangement thins out during the link from the chorus to the next verse.
Bass: notice the fills before the start of the next verse.
Drums: notice the fills before the start of the next verse.
Secondary: trumpet fills on the chorus, synth string line.

CD TRACK 23

Arrangement: this track looks at how a riff can be doubled for a hard rock song.
Guitar: guitar one is mixed in stereo (L and R). Guitar two (R) enters, after one complete riff, an octave above guitar one. Finally, guitar three (L) doubles the riff two octaves above when the riff is transposed up a tone.
Bass: bass doubles the guitar riff.
Drums: open hi-hat for a more splashy sound.

CD TRACK 24

Arrangement: this track repeats the riff of CD 23 but provides two ways of harmonizing the riff.

Guitar: guitars one (L) and two (R) play the original riff, guitar three (L) is a third above, and guitar four (R) enters a sixth above.

CD TRACK 25

Arrangement: this is an example of the 'maximal' style. The basic musical structure is first heard with guitars and rhythm section only.

Guitar: guitar one is a prominent guitar playing low notes and then chording. Guitar two is acoustic, strummed. Guitar three is a 12-string with capo at first fret. Listen for the tremolo effect on the guitar.

Bass: bass guitar.

Drums: tom fills.

Percussion: tambourine.

CD TRACK 26

Arrangement: here track 25 is heard in a more lavishly orchestrated style.

Guitar: guitar one is a prominent guitar playing low notes and then chording. Guitar two plays stab chords. Guitar three is acoustic strummed.

Keyboard: low organ, high organ chords (L), piano (R).

Secondary: synth bell sound (L) arpeggios, high string lines centre and right.

CD TRACK 27

Arrangement: this track is modelled on Bob Dylan's mid-1960s 'wild mercury sound'. The problem is that the instruments are bunching in certain frequency areas. This first version is in mono with no EQ adjustments. It isn't easy to hear the different instruments.

Guitar: guitar one, capo at the twelfth fret, guitar two, electric with a capo at the second fret, guitar three electric arpeggio in open chords.

Keyboard: organ and electric piano.

CD TRACK 28

Arrangement: here is the same mono mix of track 27 with EQ used to differentiate the instruments. Listen for whether it sounds clearer.

CD TRACK 29

Arrangement: here is a third mix of track 27, retaining the EQ adjustments, but going into stereo and removing all the guitars so that it is carried by the organ and electric piano.

CD TRACK 30

Arrangement: this track features the distinctive sound of the marimba, treated with echo.

Guitar: guitar one plays chord stabs (R).

Keyboard: the brittle harpsichord tone contrasts with the mellow marimba and the horns. Note that both are quite percussive.

Percussion: congas, tambourine.

Secondary: echoed marimba, soft horn pad (L).

CD TRACK 31

Arrangement: this track is an extended coda/guitar solo based on the sound of Dire Straits. The first arrangement is a short guitar-only mix that gives you an idea of the basic progression and what it would sound like with only guitars and a rhythm section.
Guitar: fingerstyle lead guitar (Strat bridge/middle pick-up position), acoustic rhythm guitar, clean electric rhythm guitar (R).
Drums: moving from bass-drum pattern to full kit.

CD TRACK 32

Arrangement: this is a longer version of track 31. Listen for the build-up in the arrangement as the instruments are added and the drum part develops, and especially for the dramatic organ entry using a church-type sound. The expressive signature of this organ tone (sacred, religious, faith, eternity) throws a different light on the effect of the lead guitar.
Keyboard: church organ (R), electric piano (L).
Percussion: tambourine.

CD TRACK 33

Arrangement: this is a hard-rock arrangement based on the sound of the UK band Free. It shows how to arrange a riff and leave spaces for the drums and voice.
Guitar: two guitars playing low fifth-based chords. Guitar one (L) plays arpeggios on the chorus section.
Bass: the bass guitar plays more melodically and in a higher register than usual (a trademark of Andy Fraser's bass in Free).

CD TRACK 34

Arrangement: this is the guitar break for the previous track. Notice how it is arranged to build through the solo, which is played in the slow-bend style of Paul Kossoff.
Guitar: lead guitar tone from the front pick-up of a Les Paul. Note more reverb is added to the higher notes of the guitar to increase their body.
Keyboard: electric piano (R), mellotron strings (L).
Drums: drums move from partial to full use of the kit, cowbell.

CD TRACK 35

Arrangement: this track features a minimal folk-rock arrangement, starting with only acoustic guitar and bongos.
Guitar: two acoustic guitars, with capo. Listen for variations in the strumming patterns of the two guitars. Guitar three is wah-wah lead fills with descending single bass notes at the end of each verse.
Keyboard: after a while a harmonium enters with sustained chords. They have no rhythmic value, in contrast to the strummed guitars.
Percussion: bongos only.

CD TRACK 36

Arrangement: in a late Motown/soul style.
Guitar: guitar stabs, two guitars on rhythm left and right.
Keyboard: vibraphone (R).
Bass: very mobile, syncopated bass guitar part.

Percussion: handclaps and congas.

Secondary: high synth strings (R), brass sound (R) on chorus.

CD TRACK 37

Arrangement: this track shows two guitars, one sustained, one strummed, on a pop ballad.

Guitar: guitar one, strummed acoustic, guitar two, held chords; both with capo.

Drums: kick drum, hi-hat and sidestick. Snare saved for take-off into second verse.

Percussion: tambourine.

Secondary: trumpet (L) and strings (R) for the link to the bridge.

CD TRACK 38

Arrangement: this 'indie' rock arrangement features three guitars and an accented chordal intro.

Guitar: two guitars irregularly arpeggiating chords (L and R). Guitar three adds occasional fills.

Keyboard: phased synth adds sustained sound to the choppy guitars.

Percussion: tambourine.

CD TRACK 39

Arrangement: this track spotlights stereo guitar, the effect of echo, harmonics and an altered tuning. Note the standout harmonics at end of chorus before the verse returns.

Guitar: guitar one is a clean electric in an alternate tuning. It plays echoed harmonics on the intro (L). It is phased and echoed (R) as a stereo guitar. Guitar two, also electric, plays slow bends with distortion.

Keyboard: phased electric piano, not chordal.

Bass: bass guitar stays very tight with the kick-drum rhythm. Plenty of spaces at the bottom.

Drums: the drum beat interacts with the riff, in that the snare goes into a space. Note the flam at the end of the chorus in the fill.

Percussion: tambourine enters in the chorus.

CD TRACK 40

Arrangement: this is a slow guitar riff track. Initially, the guitars only appear for a few beats but then play more of a role. Either approach could be used as the basis for the mix.

Guitar: guitars play an accented chord riff, one being a 12-string (R), the other distorted (L). Guitar three plays muted fills with echo on the verse, prominent and higher pitched.

Keyboard: electric piano.

Bass: bass guitar plays a high arpeggio on the intro.

Drums: space for the snare-drum within the riff.

CD TRACK 41

Arrangement: this is a track with multiple guitars, and a guitar-only intro.

Guitar: guitar one acoustic (R), guitar two with capo at fret two, guitar three with clean 12-string arpeggios on the chorus.

Bass: the bass enters half way through the verse.

Drums: sidestick hi-hat for verse, full kit for chorus.

Percussion: tambourine for chorus.

CD TRACK 42

Arrangement: this track has a weird intro with a backward guitar note. The verse is built on a rhythmically tight riff; the chorus uses arpeggios and expands in feel.

Guitar: guitar one provides chords, capo third fret (R); guitar two, also capo third fret (L), plays minimally on the verse with mild tremolo arm and harmonics, then arpeggiates chords on chorus. Guitar three plays backward wah-wah lead fills.

Keyboard: sustained phased synth.

Bass: the bass sticks close to rhythm of the chord riff.

CD TRACK 43

Arrangement: this track features nylon-string guitar.

Guitar: classical guitar arpeggio playing (L).

Keyboard: piano bass notes only

Secondary: synth strings for sustained chords. Plays descending scale passage.

CD TRACK 44

Arrangement: this example of 'indie' guitar-texture rock is presented in three forms. This first version has one guitar and organ to carry the harmony.

Guitar: one guitar – guitar three – playing chords with a high capo.

Keyboard: mellow organ sustained chords.

CD TRACK 45

Arrangement: here is track 44 again, minus the organ and guitar three, but with two new guitars.

Guitar: guitar one and guitar two play a twin lead harmony that spans the stereo image.

CD TRACK 46

Arrangement: here is track 44 again, with all instruments together. Tracks 44-46 show how subtle changes of instrumentation change the texture and the prominence of certain ideas.

CD TRACK 47

Arrangement: this is a middle section building up to a verse. A low string part muddies the sound, over-enforcing the saxophone and distorted guitar two. Listen for the moment when this string part is removed and the mix is suddenly clearer. The part is pulled midway through the verse sequence at 0:24 seconds. During the chorus the first four bars have strings and sax, both are out for the second, and the sax returns for the third and fourth times.

Guitar: guitar one is a single-coil pickup (L) and guitar two (R) a distorted double-coil, both playing the riff, with capos. There is a touch of harmonized guitar in thirds before the verse.

Keyboard: rock'n'roll piano eighth-notes in verse (R), electric piano.

Drums: drums develop from kick-drum and hi-hat to build up the beat.

Secondary: saxophone (R); sustained string chords (L) on the chorus, then removed.

CD TRACK 48

Arrangement: here is an unconventional multiple lead guitar break, almost but not quite in parallel phrases, emphasising the character of the electric guitar. It is also an example of implied harmony. This first mix includes guitar chords.

Guitar: two electric guitar rhythm parts, four lead guitars.

CD TRACK 49

Arrangement: this second mix of 48 omits the rhythm guitar parts. This creates a clearer mix, makes the lead guitars stand out more, and allows the lead guitars to imply the chords from their own single-note lines.

CD TRACK 50

Arrangement: here is a dramatic orchestral interlude in an acoustic ballad otherwise dominated by acoustic guitar. Two unrelated chords are bound together on a rising bass scale. The abrupt change in and out of this bridge is not only about dynamics but also timbre. This is an unorthodox variation on the dynamic contrast arrangement strategy described in Section Two.

Guitar: two acoustic guitars (L and R), one capoed at the third fret.

Keyboard: organ.

Bass: bass guitar, plus contrabass sound – more of a treble edge than double-bass.

Percussion: timpani.

Secondary: synth strings, music box arpeggio, brass, Oberheim synth octaves, orchestra 'hit', trumpets.

INDEX TO THE CD

Numbers refer to CD tracks and not pages

INDEX OF SONGS AND ALBUMS

INDEX OF ARTISTS

ACKNOWLEDGEMENTS

Most quotations are from personal interviews. Some quotations are taken from back issues of *Guitarist*, *Mojo*, *Making Music*, *Melody Maker*, *Q*, *Uncut, and Guitar World*.

For their involvement in the preparation of this book I would like to thank Nigel Osborne, Tony Bacon, John Morrish, John Ryall, Mark Brend, and Simon Smith. A special thanks is due to Robin Morris for invaluable last minute support and assistance with the compilation of the audio. The CD was mastered by Tim Turan of Tim Turan Audio, Oxford. The author would also like to thank readers who have taken the time to post online reviews of other books in this series.

About the author

Rikky Rooksby is a guitar teacher, songwriter/composer, and writer on popular music. He is the author of the Backbeat titles *How To Write Songs On Guitar* (2000), *Inside Classic Rock Tracks* (2001), *Riffs* (2002), *The Songwriting Sourcebook* (2003), *Chord Master* (2004), *Melody* (2004), *Songwriting Secrets: Bruce Springsteen* (2005), *How To Write Songs on Keyboards* (2005) and *Lyrics* (2006). He contributed to *Albums: 50 Years Of Great Recordings*, *Classic Guitars Of The Fifties, The Guitar: the complete guide for the player*, and *Roadhouse Blues* (2003*)*. He has also written *The Guitarist's Guide to the Capo* (Artemis 2003), *The Complete Guide To The Music Of Fleetwood Mac* (revised ed. 2004), fourteen Fastforward guitar tutor books, four in the *First Guitar* series; transcribed and arranged over forty chord songbooks of music including Bob Dylan, Bob Marley, the Stone Roses, David Bowie, Eric Clapton, Travis, The Darkness, and *The Complete Beatles*; and co-authored *100 Years 100 Songs*. He has written articles on rock musicians for the new *Dictionary Of National Biography* (OUP), and published interviews, reviews, articles and transcriptions in magazines such as *Guitar Techniques, Total Guitar, Guitarist, Bassist, Bass Guitar Magazine, The Band, Record Collector, Sound On Sound*, and *Making Music,* where he wrote the monthly'Private Pluck' guitar column. He is a member of the Guild of International Songwriters and Composers,
the Society of Authors, the Sibelius Society, and the Vaughan Williams Society. Visit his website at www.rikkyrooksby.com